THE
NEXT
PANDEMIC

ON THE FRONT LINES
AGAINST HUMANKIND'S
GRAVEST DANGERS

ALI S. KHAN

WITH WILLIAM PATRICK

PublicAffairs
New York

PublicAffairs
Hachette Book Group
1290 Avenue of the Americas, New York, NY 10104
www.publicaffairsbooks.com
@Public_Affairs

Printed in the United States of America

Originally published in hardcover and ebook by PublicAffairs in May 2016
First Trade Paperback Edition: September 2020

Published by PublicAffairs, an imprint of Perseus Books, LLC, a subsidiary of Hachette Book Group, Inc. The PublicAffairs name and logo is a trademark of the Hachette Book Group.

The Hachette Speakers Bureau provides a wide range of authors for speaking events. To find out more, go to www.hachettespeakersbureau.com or call (866) 376-6591.

The publisher is not responsible for websites (or their content) that are not owned by the publisher.

Editorial production by Christine Marra, Marrathon Production Services.
Print book design by Jane Raese

Library of Congress Cataloging-in-Publication Data
Names: Khan, Ali, MD, author. | Patrick, William, 1948– , author.
Title: The next pandemic : on the front lines against humankind's gravest dangers / Ali S. Khan with William Patrick.
Description: First edition. | New York : PublicAffairs, [2016] |
Includes bibliographical references and index.
Identifiers: LCCN 2016001718 (print) | LCCN 2016002627 (ebook) |
ISBN 9781610395915 (hardcover) | ISBN 9781610395922 (ebook)
Subjects: | MESH: Disease Outbreaks | Disasters | Internationality |
Personal Narratives
Classification: LCC RA441 (print) | LCC RA441 (ebook) | NLM WA 105 |
DDC 362.1—dc23
LC record available at http://lccn.loc.gov/2016001718

ISBNs: 978-1-61039-591-5 (hardcover), 978-1-5417-6864-2 (paperback),
978-1-61039-592-2 (ebook)

LSC-C

10 9 8 7 6 5 4 3 2 1

To the people and communities worldwide
struggling against infectious diseases,
and to the disease detectives who help protect them

CONTENTS

INTRODUCTION TO THE
PAPERBACK EDITION

I based this book on my thirty years of experience responding to outbreaks all over the world. The overwhelming lesson of that work, as the title communicates, is that we are always on the edge of another disease outbreak.

The events of 2020, of course, make this point obvious. Since the unrecognized arrival of COVID-19 in the United States in January, my days have been filled with efforts in responding to the pandemic on top of my usual duties managing the College of Public Health at the University of Nebraska. I've been asked to consult internationally, nationally, and locally on strategies to minimize community transmission and to work with organizations trying to figure out how to reopen schools and businesses with so much uncertainty about how this disease will spread in communities over the next few years. Despite the various lockdowns, I have still been able to do some field epidemiology work, including developing trainings for contact tracing, reviewing site preparations to quarantine rescued Americans, and visiting a meat packing plant to examine prevention strategies. There has been a mountain of public attention paid to the problem now that it is in full view.

Yet there is more we can learn by examining the work we've done—and the work we haven't. First and foremost, we were not prepared. Not just low- and middle-income countries, which often lack the resources to set aside for disaster preparedness, but the whole world. This despite the fact that we have already had recent outbreaks due to SARS (severe acute respiratory syndrome) and MERS (Middle East respiratory syndrome)—both coronaviruses. As I document elsewhere in this book, I spent time in Singapore responding to SARS and saw firsthand the importance of "superspreader events"—in which one victim is responsible for infecting an extraordinarily large number of others—in broadly disseminating the virus. Those of us who study disease have long argued that pandemics were more likely in the age of air travel and high urban population density and that superspreading events would play a big role; but worldwide, not enough action was taken to prevent such events during COVID-19. We also warned that the socioeconomic and political fallout from a global outbreak can easily dwarf the final count of dead and sick. The COVID-19 economic losses alone are being counted in the trillions with estimates that 90 percent of the world will have lower per capita income. The cost of preparedness now seems cheap: hundreds of millions, maybe billions of dollars.

Another lesson I learned from my time chasing outbreaks abroad was that magical thinking is an enemy of science. When Ebola was spreading through Sierra Leone, rumors circulated that the disease was caused by "witch guns," a kind of evil that could infect you. We have had similar rumors all over the world: a manmade coronavirus was created either for germ warfare or as part of a hundred-year plot to force people to get vaccinated; masks are a conspiracy to take away our rights and cause lung disease; the disease is less deadly than the flu; a herbal potion to cure COVID-19 was being promoted by an African president. Such rumors flourish in the absence of good information and environments where science is actively denied. The governments of China, Russia, Brazil, Mexico, the United States, Iran, and so many others failed to rapidly and transparently share data with their own populace—and in the case of China, with the global community—in the critical early days of their outbreaks. And when we needed leadership the most, both within countries and in the wider global community, too many national leaders reverted to tribalism, seeking to blame others for the outbreak or surrendering to the outbreak rather than find the means to work with them for containment.

In the midst of this chaotic mess, we saw two predominant strategies emerge. The first model was focused on a robust national response for containment and elimination of the virus as championed by China—it required extraordinary government intervention but led to the fewest illnesses and deaths. The World Health Organization heralded this model and most Asian and European countries followed this approach. After months of response, China has seen daily cases in the teens with outright elimination—as of this writing—in Thailand, Taiwan, Hong Kong, and New Zealand. The second model was a more delayed response and mitigation strategy when a country's health care system was overwhelmed with cases—the model in Italy, Spain, the United Kingdom, the United States, Brazil, and Russia. These countries have seen a large number of cases and deaths. There are mixed patterns in low- and middle-income countries that have public health systems incapable of providing good data on the number of cases; some also have low-functioning health systems that could collapse. Fortunately, many of these countries had fewer elderly in the population, who are at the highest risk of death.

One especially difficult lesson from this global disaster is that it is a dress rehearsal for a potentially more lethal pandemic. At this point, COVID-19 has not been nearly as deadly as the 1918 influenza outbreak, which is estimated to have infected one-third of the global population and led to 50 million deaths. For COVID-19, early estimates are that about 5 percent of the population were infected in the first wave, and the death rate is approximately 1 percent—still five to ten times worse than seasonal influenza. This outbreak was so challenging not because the disease was so lethal but because the surge in infections rapidly overwhelmed local health capacity to provide diagnostic testing, personal protective equipment, health care personnel, hospital beds, and ventilators. The outbreaks continue because public health has not been up to the task to Test and Trace—a successful and proven strategy.

Microbes and humans have been best friends and enemies since we first started to settle down to farm. These microbes are critical for our gut metabolism and supply us with cheese, bread, and wine. However, with large human populations in one place came the ability of infectious diseases—such as measles, which likely came from a cattle virus—to be transmitted solely between humans. The subsequent centuries have been marred by numerous plagues before COVID-19. Avian influenza viruses and other zoonotic viruses wait in the wings, ready to claim the title of the next pandemic.

It is challenging to look at all the wreckage of this disease—more than 500,000 worldwide deaths, as of this writing, along with untold economic losses—and think that it could happen again or be worse. But it will. And if we don't take seriously our responsibility to work together, to quickly and dramatically change our priorities when the early signs of the next outbreak emerge, then we will be victims once again. The principles are simple: strong leadership, data transparency, and a willingness to spend time and money on robust public health and healthcare systems, and community engagement. The countries that have followed these principles have survived with limited harm. The ones that have replaced them with hope and magical thinking have suffered. It's up to us all, collectively, to learn the hard lessons now.

As is so often the case, microbes pose a threat, but the greater and more lasting danger is us.

Ali S. Khan
July 5, 2020
Omaha, Nebraska

PREFACE

As I write this, the news is all about Zika, a mosquito-borne virus newly introduced to the Americas that causes a mild fever in millions of cases, but also microcephaly, a severe birth defect that gives rise to abnormally small heads and brain damage. Multiple nations in South America have asked their families to delay pregnancies, and the United States has asked pregnant women to defer travel to the region. Americans are also on edge because of the risk of cases from local mosquitoes. In Sierra Leone, Ebola virus has returned—likely from sexual transmission—after a forty-two-day hiatus, which extends the span of the West Africa outbreak to more than two years. Meanwhile, there are the usual myriad stories of bird flu outbreaks, food-borne illnesses, and antibiotic-resistant bacteria.

All of these epidemics and potential pandemics reinforced my initial reason to write this book: to continue to share my perspectives from twenty-five years in public health, to provide a context for all of these headlines, to help separate the hype from the facts, and to explain which diseases pose the greatest risks and why we will always be susceptible to rogue microbes. But my most important goal is to assert that not all epidemics and pandemics are inevitable; and that most are preventable if we have the will, and if we back up that determination with the allocation of resources.

Despite my lifelong interest in infectious diseases, it was an investigation in a Congolese village, looking for Ebola patients with no resources, that changed my life and determined the course of my career. That early experience showed me that people are the same everywhere in the world in their aspiration for health, regardless of their unique challenges.

I want to give thanks for my career to my professional mentors. There are so many that I can list just one set here: Geoffrey Langlands, Robert Furchgott, Bob Gaines, Nancy Cox, Larry Schonberger, Louisa Chapman, Thomas Ksiazek, Mark Eberard, Lonnie King, and Howie Frumkin. I also want to thank my wife, Kris, the artist and English major, who kept the home fires burning while I was deployed all over the world, and who reviewed and edited this manuscript with the care that only a loving spouse can give.

I also want to thank William Patrick, an amazing collaborator who took stream-of-consciousness transcripts from twenty-five years of public health case-files and turned them into a scientific adventure story. And special thanks to my assistant, Catherine Ely, and to Ben Adams, my publisher. He believed. And to magic.

In writing the book, I found it liberating to not be limited to a specific disease and the deathless prose of a journal article or press release. And to use personal anecdotes to provide a behind-the-scenes view of the work of disease detectives to identify, respond to, and stop epidemics. I could tell the stories not just of microbes and the diseases they cause, but of the actual individuals and communities afflicted with the diseases. These will always be their stories.

Ali S. Khan
February 1, 2016

1

FIRST BLUSH

If it is a terrifying thought that life is at the mercy of the multiplication of the minute bodies (microbes), it is a consoling hope that science will not always remain powerless before such enemies.

—Louis Pasteur

We had been in the jungle for about two weeks when a kid on a motorbike rode up and told us that the rebels had overwhelmed government forces and that all these combatants were coming our way: Laurent Kabila's guerrillas, hot on the heels of Mobutu Sésé Seko's army.

This was in a province called Kasai-Oriental, just about in the center of Zaire, which is just about in the center of Africa. We were there on behalf of the World Health Organization and the Centers for Disease Control and Prevention to investigate an outbreak of monkeypox, a less deadly but still highly problematic cousin of smallpox. If it could be spread indefinitely by person-to-person contact, it could become a global pandemic. So the degree of sustained transmission was the central question we were trying to resolve. But suddenly the more pressing issue was how the hell we were going to get out of there.

We called the American embassy, which advised us to wrap up our investigation and evacuate immediately. "They'll likely take your vehicles and gear," they told us. "But they probably won't kill you."

This was not an entirely reassuring assessment. We were next door to Rwanda, scene of one of the worst genocides in recent history. Mobutu's forces were known to loot, pillage, and kill in the best of times, and the word was out that they had not been paid in months. "Why do you need to be paid?" Mobutu had scolded them once, or so the story goes. "You have guns."

The nearest airstrip, a trail of red dirt hacked out of the ever-encroaching vegetation, was seventy-five miles away in Lodja. But that was our only way of making it back to the capital.

Our team of disease detectives had been spread out to interview the locals and to collect mice, monkeys, squirrels, and rats so we could take their blood. Despite the name, monkeypox is more often found in rodents, and the primary means by which people get sick is contact with the bodily fluids of these animals, often when captured for food.

I sent some of the local villagers out to round up our team, and once everyone was accounted for, we attacked our own camp, running back and forth collecting equipment. I was dumping out vials of liquid nitrogen, which filled the jungle with plumes of white vapor, then burning my fingers as I retrieved the supercold canisters to consolidate our samples into a single tank. We were looking over our shoulders the whole time, as one of my colleagues with a military background used the satellite phone to call his contacts in the US Department of Defense.

They said, "If need be, we can pick you up in a few hours." My colleague asked, "How is that possible? You don't have any assets in this part of the world." They curtly answered, "That's our business, not yours."

But we weren't sure we had two hours to spare in that location. Better to get out of there now and find a plane in a couple of days. So we left behind our trucks and piled our ten people into three 4×4s and sped off into the bush toward the nearest town, a day's drive away.

We rumbled along for two or three hours in tense silence, worried about the abrupt ending of our study, worried about our gear, worried about the villagers who might now be targeted for having helped us.

Then when we got to the river our hearts sank—there was no bridge. For a moment, it looked like were going to have to leave everything behind and swim for it. But the locals had rigged up a rudimentary ferry system consisting of a flatbed on a giant pontoon and a cable system for pulling us hand over hand, which allowed us to get to the other side.

For the next eight hours we continued through the overgrown, mosquito infested, muddy, rough terrain until we arrived at the Catholic mission in Lodja, a low cinder-block building with all the frills of a Motel 6, but to us it could have been the Paris Ritz. Hot meals with no concern about dysentery, and hot showers where accumulated dirt ran off each of us like a muddy river. The priest and novices were wonderful people, a reminder of why the human race is worth trying to help.

But first I placed a satellite call to our contacts in Kinshasa, who told us that a French film crew would be flying in the next day to shoot a documentary.

So we were ready the next morning when a thirty-seat twin-propeller plane touched down. Unfortunately, dozens of panicked villagers trying to flee the rebels and the army had also shown up hoping to get aboard. This led to a mad scramble around the airplane with security guards firing into the air to get everyone to back off.

A few minutes later our group of scientists, guides, and our single, eccentric mammologist were buckled in and ready for takeoff. But no sooner were we airborne than the skies let loose a horrendous thunderstorm with pounding rain and vicious turbulence that had us bouncing around like the passengers in *Airplane!* Then the liquid nitrogen tank we had with us in the cabin broke loose and started smashing into things.

The guy to my left was praying. I looked over and saw that the French physician sitting next to me was writing a farewell note to his family. Which got me thinking. If today was my last day, was I ready to die?

W hen I went to medical school, becoming a geek version of Indiana Jones was not what I had in mind. I'd been inspired to study medicine by my father. He'd been a fourteen-year-old peasant farmer with an elementary school education who made the multiweek trek from a remote village in Kashmir to Bombay at the beginning of the Second World War, lied about being nineteen, and joined a Scandinavian freighter as a wiper in the engine room.

My scientific interests, immunology and infectious disease, had been spurred by childhood readings of how Louis Pasteur refuted the theory of spontaneous generation. But after my residency in pediatrics and internal medicine, I was selected for a two-year fellowship to work as a disease detective at the Centers for Disease Control and Prevention (CDC) in Atlanta, or what I lovingly refer to as *CSI:Atlanta*. I wound up staying for almost twenty-five years, leaving in 2014 to become dean of the College of Public Health at the University of Nebraska Medical Center.

My job during those years took me from jungle outposts, to Chilean villages reachable only on horseback, to crowded Asian cities locked down under quarantine, to the abattoirs of Persian Gulf sultanates where migrant workers slaughtered goats and sheep under appalling conditions. My colleagues and I worked to stop the spread of Ebola, SARS (severe acute respiratory syndrome), MERS (Middle East respiratory syndrome), and lots of other scary diseases. I was also directly involved in trying to contain the spread of anthrax after the 2001 bioterrorism attack in Washington, and in rebuilding the public health infrastructure in New Orleans after the devastation of Hurricane Katrina.

I hope these tales of my adventures in public health will be entertaining in their own right. But I tell them to dramatize and particularize the disconnect between the outbreaks of hysteria that come with huge headlines, only to be forgotten within weeks, and the very real, long-term structural dangers that should, yes, genuinely scare the pants off us, but more importantly, should lead to long-term structural change in how we address global public health.

Just as we know about (but so far have done precious little to address) huge problems with our physical infrastructure—crumbling rail lines, leaking combined sewers, bridges that are on life support—we have maintained a short-sighted and fickle approach to emerging infections and possible pandemics that have us frothed up one moment, oblivious the next. I started this manuscript just as the Ebola outbreak in West Africa began to make headlines. As the book goes to press, Ebola is a distant memory, and the world's attention has shifted to Zika. Our failure to more deeply understand and more consistently attend to the bigger issues leaves us, as they say along the fault lines in California, just waiting for the big one.

———

The Centers for Disease Control and Prevention is the successor to a wartime federal agency called Malaria Control in War Areas, which was set up in 1942 to protect stateside training bases from malaria during World War II, many of which were in the South, which has been known to harbor a few mosquitoes. Just after the war, in 1946, it became the Communicable Disease Center (CDC), but was still focused on malaria and typhus. It had roughly four hundred employees, most of whom were engineers and entomologists. The following year, the center paid a token $10 to Emory University for fifteen acres of land on Clifton Road in Atlanta, where the greatly expanded CDC is still headquartered today.

The program where I got my start, the Epidemic Intelligence Service (EIS), was established in 1951 by Dr. Alex Langmuir to address biological warfare concerns that arose during the conflict in Korea. Its mission was to train epidemiologists on extant public health problems while they kept a watch for foreign germs. Since that time, the EIS has been a two-year postgraduate training program in epidemiology, with a focus on fieldwork. It's like a traditional medical residency program in that much of the education occurs through hands-on assignments and mentoring.

Rather than making rounds in hospitals, though, EIS officers evaluate public health surveillance systems; design, conduct, and interpret epidemiological analysis; and conduct field investigations of potentially serious public health problems in the United States and around the world. EIS officers have worked on issues as varied as polio, lead poisoning, cancer clusters, smallpox, Legionnaires' disease, toxic shock syndrome, birth defects, HIV/AIDS, tobacco, West Nile virus, E. coli contaminated water, natural disasters, and fungal meningitis. But my first assignment was not nearly so impressive.

I was a twenty-six-year-old rookie (I looked about twelve despite the mustache I'd grown in the hope of adding a few years) when I conducted my first Epi-Aid, an investigation of patients with chronic fatigue syndrome that eventually proved that a controversial study linking the illness to a retrovirus infection (like HIV that causes AIDS) was due to sloppy lab work.

This was the kind of thing that only a serious geek could get excited about. But immediately afterward I was summoned to my first real challenge in the field—I was shipped off to Hawaii to investigate an outbreak of diarrhea on a cruise ship.

Okay, so maybe this was still not the kind of thing that was going to win me a Nobel (either the Peace Prize or the award in medicine and physiology), but at least it was going to get me out of the office.

Now, very few cruise ships are registered in the United States, but this one sailed only the territorial waters of the Hawaiian Islands, so it flew the US flag, which meant that its owner, along with the state health department, were entitled to call up CDC and ask us to investigate. The only problem was that the viral diarrhea people at CDC didn't have an EIS officer available so, for whatever reason, they asked me to go and respond, even though I knew nothing about the subject. However, I was reminded of the suitcase lore of EIS officers: the farther you to travel to an outbreak, the bigger expert you seem.

For most of the ten hours I spent flying west I was on the phone with my supervisor, trying to get up to speed on Norwalk virus (common gastroenteritis, or "stomach flu"), which, judging from the history, seemed to be the cause of the outbreak, which meant in turn getting up to speed on projectile vomiting and the fine points of evaluating the stool quality of diarrhea. This was in the early 1990s, when the only way to make a call was from what amounted to a pay phone in the back of the plane. I tend to be an animated phone talker, and I'm pretty sure I was loud enough to be heard in the cockpit.

When the plane landed in Honolulu, the captain said, "Would everybody please stay seated. We need to allow Dr. Ali Khan to get off the plane first."

I looked around and all the passengers were staring at me, and I thought, Gee, how do they know I'm the doctor flying in on an emergency case?

Then it occurred to me that I was the jerk who'd ruined everybody's vacation by talking diarrhea all the way across the Pacific.

A bunch of tourists with the runs may sound like something out of a Judd Apatow gross-out comedy, but it was no laughing matter to those who got sick, or to the owner of the cruise line, who might lose his business.

The outbreak had occurred at sea, so when the ship returned to port the crew threw out every scrap of food on board and scrubbed down everything until the local health department gave them the okay. Then the ship took on new passengers and set sail again. But within two days (the incubation period for Norwalk virus) this entirely new set of passengers began getting sick. Which is when the crew and the health department called for help. The crew headed back into port, then waited at anchor for their consulting epidemiologist to fly in and be motored out to them in a small boat.

Despite my complete ignorance, I planned to immediately launch into a series of fourteen-hour days inspecting the ship and developing a questionnaire.

And then matters took a turn for the worse.

I am prone to seasickness, and even with the gentle rocking of the ship at anchor I became violently ill. But I was from the federal government, and I was there to help, so I spent the first few hours lying on a banquette, surrounded by all the senior staff, moaning out directives, mumbling, turning green, and rushing to the bathroom, until the ship's nurse yanked down my pants in front of all these people and gave me a shot of Compazine.

With my dignity compromised but my health improved, I collected the questionnaires and tabulated the data, which created a detailed picture of daily behavior that thoroughly invaded everyone's privacy: who ate what, how much and how often; who consorted with whom; which bathrooms they used; how much each passenger drank; and on and on.

Fortunately, a bit of statistical analysis yielded one correlation of particular interest. It was the linkage between the number of cups of ice consumed and the likelihood of getting sick.

Bingo.

The ship's ice was kept in a big open bin, then scooped up and sent to the dining room. Most likely the "index patient," the first one to come down with gastrointestinal distress, had been an infected member (or members) of the kitchen crew who went for the ice. But dirty hands came in contact not just with the scoop but with the ice itself, and the virus was transferred and preserved. And while the ship was thoroughly cleaned after the first outbreak and passengers changed, the crew members stayed onboard to infect the ice again.

As is so often the case in matters of public health, once you've isolated the problem, the solution comes down to better hand washing, and to a rather simple intervention. I got them to change over to one of those machines where the ice drops down into a bucket from a dispenser. Then they were good to go, and I was free to return to the major land mass of the US mainland, which did not wobble.

But it's funny how much our view of a disease depends on context. Among generally healthy, well-fed Westerners who can afford vacations, diarrhea may be inconvenient, and it may even be embarrassing, but generally it's no big deal. Among small children in third-world countries, however, diarrhea accounts for some 800,000 deaths each year—more than AIDS and malaria and measles combined.

It's also amazing how often something as mundane as an ice scoop can make all the difference.

In 1854, a London physician named John Snow (not the one from *Game of Thrones*) set out to investigate an outbreak of cholera in Soho. In Snow's day, the overriding explanation for infectious disease was the miasma theory, in which the source of illness was thought to be "bad air."

But by studying the distribution of disease and putting the cases on a dot map, Snow was able to track down the source to a water pump on what was then called Broad Street. Snow's chemical and microscopic examination of the water could not prove that it was the culprit, but he was able to persuade the local council to remove the pump handle and thus shut off this particular water source. His work, coupled with that of others, laid the foundation for one of the mainstays of modern medicine: "germ theory." And although he did not get the recognition he deserved at the time, Snow's study became the founding event of the modern science of epidemiology.

OUT OF SEASON

At first blush, my next assignment might seem equally as small potatoes as the outbreak of diarrhea in Hawaii. This was June 1992, when a cluster of influenza B appeared in Fairbanks, Alaska, and the state asked CDC for help.

Influenza rarely makes the list of diseases that keep ordinary citizens awake at night. In the mind of the average person, the flu fits in more easily with everyday ailments like the common cold. But while the 2014–15 Ebola epidemic, which killed 11,000 people, became a global news event, influenza causes between 250,000 and 500,000 deaths each year, every year, worldwide. The infamous influenza pandemic of 1918 sickened 20 to 40 percent of the global population and caused anywhere from 50 to 100 million deaths, including 675,000 in the United States alone. Sad to say, there is nothing to prevent a pandemic on that scale, and that deadly, from happening again. Which is why influenza is taken very seriously, and monitored very closely, by disease detectives like me.

In 1918, the victims were often young, healthy adults in the prime of life. That's why people who don't know much about history will often know about the flu that began to sweep across the continents just as the mass slaughter of World War I died down. It's the perfect plot device to kill off romantic rivals in period dramas like *Downton Abbey*. Anytime there's a pretty young thing who stands in the way of true love for the hero and heroine, you can be sure that the pretty young thing is going to be toast, and you can bet she's going to be toasted by the Spanish flu.

The US population in 1918 was 103 million people, so if a pandemic on the same scale occurred today with our current population—three times larger—we'd be looking at close to 2 million dead people in the United States alone. Which is, once again, why we epidemiologists worry about influenza, and why we're very attentive anytime it reappears with novel characteristics.

What set off the alarm bells in Fairbanks was the fact that a cluster of cases appeared in the summer, despite the fact that flu is usually a winter phenomenon in temperate countries. It's not that the bug isn't around all year. It's just that in summer people spend more time outdoors, and because they're not packed together in closed spaces, they don't infect one another as easily. There are cases, but they usually travel below the radar.

But in Alaska, in 1992, the state public health laboratory isolated the virus from throat swab specimens obtained from nine patients in the period from June 5 to July 5. The antigenic and molecular characteristics were unknown, so we thought it would be a good idea to find out more about what was going on.

Epidemiologists often refer to "epidemics," "clusters," and "outbreaks," but which term we use is more a function of art, and of the amount of attention we want to stir up, rather than some supertechnical line of distinction. Technically, a pandemic is an epidemic that spreads worldwide or occurs over a large geographical area, crossing international boundaries, and usually affecting a large number of people. Flu pandemics are usually caused by influenza A. This summer flu in Alaska was influenza B, a kissing cousin, which made the worst-case scenario unlikely, but we were still curious. And concerned. Influenza B has a habit of sweeping through nursing homes with a scythe. And when evolution rolls the genetic dice, there always can be unpleasant surprises.

Unlike Ebola, the influenza virus can travel very efficiently via large airborne droplets when infected persons sneeze, cough, and talk. So, actually, if you were out to make a horror movie about a truly scary pathogen, it wouldn't feature an exotic foreign star like Ebola, which generally requires direct contact with blood, saliva, semen, or other bodily fluids. Moreover, with Ebola, you're infectious mostly toward the end of your illness, when you're probably not in the mood to go around and do much socializing anyway. With flu, you can be infectious even before you show any signs of illness.

Yes, the lead villain in the end-of-the-world pandemic thriller would be everyday influenza, which, with its proven capacity to kill millions, can be spread by a sneeze or a handshake.

And while Ebola is scary, its terrifying reputation is out of proportion to its actual risk, in part because of the way it's been sensationalized in the media, dating back to the urtext of Ebola narratives, Richard Preston's *The Hot Zone*. There's no doubt that Ebola is a nasty disease, but influenza is not exactly your friend.

The 1918 influenza likely killed by creating a "cytokine storm" in the bloodstream and lungs, cytokines being small proteins involved in signaling, as in the immune response. When the virus infects the lung, it overstimulates the immune system, which leads to an influx of T-cells and macrophages, cells that exist to ward off invaders. But the presence of those cells activates even more of an immune response, which stimulates the production of even more cytokines. And when you have too much of a good thing too quickly, a deadly feedback loop can start to roll, and the accumulation and concentration of immune cells—free radicals, coagulation factors, tumor necrosis factor-alpha, interleukin-1, interleukin-6, interleukin-10, and interleukin-1 receptor antagonists—can damage the tissues. When this happens in the lungs, the accumulation of immune cells can block off the airways. In other words, you drown in your own fluids.

The danger from flu is that it can undergo a dramatic genetic shift so that the population has no immunity to its new structure. But the flu virus also continually drifts or mutates, which means that each year we have to update the flu vaccine we plan to manufacture and distribute. To prepare for the fall onslaught, we have to make a final decision about what is in the upcoming season's vaccine about six months ahead of time. Given that the manufacture of the vaccine relies on what is, essentially, 1940s technology—the virus is grown in eggs, inside the shell—the process is always time consuming and imperfect. So when there's an early flu outbreak, the concern is how much this new preview strain matches the vaccine that's already in the pipeline. Which means that even seemingly arcane or tangential information can be useful.

I left Atlanta at nine thirty on the morning of July 12 and arrived in Fairbanks at four thirty in the afternoon, local time. I'd never been to Alaska, and this being summer, there was bright sunshine with people out roller skating and playing in the park—it was quite lovely. But summer also meant that it was high tourist season, and the only accommodation I could find was what turned out to be a rattrap rooming house straight out of a Raymond Chandler novel. And the constant daylight meant there was no way I was going to get any sleep.

I drove my rental car to a rundown area of town that looked like Detroit on a bad day and parked at the three-story rooming house. The guy at the desk was covered in tattoos, and the only telephone and television were in the lobby. My room was on the first floor, and despite the open window and the fan, it smelled distinctly of vomit. The window being open, of course, meant that anybody could climb right in, and that included battalions of mosquitoes.

My job was to discover as much as I could about the strain of flu that had hit Fairbanks and to figure out if it was spreading. I was also supposed to send back specimens of the virus to Atlanta so researchers could compare it to known strains, to help refine the new vaccine then being prepared. Also, CDC had been running a viral surveillance system for the past five years, enrolling primary-care doctors all over the country to track cases of flu, then submit samples from their patients to a central facility. I had been asked to review how the system had been working in Alaska.

And, oh yes, I also needed to take back a photograph of a moose. I can't remember who asked for it, but somebody at the office wanted to see what a moose looked like up close.

At nine fifteen that first brightly lit morning, I met with the head of the state virology lab, Don Ritter. A Chicago native, Ritter had come to Alaska as an army helicopter crew chief, mapping the state's topography. He had developed an interest in wildlife that led to an interest in pathogens.

Sitting in his office, I listened as he filled me in on the ins and outs of the viral surveillance program: where the samples came from and how they made their way through the system. He also mentioned that they did get unusual viruses in Alaska, in part because, as Sarah Palin could tell you, they have signif-icant traffic with Russia.

If this were a spy novel, that comment would be the tagline to end the scene, after which your hero would go on to dis-cover deadly pathogens wafting over the Bering Strait in a de-vious scheme of biological warfare. But even without getting carried away into John le Carré territory, I made a note. Dis-ease detectives have to consider all the possibilities. Especially when they make you feel like James Bond.

My next stop was the office of Dr. Alan Macfarlane, a very meticulous pediatrician; so meticulous, in fact, that he was the first and only person in my career as a public health official to ask to see my identification. Maybe some people would have said he was too thorough, because he had taken a swab of any-body who came to his practice with so much as a runny nose, then sent the samples off to be cultured. It was because of this abundance of caution that he'd been the one to detect the outbreak's first cases, all children under nine, most of whom were his patients. He'd also put a complete description on file for each child that went something like this:

Case number one. Seven and a half years old, fever to 104. Stomachache for two days, occasionally dry cough, headaches, myalgias, no sore throat, red, puffy eyes, previous medical history of recurrent otitis and recurrent otitis media and sinusitis. Had taken some Tylenol. Did not remember being exposed to anybody with influenza. Was diagnosed with pharyngitis and fevers.

After he was satisfied that I was who I said I was—an epidemiologist from CDC, also a member of the US Public Health Service—Dr. Macfarlane gave me the addresses of the patients' families, as well as his permission to interview them. À la John Snow, I then marked all the addresses on the local map and started thinking about logistics.

My immediate objective was to find out more about each of the children and how their paths might have crossed. Did some of them share day care? Did they attend the same schools? How many siblings did each have, and had any of them been to a doctor?

Children with influenza B are prone to Reye's syndrome, which can cause swelling of the liver and brain, so this was also a good time to see whether or not the families knew that they shouldn't be giving their kids aspirin, which can trigger the condition.

But getting to the bottom of an outbreak is not just about medicine or virology. It's about the people and the community and the kind of social interactions taking place.

So this is when I went into gumshoe mode, following the same incredibly boring, door-to-door routine that is the daily bread of detectives, whether disease or homicide. I contacted day-care centers, hospitals, emergency rooms, HMOs (health maintenance organizations), and nursing homes, asking if they'd noticed increased signs of influenza-like illness. I also checked with tour groups, hotel doctors, and even prisons. Basically, I had to track down every damn doctor in this part of Alaska to try to find out what they knew. How many patients had they seen with bronchitis, pneumonia, pharyngitis, otitis, and so on, and where was it coming from?

But the big question underlying all my hundreds of small questions remained. Am I seeing something new? And then following from that: Is it something to worry about?

As to the cause for worry, here's the thing about influenza:

Viruses exist on the border of the living and the nonliving, and there's still some debate about which side they're on. (I firmly believe they are alive and even collectively intelligent.) Like a living thing, a virus has the ability to replicate, but that's about it. Unlike mainstream life forms, it doesn't produce all the proteins it needs to make copies of itself. That's why it invades and hijacks other cells—often yours or mine— subverting the cytoplasmic material into making more viral proteins, rather than more of whatever cellular material would have been produced ordinarily.

Migratory waterfowl serve as the natural reservoir of the influenza A virus, but it also inhabits horses, dogs, pigs, poultry, and humans, and each influenza virus, no matter which type, is made up of eight genomic segments that are very promiscuous, always mixing and matching. The other type circulating in humans is Influenza B, but it is only found in humans and seals, which limits its pandemic properties. Either way, the strain of influenza A virus that makes you sick can consist of multiple segments from multiple sources, and the virus doesn't care if its eight genetic building blocks come from birds, humans, pigs, or a little of each. In that respect, influenza is like a lazy warehouse worker at Amazon or Zappos who just grabs whatever's handy and sticks it in the box. The end result is often like a shipment of socks (for an octopus, perhaps), none of which are necessarily mates. As long as there are eight of them, however, the system still works, and the virus can pump out more virus. And if you have the right mismatch, you can have the next deadly mix for a new pandemic virus.

Influenza also wears a viral overcoat made of two different proteins: hemagglutinin and neuraminidase that are used to identify the different viruses. We give the resultant strains names that combine the letters "N" (for neuraminidase) and "H" (for hemagglutinin) with numbers that refer to the order in which the particular H or N within the strain was discovered. The result is monikers like H1N1 or H5N1. The hemagglutinin enables the virus to latch on to the cell and penetrate the surface; the neuraminidase punches an escape hole in the cell wall when it's time to get back out. Every year this overcoat changes a little, in what's called "antigenic drift."

This jumbling and tumbling produces the standard amount of novelty we see each year in the virus. Because the surface hemagglutinin, but also the components, triggers its own quite specific immune response in the host (you or me: the flu victim), we're in better shape to the extent that the components from last year show up again this year. The repeat of older elements means that our bodies will have developed antibodies to fight those elements. We call this "cross protection." But even these minor changes add up, so we are no longer protected, which is why we get reinfected with the same basic strain and why we need to get vaccinated each year. With estimates of 3,000 to 49,000 deaths from influenza in the United States each year, getting vaccinated is good sense.

And what worries epidemiologists is not so much antigenic drift as what's called "antigenic shift," which is the complete shedding of the overcoat of influenza A viruses with a new hemagglutinin (HA) or hemagglutinin and neuraminidase (HA/N) combination. A wholesale transformation that carries with it the risk that the target population (you and I) will have no immunity whatsoever, because everything coming at us will be brand new. This total makeover happens once every couple of decades. It's what happened in 1918, and it's a big part of why 50 to 100 million people died. Invariably these new human viruses have an avian origin, but it can also be pigs, as we saw with the 2009 H1N1p ("p" for pandemic) outbreak.

A primary focus of all the various influenza disease-monitoring systems is to identify any such brand-new influenza viruses that may be infecting humans or causing epizootics in animals, assessing whether they pose a threat for a human pandemic, and getting a head start on producing a vaccine. The proclivity of flu viruses to swap genetic material especially if a pig is infected with more than one virus, and for the origin in animals of pandemic viruses, explains the laser-like focus on bird and pig influenza outbreaks, and the need to keep people from becoming infected with these viruses.

Humans are a natural host for influenza, so it's not as if the virus just dies off completely when spring comes and is then reborn the next fall and winter. Flu is always being transmitted from person to person, year round, year after year.

I stayed in Fairbanks for a total of two weeks, but I left my film noir flophouse after only a couple of days. Unfortunately, the next place I stayed was even worse, a really creepy bed and breakfast run by a survivalist couple whose home-schooled children never left the house. As I recall, these people were not terribly thrilled at the idea of having a federal agent present in Alaska, let alone in their own kitchen. And I was a Pakistani American to boot. Back in the early 1990s, people weren't as quick to suspect that someone who looked like me was a terrorist. (That would come later.) But I think my survivalist hosts were pretty sure I wasn't a Christian, and they kept an eye on me just in case I was up to something fishy.

My detective work in Alaska was ultimately reassuring rather than alarming. There was no epidemic; there were no headlines, no radical shift in the makeup of the virus. It may have been simply that with a finer filter, in this case Dr.

Macfarlane, we caught more cases. The vaccine that was in the works for that year was a strain called influenza B Panama, and our Alaska cases were right in that groove. And the minute I got a break, Don Ritter took me out into the woods and I took a picture of a moose, animals which, in case you're interested, are huge.

But the sad truth is that the influenza vaccines we produce each year are never very good, especially among the elderly, who are at the highest risk of complications or death. We even have a special high-dose vaccine for this group. Our vaccines are better than nothing, but their narrow range of effectiveness demands such a high degree of predictive ability on the part of public health officials that we always run the risk of catastrophic failure. What we need in order to lower the stakes is a universal flu vaccine that will protect against all strains based on a different mechanism of action, or by targeting more of the conserved past of the virus.

Setting aside cytokine storms, when flu is fatal, it's usually because it has led to pneumonia. Since 1918, we've developed the ability to treat pneumonia with antibiotics, once so precious that we saved the urine of those receiving penicillin in order to crystallize it back out.

Still, it's always better not to get sick, which is why vaccines were developed.

But as I mentioned earlier, these preventive measures are still primitive, involving a highly imperfect process of picking just the right strain to replicate, then growing it in tens of thousands of eggs, and more recently in cell cultures.

The need to track viruses in order to anticipate what's coming down the pike is why we try to gather all the information we can, including long-shot investigations like the one I conducted in Alaska. The more data we have, the less we have to rely on guesswork. But it remains a high-risk proposition, because while you don't put all your eggs in one basket, you do put 90 percent. And we see the consequences of trying to guess the next year's predominant influenza strain months in advance in years when we have a mismatch between the vaccine strain and the circulating flu virus. The same mistake can be made when predicting the next pandemic virus.

In 1976, a new swine flu virus was detected out of the blue in a single death and thirteen ill soldiers in Fort Dix, New Jersey. This virus was similar to the dreaded 1918 influenza virus and was feared to be the harbinger of the next global pandemic. However, the virus never persisted, but the ensuing national vaccination campaign led to about five hundred cases of a severe paralyzing neurologic illness and twenty-five deaths from Guillian-Barré syndrome—the same illness associated with Zika virus. The incident is remembered as the swine flu fiasco, and the CDC director was fired for his abundance of caution. This degree of vaccine side-effect has not been reported with other flu vaccines, and had there been an influenza pandemic along the lines of 1918's, it would have been an acceptable outcome compared to the number of deaths that might have otherwise ensued. It's a stark reminder that public health actions have major import, and it underscores the importance of correctly determining which of the many circulating zoonotic or animal flu viruses poses the risk of a global pandemic.

———

In 1918, the flu that killed 50 to 100 million people was a strain first called H1N1. Known variously as *la gripe, la gripe española*, or *la pesadilla*, it was mostly called the Spanish flu, but only because Spain was not involved in the war, which meant that it was the only European country in which the press was open about the outbreak that had been killing thousands of soldiers at the front. All the combatant nations suppressed the news to protect morale.

At some point, H1N1 made the jump from animal host to human, but at any given time multiple viruses might be invading your cells and competing to assemble the eight pieces of protein they need to create a new model of themselves. One will be better at this replication, or maybe better at getting in there in the first place, or maybe it will trigger less of an immune response. The one that does the best job of doing what viruses do will be the one to prevail against the others and make the charts at CDC and the World Health Organization.

The H1N1 from 1918 held out in the competition for forty years, replicating in humans and sometimes in pigs. But because we develop partial immunity each time a virus passes through, it became less of a threat over time, and we could think of it more like the common cold.

Then, in 1957, there was a complete shift to H2N2 prompting what became known as the Asian pandemic. While it affected mostly young children and pregnant women, it killed one to 2 *million* people, including 69,000 in the United States.

H2N2 remained dominant in the flu world until 1968, when H3N2 came along under the alias of "Hong Kong flu," causing between 1 and 4 million deaths, mostly among the elderly. Absent a completely new viral overcoat, that's the common pattern: the flu kills babies and weakened senior citizens, those who are asthmatic or who have chronic heart disease.

Then, in 1977, the old H1N1 resurfaced, probably through some sort of medical misadventure—meaning an accident in a lab, or a misguided live vaccination campaign gone astray—and it started infecting people again. Fortunately, after sixty years of cohabitation, we'd developed pretty strong immunity to it, so it was not a major pandemic.

———

Back in 1918, when this modern progression of influenza began, all we knew about viruses was by inference. We could tell that something other than bacteria caused certain infectious diseases but that was about it. In 1892, a Russian named Dmitry Ivanovsky had poured an extract of a diseased tobacco plant through a ceramic filter fine enough to remove all bacteria, and yet the extract remained infectious. Ivanovsky thought the infectious agent might be a "toxin" caused by the bacteria. Subsequent work by others on foot and mouth disease, and on yellow fever, gave rise to descriptions like "soluble living germ" for this mysterious infectious agent. It wasn't until improvements in optics led to better microscopes in the 1930s that true virology got under way. In 1931, the first vaccines were cultured using fertilized chicken eggs.

In the West, the vaccines given therapeutically have relied on viruses that have been killed, leaving only the residue of proteins to trigger the immune response.

In Soviet Russia, however, virologists have followed a completely different and largely isolated course: administering viruses that were alive but "attenuated," meaning weakened. Aside from perhaps giving more of an immunologic boost, this technique appeared advantageous in that the patient could simply inhale a tiny whiff of the vaccine rather than have an injection. Not only might this be less problematic in terms of skin reactions, but it might also be vastly cheaper for massive immunization programs, especially in developing countries.

Virologists and public health officials in the West had been wondering for quite a while if the Soviet approach made more sense. In the early 1990s, with the collapse of the USSR, we finally had a chance to compare notes, and I was the one who went over to make the comparison.

In the early nineties, CDC and Baylor College of Medicine began collaborating with the Research Institute of Influenza, St. Petersburg, and the Tarasievich State Institute for Control of Biological Products in Moscow to conduct a blind placebo-controlled study that compared the effectiveness of US inactivated split-virus and Russian live, attenuated, cold-adapted vaccines. Their test subjects were 555 schoolchildren in Vologda, Russia.

In 1992, I flew to St. Petersburg to meet with our Russian colleagues, and I was struck by how poor the country was, and how disoriented, still reeling from yet another cultural and political upheaval. Having spent seventy years in relative isolation, Russia was to science what Cuba is to 1950s American cars—a kind of living museum. And yet, the men and women in these crumbling and drafty laboratories in pre-Soviet buildings were doing good science. I had been instructed to bring along panty hose, ballpoint pens, and calculators as gifts, and as a way of greasing certain wheels. I'd also been told that sometimes getting anything to eat could be problematic.

Vologda is just south of St. Petersburg, but just east of Moscow, and several of us took the twelve-hour train ride, like characters out of *Dr. Zhivago,* traveling all night through forests and swamps, munching on whatever we'd brought along in paper bags.

Once we got to Vologda, we visited the schools where the studies were being carried out. When all was said and done, our technique of using killed virus led to local reactions (primarily redness at the injection site) in 27 percent of the kids. Kids in the attenuated vaccine group had coryza (inflammation around the nose) only 12 percent of the time and sore throat 8 percent of the time, so in terms of avoiding complications, score one for the Russians.

Four weeks after the vaccination, the children who'd receive our killed vaccine showed roughly 20 percent more antibodies. But on the acid test of preventing school absenteeism due to acute respiratory illness during flu season, the outcome was 56 percent for killed vaccine and 47 percent for attenuated vaccine, suggesting that the two approaches are roughly equivalent.

Ten years later, in January 2003, a live influenza vaccine was introduced in the United States. I was acting as the infectious diseases associate global director, deploying epidemiologists to investigate a marked expansion of influenza A H5N1 among birds in Eurasia and Africa with cases of severe human infection. The virus had reemerged for the first time since the deadly poultry outbreaks in Hong Kong in 1997. This is a highly pathogenic, fast-mutating strain of bird flu that continues to be found in multiple species, as well as in humans. It would go on to kill 60 percent of the 638 people infected. There is clear evidence for a handful of cases of secondary but limited human-to-human transmission, but if this had gone viral, literally and figuratively, it would have been a horrific pandemic. This one was scary given that 2.5 percent of people infected with the 1918–19 influenza pandemic died.

The pattern of bird migration back and forth to Africa put Europe squarely in the crosshairs, and part of my job was to assess how well the European Union countries were prepared in terms of surveillance and disease detection and laboratory systems. Tens of millions of birds died of influenza A (H5N1), and hundreds of millions were slaughtered and disposed of to limit the spread in Southeast Asia, Russia and Central Asia, the Caucasus, the Balkans, the Middle East, West Africa, and throughout Europe.

One thing about tracking disease outbreaks is that it teaches you humility. In the years after the influenza A (H5N1) outbreak began, we figured another outbreak was only a matter of time, and we expected it would be bird flu and that it would start in Asia, as it often had in the past.

So we were keeping an eye on the Eastern Hemisphere, waiting for bird flu, when a different strain came from the opposite direction—Mexico—and clobbered us with a variant of influenza A (H1N1)p that had originated in pigs. The strain contained genes from four different viruses: North American swine influenza, North American avian influenza, human influenza, and swine influenza viruses typically found in Europe and Asia.

This was in 2009, and it spread up to San Diego and Texas and then across the United States, where it led to seventeen thousand deaths. In Mexico, the disease was much deadlier and led to a five-day shutdown of the whole country to contain the outbreak. We had been dreading one thing and we got another, and it caught us completely by surprise.

This strain is still out there, by the way. In 2014, there were more than thirty thousand cases in India, with more than two thousand deaths. There were also deaths in California and Texas, and in Canada.

It is possible that this strain of swine flu did indeed originate in Asia; we don't know. Either way, it drove home the point that no country can afford to isolate its public health system. It has to be part of a global public health infrastructure. You can't get away with saying, "We're the richest country in the world. We have good doctors and a solid health care surveillance system. We're safe." It just doesn't work that way.

2

SIN NOMBRE

Even a small mouse has anger.

—Chukchi proverb

In May of 1993, nineteen-year-old Merrill Bahe was in a car with family, heading into Gallup, New Mexico, when he suddenly had trouble breathing. His family stopped at a convenience store to start CPR and call for help, and an ambulance came and took him to the Gallup Indian Medical Center. By the time he got there, his lungs were so full of fluid that the doctors there were unable to revive him. And yet, other than a fever and some mild flu-like symptoms, Merrill had been an otherwise healthy young man, a track star on the Navajo reservation.

This kind of unexplained, sudden death of a seemingly healthy young adult is dramatic enough, but the reason Merrill had been going into town was to attend the funeral of his fiancée, twenty-one-year-old Florena Woody. She had died under similar conditions five days earlier at the nearby Crownpoint Medical Center.

George Tempest, an officer in the US Public Health Service, as well as chief of medicine at the Indian Medical Center, quickly got on the phone with other doctors who tended to the Navajo Nation. He discovered that within the Four Corners region, where the boundaries of New Mexico, Arizona, Colorado, and Utah intersect, five people had died under similar circumstances during the previous six months.

In keeping with a law that required all unexplained deaths to be reported to a central registry, the local investigator for the New Mexico Office of the Medical Investigator was also alerted. For his own part, this investigator had been perplexed by a similar case of a young thirty-year-old Navajo woman who arrived at the same emergency room complaining of flu-like symptoms and sudden, severe shortness of breath, followed by rapid death soon after arrival. At autopsy, her lungs were almost twice the normal weight for a woman her age. During the postmortem, the medical examiner ladled out liters of fluid.

Public health officials thought this might be the plague, which is endemic to the region, but tests ruled it out. This was something distinctly new and different, yet within a short time a dozen more people had contracted the mysterious illness, most of them young Navajos in New Mexico. News outlets began reporting on the unexplained deaths, often using the pejorative term "Navajo flu."

That spring, I was completing my second year of the Epidemic Intelligence Service program. As advertised, it had been an amazing experience that allowed me to see a greater variety of outbreaks than most doctors see in a lifetime, ranging from vertigo linked to a gut virus in Thermopolis, Wyoming, to viral meningitis (a brain inflammation) in wealthy parents of young children in a day care in California, to measles on a college campus in New Jersey. My wife had just given birth to triplets, and I had to make critical decisions about my next job. Plan A was to take an infectious disease fellowship, but that prospect dimmed as I thought about supporting a family as a clinical trainee. But more than that, I had fallen in love with public health, the people I worked with, and the work that we did.

There was a moratorium on hiring people at CDC, but when I approached my division director, Dr. Brian Mahy, he said, "Don't worry about it. We'll get you a job."

I said, "Well that's very kind of you, but there's this hiring freeze."

He said, "Don't worry about it. That's my problem."

I never asked another question and took it on blind trust. On July 1, when my stint at the EIS ended, I simply showed up for work with CDC's Special Pathogens Branch.

One of the reasons there was space for me in Special Pathogens was this strange outbreak that seemed to be expanding across the 27,000-square-mile region that's home to the Hopi, Ute, Zuni, and Navajo Nation reservations. Adding to the mystery, reports of other suspected cases were coming in from across the United States.

The first clue to solving the puzzle came when Tom Ksiazek, who had been recruited from the US Army Medical Research Institute of Infectious Diseases to the Special Pathogens Branch, ran the patient samples against a battery of infectious agents. He found an unexpected immune response against certain Old World viruses known to be transmitted by rats.

These so-called hantaviruses, named for the Hantaan River in South Korea, were first identified during the Korean War, when American soldiers were getting infected with something called Korean hemorrhagic fever. A collective term for infections from any of a number of related viruses in Eurasia and Africa, this illness was commonly known as hemorrhagic fever with renal syndrome (HFRS), but the illness we were seeing in the Four Corners area did not involve the kidneys.

While one of the infected rodent reservoirs or natural host (and vector for transmission), the common rat, had spread worldwide via shipping lanes, it rarely if ever caused disease. Even so, our lab people began using genetic methods to probe the blood of various rodents throughout the New World.

More definitive lab evidence trickled in from genetic studies of this new virus's genetic material in the blood of infected persons, and this allowed CDC to develop more sophisticated diagnostic tests. It turned out that what we were seeing was a rare New World virus, closely related to the Old World hanta-viruses, that had never been associated with disease.

So forty years after its first appearance in Korea, this appeared to be a pulmonary version, hantavirus pulmonary syndrome (HPS). But what was the specific agent? Where did it come from? And what was the rodent host?

We launched multiple lines of investigation, but this was before CDC had established incident management systems. We had no task force structure and no emergency operation center for coordinating large outbreaks, so it was more chaotic than it should have been. Even so, we kept the focus on the patients.

During the Korean War, when our soldiers starting coming down with Korean hemorrhagic fever, researchers identified the antiviral drug ribavirin as a fully effective treatment.

So our first line of action in the Four Corners region was to put together a ribavirin trial in patients to see whether or not this drug was a therapeutic option. That task was entrusted to a team led by Dr. Louisa Chapman.

Our second objective was to more sharply define the clinical illness. That meant going to all the hospitals where these potential cases came from and observing firsthand the clinical spectrum, which is the only way you can know what you're seeing when you see it and thus identify new cases. The next step was to talk to survivors, and to the family members of those who didn't survive, visiting their homes and trying to identify the risks, while also trying to understand the course of the illness.

Our goal in all of this was to keep new cases from happening. Which necessarily involved finding the virus's natural host or reservoir, and determining the risk factors and behaviors of the virus, the rodents, and the infected people that accounted for infection. It also demanded that we create diagnostic tests and figure out the laboratory tools we were going to need to identify the disease.

The parallel phase of our job for the mammologist was to try to figure out where the reservoir of the disease was located. For hantavirus, this required trapping and studying rodents all across the southwestern United States to try to nail down everything we could about the disease vector. (In the case of hantaviruses the terms "reservoir" and "vector" are often used interchangeably because the rodents serve as both: the natural host and the direct source of human infection. In other diseases such as West Nile, the natural reservoirs may be birds, but mosquitoes act as the vector.)

Once we'd assembled all these pieces of information, the task was to link them together to create a final prevention strategy that would work in the specific communities affected.

That was an incredible amount of work in and of itself, but then we also needed to review patients' charts and get details on every individual, right down to their temperature, respiratory rate, and heart rate. What was the history of the current illness? What was the previous history? What was their travel history? What were their hobbies? What were potential exposures? What medications were they on? What about their surgical history? And then all of their lab values: sodium, potassium, chloride, liver function tests, platelets, white count, red cells. And all this updated on a daily basis.

Out of this welter of information you try to put together a picture of the disease so that you can be better at identifying additional cases, and then deduce the effectiveness of various treatments to try to arrive at the best way to manage future cases.

In early June, I joined the response team to try to establish a case definition for the initial ribavirin study in order to determine whom we should treat. This is the difficult work of making those clinical decisions, because you don't have a diagnostic test yet, and often you want to treat sooner than later, so even if you have a diagnostic test, you might not want to wait for the results to come back before you start a regimen for your patients.

Our first condition for possible treatment was that you had to be from the Four Corners region, and that you had to have fever. You could not be immune compromised, and you had to have pulmonary infiltration in both lungs. For comparison, we looked at the cases of hemorrhagic fever with renal syndrome that had occurred in Korea forty years earlier.

Since we had gotten this early signal that it was hantavirus, we thought that even though we had pulmonary involvement, maybe there were renal cases as well that we just hadn't picked up on.

Traditionally, you name a virus after the place where it is first identified. Needless to say, the local residents weren't very happy with calling this deadly microbe "Four Corners virus." Not just because the bad publicity would cause vacationers to drive their RVs elsewhere, but because of the more general stigma. Already, a group of Navajo children visiting the state capital had been discriminated against because they happened to come from the Four Corners area.

So then we suggested "El Muerto virus," after the Canyon del Muerto that was close to the site of capture of the rodent from which the virus was isolated. Unfortunately, this was near the site of a pivotal battle between the Navajo and Kit Carson's US Army. When people understood the history of what had actually happened there, we decided that maybe this wasn't such a good name either. Then there was the internal bickering among the scientists about who was the first to identify the virus, who had the right to name it, and so on. After this experience, there has been a gradual trend toward not naming diseases after places but to be descriptive about the nature of the clinical illness.

In the end, the decision was made to call it *Sin Nombre*, which is Spanish for "no name." You'd never have gotten away with calling it No Name in English, but somehow the Spanish gave it a little flourish, and the name stuck. And nobody caught the irony that a virus that was killing Indians was called No Name for a people who have had no voice.

After setting up case definitions in order to begin treating patients, I began working on a clinical database. I also worked with CDC Drug Service to figure out how to enroll patients, and I worked with the Food and Drug Administration to get this done as quickly as possible.

Setting up a clinical database meant sorting cases into three groups. The first were those residing in the Four Corners area; the second, people residing outside the area who had traveled to the Four Corners in the previous six weeks; and the third group, those who had neither resided in nor traveled to this region. We did not give drugs at this time to the third group but focused on soliciting samples and reevaluating lab results in light of any newly available data on rodents and their distribution in that locality.

As the database grew, we began revising the case definition. To accurately identify cases based on a clinical description to quick-start a drug, you need to figure out exactly who you're looking for, and this often means excluding cases that are not typical. Our case definition excluded people who might have had a hospital-acquired pneumonia, people who had been sick for more than two weeks, and people who were immuno-compromised. This would help us zoom in on the people we should be looking for, the ones who might benefit from ribavirin therapy. This became much simpler as diagnostic tests were distributed by CDC to all the state health departments.

Media attention had prompted clinicians elsewhere to rethink signs and symptoms in light of this new disease. Unlike those of us in the center of the storm, they didn't limit themselves to searching for cases within the Four Corners area.

It's routine for clinicians to identify cases of established diseases. But for novel diseases, you're dependent on the astute clinician who says, "You know what? This patient's symptoms sound like what I just read about in the newspaper."

One such case occurred in Lufkin, Texas, where a patient had died at the end of June with acute respiratory distress.

Records indicated that she had tested positive on our rudimentary test with Seoul virus, one of the Old World hantaviruses. She had an antibody count of 1:1,600, which is high, but a negative immunofluorescent assay, a test that lights up infected cells with your tagged blood if you have antibodies from a current or previous infection.

I flew into Houston at seven in the evening and picked up my rental car, then began the two-hour drive into the Piney Woods area of East Texas.

In Lufkin, a town of about 35,000, built around forestry, oil field equipment, and poultry, I met the state epidemiologist at seven thirty the next morning. I talked to the parents of the victim. I talked to her husband. I talked to the daughter, a nurse at the same hospital where the patient had been treated, and tried to solicit as much of the health history as I could. I needed to know about her habits, hobbies, and especially travel, trying to figure out how she might have gotten infected and by what sort of rodent. She wasn't a gardener. Apparently she was only a so-so housekeeper, but reportedly there had been no mice in the house for over a year. However, there were seeds and squirrels out back, as well as rats.

The next task was to review reams of records, looking for any other potential cases in the nearby area. I looked through the charts of anyone who might have had a similar disease, hoping to locate blood or autopsy samples that might have been preserved, in order to retroactively investigate these patients.

The case in Lufkin seemed like it made sense as soon as we tentatively identified the rodent reservoir for this disease: *Peromyscus maniculatus,* the white-footed deer mouse. This little beast was widely distributed throughout the Southwest—in Texas, Nevada, and California. But soon we started seeing cases as far away as Louisiana and Florida. Which led us to wonder if there were other pathological virus and rodent species.

Eventually, from these cases we found outside the distribution of the white-footed deer mouse, we discovered that there were numerous other rodent species in the same family that had their own hantaviruses.

Having followed the media attention, a doctor in Dade County, Florida, suspected hantavirus as the cause of illness in one of his patients. He sent us a sample, and he turned out to be right. But this wasn't the Sin Nombre virus we'd seen in the Southwest; it was a completely different strain, called Black Creek virus.

Our biggest concern with this Florida case was that the infected individual happened to be staying at a treatment center with thirty other people. So next I flew to Dade County and met with the administrator for District 2, the environmental administrator for the Dade County Public Health Unit, the deputy district administrator for health, and the public information officer. My job in those days involved managing the hantavirus disease-monitoring databases during the weekday, and spending the weekend investigating unusual cases. This work load was typical of the scientists in Special Pathogens— my mentor's wife actually took to visiting him at CDC on weekends—but the intensity took a toll on my family, given that I was leaving my wife alone with six-month-old triplets.

As usual, a big part of my job in the field was to determine the risk of exposure, so I needed to see who else might have gotten sick, while also making sure that investigators were on the lookout for a novel type of rodent. And we quickly found one.

The culprit for Black Creek virus wasn't the usual deer mouse, but a cotton rat. So our task was no longer a question of tracking down and isolating one rodent with one virus. This was a scenario involving multiple rodent species, each with its own, somewhat related hantavirus.

As we delved further, what we discovered was that these North American variations on the disease were not even new.

In 1978, a young man from Preston, Idaho, population 3,170, had died so abruptly and inexplicably that the attending physician contacted CDC. That must have been a slow day in Atlanta, because they sent both a CDC officer and an EIS officer, Dr. Rick Goodman, to investigate. After they completed their work, though, they were none the wiser about what had actually happened.

But then fifteen years later—again, amid the media swirl—the doctor who'd initially called CDC about the Preston case said to himself, You know what, I think this guy had hantavirus. So he contacted us again.

Fortunately, the paraffin blocks from the victim's autopsy had been preserved, and they were transferred to Dr. Sherif Zaki, CDC's chief pathologist, who looked at them under the microscope, applied a serum containing the right type of antibody/immune marker, examined the results, and concluded, yep, this patient died of hantavirus pulmonary syndrome way back during the Carter administration.

I had an opportunity to talk to the individual's dad, mother, brother, and sister, as well as his wife. They all came to Preston to chat with me, and their memories of the event—it was the death of a loved one, after all—were very fresh and vivid.

"Oh yeah, middle of summer. Temperature hitting a hundred and four that day, I remember, and he started getting fatigued and tired, his neck was sore. First he was taken to a chiropractor. He was sleeping all day. He wasn't eating. Cold sweats and fever."

They remembered the doctor who'd initially diagnosed him with flu. But then he didn't get better. He developed a cough and went to a different hospital, where they gave him a shot and some suppositories. He had trouble breathing.

Four days into it, his feet and legs were cold, and his cough was getting worse. He had difficulty breathing, so maybe he had pneumonia. By the time he went back to the county hospital, he looked blue-gray and he was gasping for breath. They found out that his lungs were filled with fluid, and shortly thereafter he died.

It turns out that the victim had been a welder in Logan, Utah, who'd lived in a prefab home with crawl space. He'd hunted elk and deer, but he also spent a lot of time going after mice in and around, and underneath, his house. According to his family, he not only shot them but stomped on them, sometimes even picking them up and throwing them against his truck to smash them.

What this case showed us is that, just because a disease hasn't been identified, doesn't mean it isn't there. It's just that it usually takes a cluster before something shows on the radar, because it takes a reasonable amount of diagnostic evidence to tie cases together and recognize that you have something new.

If we'd never had the hantavirus test from Korea, it would have taken much longer to understand the scope of the outbreak in 1993, which took place not just in the Four Corners region but well beyond it.

The confluence of factors that allowed us to identify it were, first of all, enough typical cases that people were concerned about, and a diagnostic methodology that allowed us to figure out exactly what it was. The moment we identified it, it became very clear that this disease very likely had been in the United States for thousands of years, because these viruses likely had coevolved with a variety of rodent species and had cross-species infections. The likely ancestral rodent host for virus for both the New and Old Worlds was a shrew or a mole.

Zoologists talk about how the search image affects perception. For example, a certain kind of bird will be extraordinarily adept at spotting a certain kind of bug that it feeds on, but we humans won't normally see the bug. However, if we are conditioned to look for the specific pattern of that bug on a specific kind of leaf, we become much better at being able to see it.

Before the outbreak in the Four Corners, there was no search image for hantavirus pulmonary syndrome in the United States. Physicians saw random cases with seemingly random symptoms that didn't add up to any larger pattern. This is not surprising since we have only so many ways to be ill and die. These cases had been occurring for decades, but there was no vocabulary and there was no scientific framework. Until somebody could imagine it, it remained invisible. Sometimes you need a theory before you can find the facts, because otherwise the facts are random signals, needles scattered in a haystack.

Before Four Corners, we also never would have considered that rodents carrying hantaviruses might be distributed throughout the New World. And without that awareness, we never would have observed that hantaviruses can, in fact, be spread from person to person.

In 1996, we sent a wonderful epidemiologist, Rachel Wells, down to Brioche, Argentina—a lovely Patagonian ski resort town from what I've been told—to do an investigation of what appeared to be a new hantavirus. When she came back she said, "Okay, based on my findings I think this may be transmitted person to person, because a lot of these people are closely linked."

My message back to her was, "Based on our extensive experience of forty years, that isn't the case with these viruses. These people may appear to share a link in transmission simply because they all live in proximity to one other, and thus have the same set of rodents in their homes."

We told her to go back and look at her data, which she did, and due to some of the unique relationships among these individuals, she was still convinced that person-to-person transmission was taking place.

Then, out of the blue, in December 1996, we were told that two cases of hantavirus pulmonary syndrome had been diagnosed in Buenos Aires at the Malbran Institute. That made no sense, because we'd been studying the distribution of the infected rodent species in the district of Bariloche.

The story became even more interesting when we were told of an infected physician, Monica, who'd traveled to Buenos

Aires from Bariloche after her husband became ill. She was accompanied by her good friend, Marina, also a physician. Marina in turn became ill and died at the end of the month, while a second physician who tended to Monica, who'd never set foot outside Buenos Aires, also became ill. Both of these cases occurred twenty-seven and twenty-eight days after first contact.

Even with this information staring me in the face, including some history of arterial blood exposure of the first attending physician friend, I still wrote a note recorded in my green logbook: "Could this not have been a needle stick involving the patient?"

Working with our colleagues in Argentina, we did a bunch of studies to see if anybody else was infected. We drew blood at all the clinics where these individuals had been, and at various other hospitals, identified clinicians who might well have been infected, and asked them to suggest patients who might be at risk. At that point, we knew to look for relatives who had nursed these patients in the hospital, as well as sexual partners—which was one of the things that Rachel had figured out: a number of these people had been intimate with those who had become infected in Bariloche. Subsequently we determined that this type of hantavirus, called Andes hantavirus, could indeed be transmitted among people by large particle droplets in the air.

This is a great example of a new researcher teaching an experienced virologist and epidemiologist (namely me) new tricks. Even though none of the other strains of the virus seemed to be associated with person-to-person transmission, this one was. The case reminded us how you have to be careful about your assumptions whenever you're dealing with emerging infectious diseases, because there is always room for surprises.

The Sin Nombre virus, the infection from the Four Corners, has to date never shown a human-to-human transmission. Which is a gigantic difference. Same virus, same rodents, or very closely related, but a gigantic difference. This is why, when discussing a disease that people are worried about and asking, "Well, could this go airborne?" we try very carefully to explain that this is not what usually happens. Rabies, which has persisted for hundreds of thousands of years, has never become airborne. Diseases usually have a typical way of transmitting themselves, and they stick to it.

However, given the fact that there is continuous gene shuffling every time a virus goes through its cell cycle and replicates, you can never rule out something novel—and perhaps deadly.

The classical investigative model is to examine personal factors, pathogen factors, and environmental factors, then determine how they come together to define what we should say to the public. After all, the individual doesn't know until after the fact that there's an outbreak of something deadly, whether it involves rodents or mosquitoes or birds. So it's essential to get the information out there as soon as possible, but also to be clear on the interplay of factors that affect the disease's transmission.

At first you have to ask, Is this the right carrier? It's not fair to pick on chipmunks if the culprits are gray squirrels. Once you establish the vector, it's a question of whether that rodent might spray you, or if you could contract the disease by sweeping up some dust contaminated with rodent urine, and thus inhaling the pathogen. (We always recommend to anyone who needs to sweep up rodent droppings that they first spray it down with Lysol.)

Then there's also the host factor. How much of the infectious agent is entering your body? What is your innate susceptibility to this pathogen?

All these variables come into play in determining whether or not an individual becomes sick. Sometimes it's simply the luck of the draw. Some smokers die of old age. Other people who never smoked a day in their life die of lung cancer. Sometimes the media is ahead of the medical community and drives the public health response. That's what was going on when a reporter from *Quepasa*, a science and tech magazine in Chile, contacted me, asking, "Help me understand how person-to-person transmission occurs with hantaviruses."

He was concerned about the city of Coyhaique, in Aisén province in the south of Chile. A case of what appeared to be hantavirus had occurred in a desert area with no woods and no rodents, yet the patient died. "This city has lots of rodents," he said, "but health care workers aren't taking any precautions. What are you at the CDC doing?"

Chile is obviously a sovereign nation, and CDC doesn't have the responsibility for protecting the whole world; that's the mandate of the World Health Organization (WHO). But CDC is often called on to help with outbreaks outside the United States.

A couple of days later, I spoke with Dr. Jeanette Vega from the Pan American Health Organization in Chile. She served in the Chilean Ministry of Health, and later as well at WHO as managing health director of the Rockefeller Foundation.

She led us to the case of a male individual who'd had onset of disease on September 5, 1997, and died six days later. What had attracted media attention was that his sister, mother-in-law, and brother-in-law had also died of hantavirus pulmonary syndrome. It was this cluster that got everybody involved.

Dr. Roberto Belmar had already been set up as the chief of the Hantavirus Commission in Chile, trying to determine how to respond to this outbreak. We had a series of conversations back and forth with our colleague, Dr. Elsa Salguero, and others in Argentina, trying to find useful comparisons. A week later, we were again on the phone with Dr. Vega in a conference call with many other practitioners.

They had determined that the first cluster had occurred in an area called Lagos Verde, with five deaths in three months. But then they had a second cluster in Coyhaique, with four deaths within four days!

When you look at the first and second clusters so concentrated in time, you have to assume that the most likely reason all these people got infected was exposure to some common source. When you look at the first cluster, though, where onset was spread out over many months, there's far greater likelihood that this was person-to-person transmission from one case to the next. It was this possibility that really had us intrigued.

Once again, the moment you identify the cluster—the search image—all of a sudden cases start coming out of the woodwork. We began to hear of suspected cases from all over the country, and we began to worry.

As of that time, 1997, we had been in the hantavirus business for four years, and we knew that some previous surveys had been done in this community, with rodent studies that followed up on the possibility of person-to-person transmission.

When we got there, we helped establish the National Surveillance System, then tried to compile everything that could be known about the clinical illness, focused on the Aisén province where this was going on. We wanted to describe the epidemiologic condition, who lived, who died, and then maybe do a couple of studies—some cohort studies among the family members, among the health care workers to see who was and who was not infected, and maybe some community survey work in the rural area to see whether maybe this disease was just a lot more prevalent there than elsewhere.

We met at Christmastime with the acting minister of health, the head of the health system from that province, the head of environmental health in Chile, and the Epidemiologic Surveillance Unit, as well as WHO representative Dr. Piña, who was there in Chile.

We learned that there were 14,622,354 inhabitants, 84 percent rural, living in thirteen regions, with twenty-nine health service units. At this point, they thought there were twenty-six cases, sixteen of them male, ranging in age from one year eleven months to forty-six years. Twelve of these cases happened to be in the province of Aisén. People were dying within one to eight days from the onset of symptoms.

We headed down to Coyhaique and started going to the villages, sometimes on horseback, trapping rodents, trying to get a better sense of what was going on.

We were there for two or three weeks, keeping track of which rodents were going into what box, checking the databases to make sure we'd aligned the right rodent type to the right place. We learned very quickly that there were a lot of rodents: over 40 percent of the traps were coming back positive. We were also investigating tons and tons of suspect cases to try to help the local health authorities put together a system for determining who needed to be tested and who didn't.

Aisén was 515,000 square kilometers and contained five provinces, with a population of 84,000, or 1.7 inhabitants per kilometer square, which was pretty rural. Forty-two thousand of those people resided in Coyhaique.

Lagos Verde, where our target family lived, had fifty homes and approximately one hundred inhabitants. We wanted to determine what percentage of the population was infected with hantavirus, and of that, how many people actually got the disease; and of that number, how many got severe disease and died.

Along the way, we were able to connect the everyday patterns of life in that region of the world to the spread of the disease. For example, I saw data that indicated one of the clusters, where those infected were all next to each other, was a family that had opened up a house before the rich owners came to live there, and that's probably how all those people got infected at one time.

In four of the twelve cases in that area we got a history that looked more like hemorrhagic disease, which affects multiple organs, damages the blood vessels, and affects the body's ability to self-regulate. The patients also seemed to have more kidney disease. The doctors already were trying to be very proactive in what they were thinking about treatment. If patients had low blood pressure, doctors gave them plasma from someone who had survived the disease as a way to help them respond and get better. In all ten to eleven of the cases where they could, they actually gave patients plasma therapy, an experimental technique that would reappear later when we were confronting Ebola.

In late spring and early summer we got calls about another cluster of cases in Brazil near the capital, São Paulo, suggesting person-to-person transmission, and I flew down on June 10, 1998.

The government wanted assistance not just from CDC, but also from the Pan American Health Organization, to try to understand what was going on and to try to improve their public health measures.

There were twenty-four health regions in São Paulo, overseen by the Adolfo Lutz Institute of the Brazilian Ministry of Health. They already had a surveillance system for dengue, a viral disease spread by mosquitoes within the genus *Aedes*, principally *A. aegypti*, as well as for leptospirosis, caused by a bacteria carried by a variety of animals, especially rodents. Now they were developing a separate surveillance system for hantavirus pulmonary syndrome.

They had a handful of cases in 1996, and then they had this cluster two years later, in roughly the same area, which is why we were called in.

Clinicians may see tens of thousands of patients during their career, but there will be one or two cases strange enough that they call the health department for assistance. This is especially important in developing or low- to middle-income countries where there's not necessarily great diagnostic support, and autopsies are rare. You really are depending completely on clinical acumen, and intuition, to discover the anomalies. Once there's a big outbreak everybody realizes it, but the initial ones—you need to find them and put prevention measures in place if you want to decrease the size of the outbreak before it gets out of hand.

Very often, it's when a prominent member of the community gets sick that doctors take note of special cases.

In the São Paulo region, it was a fifty-one-year-old woman named Palusta who triggered concern. She got sick and was dead six days later, which was quick for an otherwise healthy, relatively young woman. Her doctors initially suspected dengue, but when her blood sample was sent off for diagnostic testing it came back negative. But the blood was positive for hantavirus.

Palusta owned a fifteen-hectare farm with grazing land for cattle. She went there about twice a week to oversee operations, and three times a week she went to visit the home of a woman who'd once worked for her, but had died in the local hospital while being treated for pulmonary heart disease.

Another subsequent case was one of Palusta's employees on the large plantation she owned that produced sugarcane for alcohol. He had stomach pain and so much chest pain that his physicians thought he'd had a heart attack. His electrocardiogram was normal, but his blood pressure was so low that it was difficult to put in an IV. He was throwing up coffee-ground vomitus, which often suggests bleeding inside the stomach. He had very little shortness of breath, but he also died in shock. So in this case the symptoms pointed toward dengue.

Palusta's clinical history was that she had a fever on a Saturday, with headache, muscle aches, and pain behind her eyes, but no real shortness of breath. Four days later, when she returned to her doctor, he said, "You've got some protein and some white cells in your urine," and diagnosed her with dengue. She also had bruising all over her body, which contributed to the diagnosis of dengue.

The next day, Thursday, she was feeling better, but later that afternoon she deteriorated. On Friday she was back at the doctor's office in shock, with significant shortness of breath and lots of fluid in her lungs. She died within three hours.

In trying to figure out how one individual got sick, you couple the individual clinical investigation with the epidemiologic investigation. Then you align that with the entomology, or in this case the mammology, and go out and see which animals are there and which are potentially infected. Then you put these three pieces together to think about what is the right set of prevention strategies to try to keep other people from getting sick. This approach is a "One Health" approach to emerging infections. Not just to focus on humans but also the implicated animals and the environment to identify potentially novel prevention strategies. This is the pattern we follow when we prevent rabies in humans by vaccinating dogs.

Given this cluster of cases, CDC was invited to come and investigate. So we went out to see this farm of Palusta's, which was a brick building surrounded on three sides by fields. There was a concrete floor, as well as an indoor bathroom, but some of the roof tiles were missing. There were also a large shed for grain, a wood pile twenty feet from the door, and the sugarcane blocks called *rapadura* that were made on the property. I also noted a vegetable garden, chickens, turkeys, guinea hens, pigs, cattle, bananas, oranges, beans, corn, and coffee being produced. Eight people lived there, and all tested negative for hantavirus. Palusta also had another five-hectare farm where there was a grain silo. All seven household members found there also tested negative.

When Palusta first got sick and was diagnosed, the Ministry of Health sent a trapper who found two types of rodents—*Rattus rattus*, the common rat, and *Mus musculus*, the common house mouse—which usually aren't infected with hantavirus. It seemed highly unlikely that these were the culprits.

So we put down traps and captured twenty-eight rodents on our first night, and had forty captures the second. They turned out to be *Calomys*, also known as vesper mice.

In part, what we were seeing was the tremendous diversity of the family of rodents called *sigmondontinae*, which invaded the New World about 5 million years ago, then radiated out into nearly four hundred different species. What probably happened is that an ancestral virus infested a *sigmondontinae* rodent, and as the rodents evolved over time, the viruses co-evolved and diversified with cross-species infections as well.

After we assessed the farm, we went to Palusta's primary residence, which was a beautiful house in the center of town, surrounded by paved streets in a gated community with an electronic front gate, five miles from her farm. The kitchen had granite butcher-block countertops with Italian tiles up to the ceiling, and there were polished terrazzo floors throughout.

Only three months after her death, we began trapping in this area: 130 of our 160 traps had captures in them, and all were along the edge of a plowed cornfield where the brush had been allowed to grow. I had put the traps out myself the night before, one by one, and went with my team personally to pick them up. Early the next morning—before the rodents had time to bake in the sun in the metal traps, which is never good—I took them to the processing site, occasionally putting on protective gear and doing the dissections myself. The team taught me how to do orbital bleeds: you take a little capillary tube, put it right through the top of the mouse's eye, and break all the little blood vessels so that the blood drips out. We then euthanized them, harvested their organs, and placed the organs in liquid nitrogen.

A lot of these diseases had similar signs and symptoms, and we followed up with dozens of potential cases, trying to pin down the diagnosis so we could have better guidance in what to do for these patients.

We spent most of our time looking out at these large sugarcane farms and thinking about what might have changed the ecological balance to give rise to a new species of rodents, which just happened to be carrying a deadly disease.

Eventually we focused on those rough borders left around the corn and the sugarcane, which turned out to be a rodent paradise. The government had been trying to reduce the burning of cane fields because of environmental concerns—smoke equals air pollution. In 1998, three-quarters of the fields were not burned.

Which is where the law of unintended consequences came in. The government had tried to do something good, and it wound up causing a spike in a deadly disease.

This is why we always need to think long and hard about the impact of any man-made changes. Sometimes the danger is not the primordial mysteries of nature. Sometimes the danger is us.

3

THE FACE OF
THE DEVIL

*There have been as many plagues as wars in history; yet
always plagues and wars take people equally by surprise.*
—Albert Camus, *The Plague*

"I'm holding my cigarette outside the car," said Dr. Abdul
Noor, in answer to my repeated complaints. We were driving
in a small car across the salt-pan desert at the southeastern corner of the Arabian Peninsula, visiting every slaughterhouse in
each of the seven United Arab Emirates (UAE).

Dr. Noor, an Egyptian, was director of the UAE Public Health
Program. I was there to assist the Ministry of Health with an
outbreak of a bloody fever among guest workers from Southeast
Asia, mainly Indians and Pakistanis, who killed animals and cut
meat in these abattoirs. Listening over the phone as the ministry
representative told the story, I knew it could be malaria or severe
dysentery. Then again, it could be Crimean-Congo hemorrhagic
fever (CCHF). The typical pattern was a shepherd showing up
at the hospital vomiting blood. Surgeons would think he had a
bleeding ulcer, open him up, see that he was too far gone, then
close him back up. He would die, and then about five days later
the scrub nurse who'd cleaned up the patient's blood and the
bloody surgical instruments would fall sick and start bleeding,
followed by others on the surgical and clinical teams.

Crimean-Congo hemorrhagic fever is a viral illness that can cause blood to spill out of your gut and large bruising under your skin, as well as mental confusion, coffee-ground vomiting, and black stools. CCHF is only one of about twenty viral hemorrhagic fevers that can pop up anywhere in the world, but it is the fever of choice in pulp fiction, even if misattributed, since it is the bloodiest of all. And whereas the bleeding in most viral hemorrhagic fevers (VHFs) is rarely life threatening, it is with CCHF. Over a third of those infected with Crimean-Congo hemorrhagic fever die within two weeks, often quite dramatically.

VHFs occur from four distinct viral families, with distinct animal vectors. Yellow fever, Rift Valley fever, and dengue are all carried by mosquitoes. For Crimean-Congo, as well as Omsk and Kyasanur Forest diseases, the natural host is ticks. For Lassa, Bolivian, and Argentinian fevers, as well as hemorrhagic fever with renal syndrome and hantavirus pulmonary syndrome, it's rodents. And then there's the hemorrhagic fever that's gotten the most attention lately, Ebola, which is borne by bats.

Despite the different reservoirs and vectors that define the geographic range of these conditions, the VHFs are lumped together because they are all characterized by a similar illness that affects almost all human organs: blood vessels become leaky and the patient has trouble maintaining blood pressure.

Along with the grotesque symptoms, not to mention the risk of death, VHFs are of great concern because many are associated with person-to-person transmission, and they rarely have effective therapies or vaccines. Most are infectious even by small aerosol particles in the laboratory setting, so work with any of these viruses is generally contained in biosafety level 4 conditions with moon suits or large airproof cabinets. The clinical diagnosis remains difficult because the frank bleeding does not always appear and, as I mentioned, the other symptoms are similar to those of malaria, dysentery, and a number of other diseases.

The government of the emirates had invested tremendous resources in a modern health care system, which was a good thing, otherwise they would have been seeing infected health care workers. Unfortunately, they showed remarkably little concern for guest workers like these meat cutters, or for the lower classes in general.

Of the UAE's population of 9 million, 7 million were noncitizens, mostly from India. And in a country like this it was difficult to separate public health problems from social and political problems—they were all one and the same.

And yet the embrace of modernity in the emirate of Dubai, for instance, had been stunning as it redefined itself as a global banking and transportation hub. In the market, you could see women in burqas and women in short skirts, side by side, and those in the short skirts went from the mosque to the nightclub across the street.

Happily, American consultants, like me, were treated very respectfully. When the emir asked for your help, you could count on a first-class airline ticket and a room at a five-star hotel.

At the first slaughterhouse Dr. Noor and I came to, it took me about twelve seconds to come up with a theory for why the butchers were getting infected. As "protective clothing" they wore blood-smeared sleeveless undershirts, dhotis, and flip-flops.

You'd have thought the ministry would have come out sooner for a look, but there were other cultural chasms to be bridged—classic problems in developing countries. Aside from a lack of concern for the lower orders, there was also no tradition of interventional or hands-on epidemiology: the idea that practitioners go out and try to solve problems rather than sit in an office and tally up the sick and dead toll. My colleague from the Ministry of Health, Dr. Noor, the heavy smoker, couldn't understand why I wanted to be out in the blinding heat amid the dust storms and the thorn bushes, going from one stinking abattoir to the next stinking animal pen to actually observe and gather data.

The UAE, which includes Abu Dhabi and Dubai, was established as a country of sorts in December 1971, but it's really a federation of seven absolute monarchies stretching for more than four hundred miles along the southern shore of the Persian Gulf. It borders Oman to the east and Saudi Arabia to the south. It also shares sea borders with Qatar and Iran.

The emirates emerged as a British protectorate out of the defeated Ottoman Empire after World War 1. The Brits were hoping for another "black gold" rush, as in Baku or Mosul, but for all the efforts of the Anglo-Persian Oil Company and the Iraq Petroleum Company, oil did not begin to flow until the 1960s. The UAE is now recognized as having the seventh-largest oil reserves in the world, and the seventeenth-largest reserves of natural gas. With those resources, as well as its strategic location adjacent to the Strait of Hormuz, the UAE has prospered.

But there were more subtle problems for us in trying to remediate this outbreak. Aside from the rather abstract approach to public health and lack of concern and protection for little people, there was the turf war going on between the Ministry of Health and the Ministry of Agriculture. And CCHF, like most other emerging infectious diseases, had to be addressed not just as a human disease, but as a question of animal-human interaction; in this case, an issue of how livestock and animals were handled. This is called the One Health approach.

Over three quarters of emerging diseases are zoonoses (meaning transmitted to us through contact with animals). These include CCHF, hantaviruses, henipavirues, and Ebola; others, like seasonal human influenza and HIV, started as zoonoses. Due to a perfect storm of genetic, ecologic, behavioral, and political factors these pathogens emerge from their natural environment in the wild and infect humans. So One Health is also an approach to hunt for these microbes in and near their natural environment to identify those that have the potential to get a foothold in humans.

Our investigations also took us down to the docks to see how the sheep were brought in and where they were housed. We knew that 80 percent of the animals in the emirates came from Australia, where there were no deadly Hyalomma ticks or their resident CCHF virus, and that as such they were disease free. But it turned out that those sheep were being mixed in with naturally infected animals from Somalia and Iran; the virgin Australian sheep would pick up a primary infection with CCHF from ticks coming off these other animals or the pens themselves, and they would have extremely high levels of virus in their blood as they went to slaughter. The tick-infested animals were being smuggled in on little dhows across the Persian Gulf, making import bans meaningless. The obvious solution was to stop mixing animals, but there was nothing we could do about local preferences. The face of an Australian sheep, the locals said, looked like the face of the devil, so they preferred the animals from their own region.

We made a series of recommendations starting with protection of the butchers and other animal handlers, as well as implementing a monitoring system for new infections. We also recommended that Australian sheep be segregated from the other local animals, and that the local animals be dipped for ticks before entering holding pens, and that holding pens be treated with disinfectant each time the population of animals changed. We also left the drug ribavirin, which had been shown to work in small studies, in the local hospitals for use with any new suspected cases.

The outbreak in UAE was the largest ever reported, but it represented a persistent phenomenon across the region. While I was in UAE, the Saudi Ministry of Health invited me to advise them on their own cases of CCHF among guest workers. So I got a visa in Dubai and flew over to Riyadh. Unfortunately, my local contact decided to skip picking me up because it was late and it had rained, so I had to negotiate customs and immigration on my own. The immigration officer asked for my passport in Arabic and when I didn't understand, he saw it in my hand and asked me for it in English. So I handed him my official US passport.

Then he asked me, "Are you a Muslim?"

"Yes," I replied.

"What sort of Muslim does not speak Arabic?" he responded.

Then, even though he had my official (not personal) US passport in his hand, which lists my birthplace as New York, New York, he asked me if I was an American.

"Yes," I told him.

"No, you are just a Pakistani with false documents," he said with disdain. At which point he began to tear through my suitcase, throwing my stuff all over the inspection station. And do remember that I was an invited guest, entering the country on official business.

Lo and behold, he found fifty vials of a white powder tucked inside my field gear. There was pure glee in his eyes, so it seemed. Evidently he relished the thought that I would be executed by the following Friday. Saudi Arabia had one of the worst human rights records in the world. Based on Sharia law, its legal system included flogging and stoning, and apostasy was punishable by death. Systematic discrimination against women and religious minorities continued, as well as lack of protection of its guest workers. It also had the strictest drug laws in the world, with perfunctory trials, swift injustice, and public beheadings after the holy Friday prayer. My annoyance turned to pure fear as I stammered that the vials contained ribavirin, an antiviral drug I'd been asked to bring into the country.

The airport doctor was called, cooler heads prevailed, and I was allowed to keep mine. I was released two hours later.

The conditions of the outbreak in Saudi Arabia were the same as those in the UAE, including the same rift between the animal and human health ministries. I made essentially the same recommendations and left the ribavirin for use.

Shortly afterward, I was asked to consult in Oman for more CCHF cases. Unlike the Saudis, the Omani people were super-friendly and progressive in all matters, including their public health system.

In Oman I also had the pleasure of working with a new EIS officer, Dr. Joel Williams, a US Air Force veterinarian, along with Gary Maupin, a great mammologist and budding tick expert. This investigation was something of a trial by fire for Joel, whose luggage traveled the Middle East in search of him throughout the mission. I also remember him trying his best to draw blood from the neck of a goat while another started to eat his field notes. Gary and I had to restrain him from shoving his hands down into the stomach of the critter to retrieve them, and then from serving roasted goat that night!

Our series of recommendations seemed to work—or the ecologic conditions driving the ticks and CCHF infections of animals in the region subsided. There have been few subsequent cases.

———

On May 6, 1995, just a few weeks after I returned from the Middle East, Julia Weeks, medical director of the Zaire American Clinic, placed a call to CDC from a lawn party at the British embassy in Kinshasa. She'd just heard from a missionary that a hospital in Kikwit, a city of 400,000 in the Bandundu region of southwestern Zaire, was reporting an outbreak of the red diarrhea, caused by shigella.

Given that May 6 was a Saturday, CDC offices were closed, and even though I was still pretty junior, having been at CDC for only four years, her call was directed to me at home. We talked for about half an hour, until the batteries in her cell phone began to fade.

Central Africa is rife with malaria, sleeping sickness, yellow fever, cholera, yaws, and typhus, but this situation sounded much more dramatic. Reportedly, as many as two thousand people had been infected, with fever and massive hemorrhaging, and they had not responded to ciprofloxacin or to any of the other usual antibiotics. Twelve health care workers had already died.

I called my boss, Clarence James "CJ" Peters, head of the Special Pathogens Branch, and we arranged to meet first thing the next morning in his office in the basement of Building 3 at CDC. He'd seen this sort of thing before. In 1989, Dr. Peters had been head of disease assessment at the US Army Medical Research Institute of Infectious Diseases, Fort Detrick, Maryland, when dozens of macaques imported from the Philippines and destined for use in medical research suddenly died at Hazelton Research Products' primate quarantine unit in Reston, Virginia. His efforts to contain that outbreak were chronicled in Richard Preston's *The Hot Zone*. CJ had also tracked the Bolivian hemorrhagic fever known as Machupo in South America.

We were joined by Tom Ksiazek, CDC veterinarian and virologist who'd helped unravel the mystery of hantavirus, and we agreed that our first objective should be to obtain blood samples. Our second task should be to fax Kinshasa with instructions for diagnosing viral hemorrhagic fevers and for managing patients.

In 1988, CDC had printed a procedures manual for dealing with this sort of thing in a special issue of *Morbidity and Mortality Weekly Report* (*MMWR*). It called for double gloves, surgical caps and gowns, waterproof aprons, shoe covers, and protective eyewear. Every object that came in contact with the patient had to be put in double airtight bags, sponged with disinfectant, and then incinerated. The patients themselves were to be isolated in a single room with an anteroom equipped with hand-washing facilities. Procedures also called for minimal contact with corpses, which, given African funeral customs, was highly problematic.

We also needed to inform the upper ranks at CDC: our division director, Dr. Brian Mahy, and the head of the National

Center for Infectious Diseases, Dr. Jim Hughes. CDC requires an official invitation from a local or national public health agency before launching an intervention, so we would have to wait for a request from the government of Zaire, which, inconveniently, maintained strained relations with the United States. Helping out in Kikwit would be further complicated by the fact that there was no reliable telephone service, and resources for sanitation and barrier nursing were minimal.

As we began to investigate, we learned that the outbreak was much more convoluted than originally reported, and that our call was only one strain of the conversation. The outbreak had first surfaced on April 9, when a thirty-six-year-old male laboratory technician who worked at Kikwit II Maternity Hospital went to Kikwit General Hospital with fever and bloody diarrhea. Suspecting a perforated bowel from typhoid, surgeons with shoddy infection control operated on him on April 10, but he died three days later.

By that time, the medical personnel who'd cared for him began to evidence fever; headache; back, joint, and muscle aches; and in some cases hemorrhagic manifestations.

These caretakers included nuns belonging to the order of Little Sisters of the Poor, based in Bergamo, Italy. The head nurse, Sister Floralba Rondi, seventy-one, who had come to Kikwit by boat in 1952, died on April 25 of what was thought to be a malarial fever. It was when the second nun, Sister Clarangela Ghillardi, a sixty-four-year-old obstetrics nurse, died on May 6, that authorities realized this was not malaria. Reports of these deaths were relayed to Italy and then back to Kinshasa and various other places that were searching for answers. But the small outbreak in Kikwit had gotten mixed in with a regional outbreak of Shigella and had led to Julia Weeks's call to CDC. It also brought up eerie reminders of the "sentinel nun" monitoring system for Ebola since the original 1976 Yambuku outbreak was identified by dead nuns.

Already on the scene was University of Kinshasa virologist Jean-Jacques Muyembe-Tamfum, who'd been in Yambuku,

Zaire, in 1976, when Ebola hemorrhagic fever was first recognized. He instructed a military nurse to draw blood from fourteen patients known to be infected, then arranged to have the samples flown to the lab of Belgian virologist Guido van der Groen at the Institute of Tropical Medicine in Antwerp. Zaire, once known as the Belgian Congo, still had close ties with its former colonial overlord, and Van der Groen had been the scientist who analyzed the first specimens from Yambuku in 1976.

Dr. Muyembe-Tamfum put the fourteen vials of blood in a metal canister, put cotton in for padding, put the canister in a plastic box, filled it with ice, and sealed it up. Then he gave it to the French deputy bishop of Kikwit, who flew the 240 miles to Kinshasa in a Mission Aviation Fellowship Cessna, and delivered the samples to Dr. Jean-Pierre Lahaye, chief of the medical section at the Belgian embassy. Dr. Lahaye replenished the ice in the box, then set about trying to find a way to get the blood to Antwerp. Which led him to an employee of Sabena Air Lines who frequently traveled between Zaire and Brussels, and who agreed to transport the samples in her carry-on. He also persuaded the Belgian ambassador, Andre Moens, to draft an official letter requesting that the blood be allowed to pass through customs without question, and explaining that no one should open the container except doctors at the Institute of Tropical Medicine.

The courier arrived in Brussels at six in the morning on May 6, the same day that Julia Weeks and I spoke over the phone. She breezed through passport control, then handed her package to a doctor from the Belgian Development Corporation, who drove the samples to Antwerp. As it turned out, though, Guido van der Groen no longer had the biosafety level 4 containment facility required for working with a risk group 4 pathogen. So he opened the box, refreshed the ice once again, and sent it on to Atlanta.

We received the samples on May 9, and tested them with enzyme-linked immunoabsorbent assays to detect viral markers (antigens) and virus-specific antibodies. We found evidence of Ebola virus infection in all fourteen patients. Additional assays, including viral isolation and RNA analysis, were consistent with the diagnosis of Ebola hemorrhagic fever, perhaps the most dreaded disease in the world.

Named after the Ebola River, a tributary of the Congo, Ebola virus is another zoonotic pathogen first thought to be a new strain of the closely related Marburg virus. Marburg first appeared in 1967, in the German city for which it's named, when laboratory technicians at the Behringwerke and the Paul Ehrlich Institutes were exposed to infected tissues from vervet monkeys imported from Uganda. Twenty-five technicians and six of their contacts, in Marburg and Frankfurt, Germany, and in Belgrade, Yugoslavia, fell ill. Seven people died.

Then, in 1976, a teacher at the mission school at Yambuku, 621 miles north of Kikwit, sought medical intervention for what appeared to be malaria, and he received an injection of chloroquine at the mission hospital. But they did not use disposable needles, or even sterilize the needles they did use. They had five glass syringes for a 120-bed hospital. Twenty-nine days later, and after eleven of its seventeen staff members fell ill, the hospital closed. Ultimately, 318 people were infected and 280 died. Among the dead were, once again, two Catholic nuns. This gave rise to the dark humor reference to there being a sentinel nun disease-monitoring system for Ebola.

The scope of the outbreak was limited, very likely, because this was six years after eradication of smallpox and the locals still knew how to isolate people with presumptive communicable diseases. Even so, Ebola hemorrhagic fever was something new in the world of emerging infections. There was a simultaneous outbreak in southern Sudan that originated in a cotton-manufacturing factory, and which led to 284 infections and 151 deaths. Despite the geographical and temporal proximity, the outbreaks were actually due to two different strains of Ebola virus: Zaire and Sudan. The ecologic conditions just happened to be right for both strains of these ancient viruses to emerge simultaneously. Ironically, the outbreaks were helped along by just enough development to create health care centers with insufficient infection control practices. In other words, the hospitals themselves became force multipliers for the spread of the infection among humans, via direct contact or large droplets from coughs and sneezes or contaminated materials such as needles, beginning with the doctors and nurses or family members providing care.

The next year, a nine-year-old girl with fever and abdominal pain, and vomiting blood, was admitted to Tandala Mission Hospital, also in Zaire. She lived with her family in a small village twelve miles away, had been in good health and had not traveled outside of the area. She was diagnosed with the newly described disease, and twenty-eight hours later she died.

This case prompted a reexamination of the death of a physician from Tandala, five years previously, who'd nicked his finger while performing an autopsy on a Zairois Bible school student. The student had been diagnosed with yellow fever. The physician became ill twelve days later. When his hospital records were reviewed in 1977, it appeared that Ebola might have been around as early as 1972.

For nearly twenty years after the little girl's death in Tandala, the virus seemed to have receded into the jungle, where it lived between human outbreaks. We didn't know then that bats were the natural reservoir, and that humans got infected either directly or through consumption of "bush meat" such as the tiny deer called duikers, or chimpanzees. The great apes are actually more severely affected than humans, with some specialists recently estimating that Ebola may have recently wiped out a third of the world's chimpanzees and gorillas.

Then, at the beginning of December 1994, in the Minkebe and Makokou regions of Gabon, prospectors from three gold-panning encampments located in small clearings in the rain forest got sick with a bloody fever illness. Eventually, thirty-two people traveled sixty-two miles south via boat to Mekouka General Hospital for medical treatment.

At the end of the month, in another small village far from the gold-panning encampments, a second wave appeared. The first victim lived near a *nganga,* or traditional healer, who naturally attracted sick people, some of whom had previously been treated at the hospital. Another sixteen cases occurred in January, none of whom had been in the area affected by the first wave. All sixteen patients had been either in direct contact with patients hospitalized at Makokou General Hospital, or with the *nganga,* or with people caring for patients.

Only eight days after the last case, mistaking this for an outbreak of yellow fever, Gabonese health officials declared the epidemic officially over (even though established procedure for Ebola would have been to not give the all-clear until forty-two days after the last case died or was discharged from the hospital [twice the longest incubation period]). Overall, forty-nine people were admitted to Makokou General Hospital and twenty-nine died. The diagnosis would be reexamined and revised in light of Kikwit, drawing parallels with the original Ebola outbreaks. When the conditions are right, the virus can easily emerge in multiple countries at the same time.

———

Six days after the phone call from Julia Weeks and a day after receipt of the samples, CDC relayed the diagnosis from the Kikwit outbreak to the US embassy in Kinshasa, and to the World Health Organization in Geneva, both of which notified the Zairian Ministry of Health. The Zairian government immediately quarantined the city and closed the road leading from Kinshasa to Bandundu Province. The US embassy declared the outbreak a disaster, and the Office of Foreign Disaster Assistance of the US Agency for International Development authorized the payment of $25,000 to local nongovernmental organizations for the purchase and transport of essential medicines and supplies. Although air as well as road traffic were restricted, the government of Zaire, not known to be overly cooperative with the Western democracies, allowed the Mission Aviation Fellowship to provide transport.

Through the US embassy, the Zairian government also requested that CDC send in investigators. At the same time, the World Health Organization asked CDC, which supported a WHO collaborating center for virus reference and research on special pathogens, to join its team. Also providing assistance would be Médecins Sans Frontières (MSF), the National Institute of Virology in South Africa, the Pasteur Institute in Paris, and the Institute for Tropical Medicine in Antwerp. To oversee the response, WHO set up an international committee on scientific and technical coordination, chaired by Dr. Muyembe-Tamfum.

To head our own effort, CJ chose Dr. Pierre Rollin, a French clinician, virologist, and historian who was a leading expert on hemorrhagic fevers, and who'd also participated in the Ebola Reston investigation in 1989. I don't think Dr. Rollin saw the point of including a newbie who didn't speak French, but I went along as the junior epidemiologist. He told me not to get in the way and not to bother bringing a computer: there would never be enough electricity and no way to collect data. But to make sure I pulled my weight, he gave me the job of lugging the thirty-pound satellite phone (this was before these things had shrunk to cell-phone size) everywhere we went. My arms and back ached for weeks afterward.

It also did not endear me to Pierre that I have severe motion sickness. When you're prone to headaches and nausea on long rides, and you find yourself squeezed into the back of a crowded car on bumpy roads in sweltering weather for hours on end, the best you can do is say, "Please don't talk to me— and could you please turn off that radio?" It's as if you need to close down all your sensory inputs as a survival mechanism.

---

*Z*aire *ebolavirus*, of the family *filoviridae*, or filoviruses, is actually one of five members of the genus *Ebolavirus*, each named for the region in which it was originally identified, the others being *Bundibugyo ebolavirus*, *Reston ebolavirus*, *Sudan ebolavirus*, and *Taï Forest ebolavirus*. Reston is the oddball one, identified in Philippine monkeys, that doesn't cause disease in humans. The Zaire strain is the deadliest, both in terms of number of outbreaks and of mortality, averaging 83 percent since it first appeared.

While Richard Preston overdid it with his gory descriptions in *The Hot Zone*, Ebola hemorrhagic fever is terrifying. The virus eats microscopic holes in the endothelial lining of the blood vessels, and as the holes enlarge, blood seeps into the intestines, bowels, and respiratory tract. The fever can bring on hallucinations, and the victim's tears can turn red with blood. Ebola has been known to cause bleeding from the nose, ears, bowels, bladder, and mouth. But bleeding occurs in only 10–15 percent of patients, and most often this is simply bruising and oozing from mucous membranes, and from the site of needlesticks. Hiccups, suggesting your diaphragm is calling it quits, are likewise an ominous but rare sign. Most characteristic for the patients I saw was a mask-like expression on the face.

Like other RNA (ribonucleic acid as opposed to the larger DNA, deoxyribonucleic acid) viruses, Ebola mutates rapidly, at a rate similar to that of influenza virus, both within a given person during the progression of disease and in the reservoir provided by the local human population.

Viruses don't replicate through cell division, though. Instead, they hijack host enzymes and cell structures to produce multiple copies of themselves, self-assembling into viral macromolecular structures within the host cell.

When you're infected, unless you develop an unusually powerful immune response, the disease co-opts your body and turns it into a virus factory. Then, even if you're lucky and recover from the acute phase of the infection, you can have long-term complications from muscle aches and joint pains, and you continue to have virus in sites that are protected from you immune system like the brain, the back of your eye, and, if you're of the male persuasion, your testicles. Virus can then spill out from these sites back into your system to make you sick again. Given the way the virus can linger in the male reproductive system, men can spread it as a sexually transmitted infection for up to nine months after they recover.

O n May 11, we arrived in Kinshasa, which had to be the most disorganized place on earth, a city of 10 million on the south bank of the Congo River, combining modern high-rise buildings and sprawling slums where people lived under tarps or pieces of corrugated tin. We spent a week there, hacking our way through the bureaucracy and the tangled vines of third-world corruption.

I had seen the dismal results of British and French colonization, but at least in the latter case you could usually get a good baguette. Belgian colonization, however, had left an implacable scar on the people and country. Nothing got done in this part of Africa without bribes and various under-the-table dealings, because Zaire, the former Belgian Congo, had set the gold standard for corruption since the days when it was the personal property of King Leopold, whose overseers incentivized workers on rubber plantations by chopping off their arms if they failed to meet their quotas. When the Belgians pulled out in the 1960s, supposedly they left behind all of thirty home-grown university graduates in a country two-thirds the size of Western Europe. Even in 1996, this was still Conrad's *The Heart of Darkness*.

We met with the WHO representative, who had managed to provide a computer and printer. USAID provided bikes and motorcycles. Chevron, which had been drilling oil in the region for twenty-five years, agreed to send us a jeep and gasoline, as well as liquid nitrogen. These contributions surged from numerous NGOs (nongovernmental organizations) and governments once the scope of the outbreak was clear. However, during the final accounting, the main contribution of Zaire, a country with immense wealth in diamonds, gold, and oil, but with an impoverished civic life—thanks first to the Belgians, and then to the kleptocracy set up by Zairian president Mobutu Sésé Seko, said to have personally stolen between $5 and $15 billion during his tenure—was to not charge custom duties on the charitable supplies coming in.

Kikwit's airstrip was a repurposed soccer field, and we were set to fly in on a cargo plane that must have been built around 1940, but our departure was held up by journalists paying $500 to $10,000 to the Ministry of Information for transport despite the travel ban, which meant that they got priority well ahead of us nonpaying humanitarians. I understood the power of the media when I had to wait on the plane in Kikwit until the journalists had gotten off so they could *take our picture getting off*.

We still managed to arrive at the 350-bed Kikwit General Hospital on May 12, with our supplies of surgical gloves, gowns, rubber boots, duct tape, face masks, bleach, and body bags. Accompanying Pierre and me was Dr. Philippe Calain, a Swiss physician and excellent research virologist who was completing a molecular biology postdoctoral fellowship at CDC, but changing his whole career path after this outbreak to focus on this kind of work in the field. We were met by the hospital's medical director, by a representative of the Institut Pasteur, and by Colonel Dr. Nsukami Zaki from the Zairian army, perhaps the government's only functional element. Dr. Zaki had been recruited by the Zairian Red Cross to organize the work of their volunteers, which included procuring a truck for carrying the dead to burial and a bulldozer for digging mass graves.

What would have been a sad and depressing facility under the best circumstances had been turned into a tropical hell. Most of the staff—as well any patients who could—had fled, adding to the spread of the disease. This left only the critically ill, including one man in a full body cast. And the dead. We had to step around the corpses of the patients who'd died, now stinking and swollen on the floors and in the beds. There was extensive contamination by blood, vomit, and excrement, and needles and syringes lay underfoot. There was no electricity, lighting, or running water. And there was no latrine.

My job was supposed to consist of establishing disease surveillance, determining transmission factors, and implementing measures to help control the outbreak. Pierre—the true hero of this and many Ebola outbreaks in the future—along with Philippe were to focus on gathering clinical information and setting up a portable laboratory. But it was painfully obvious that, whatever our plans, their priority now had to be cleaning up the squalor and providing care for the remaining patients.

Four separate hospitals had been implicated: the center of the outbreak was Kikwit General, and then there was Kikwit II Hospital, as well as the hospital in Mosango, where one of the medical personnel who cared for the laboratory technician had been transferred. Mosango was interesting since the only infection control taken by the lone doctor who never got infected was to rigorously wash her hands. The fourth hospital was in Yassa Bonga, approximately 155 miles away.

We turned our attention first to Kikwit General, which had 326 beds in twelve separate buildings called pavilions. Patients slept on thin mattresses with no sheets, on metal bed frames coated in chipped white enamel paint. The hospital did not provide meals, so what food there was had to be brought in by families.

On the first day, we remained outside to ferry medical supplies and protective gear to the door. On the second, wearing plastic gowns, glasses, boots, and gloves, we entered the hospital to help colleagues provide medical care and to remove dead bodies from the wards, burn mattresses, and institute basic hygiene. The team from the Belgian branch of Médecins Sans Frontières, which maintains a permanent office in Kinshasa, included two sanitary engineers, one of whom could speak the local language. They installed a water tank and a waste disposal system, provided an electric generator, and supplied sterile water filters.

The Zairian Red Cross also played a vital role in burying corpses, but until we arrived their volunteers lacked protective clothing, and six of them became infected and died. We supplied them with orange biohazard jumpsuits, rubber boots, and masks, as well as miner's lamps to strap to their heads for lighting in areas where there was no electricity. They truly looked like creatures from a horror film, or the devil's own henchmen, as they sprayed each body with bleach, placed it in a white plastic bag, then sprayed it again. They would then put it on a gurney and take it through the covered walkway that led from Pavilion 3, the quarantine ward, to the small concrete building that housed the morgue.

Once the hospital was in better order, the Zairian Red Cross began taking trucks to the surrounding villages to collect the dead, which was incredibly dangerous work, made worse by the hostility of Zairians, who wanted to deal with the dead in their own way, which involved a great deal of touching, kissing, and washing. Sadly, some of these young men were beaten for their efforts.

Ordinarily there would have been twelve physicians at Kikwit General, two hundred nurses or midwives, and sixty room attendants. But of the remaining doctors, three were ill: one recovering at home, two in the hospital ward. Only three nurses and one ward attendant, or orderly, remained, and they had been working without rest for several days, unsupervised and unprotected.

The hospital director recruited two more nurses and one more orderly, and one nurse from the existing team kept working until the next morning, when a third volunteer nurse joined them. So for the first week, the hospital was staffed by a rotating team of only three nurses and one ward attendant. A third nun from the Little Sisters of the Poor of the Palazzolo Institute, forty-eight-year-old Sister Danielangela Sorti, died shortly after our arrival. A total of six would die. The last was Sister Vitarosa Zorza, fifty-one, a nurse who had traveled to Kikwit to help the infected of her order in their compound. She likely died from the smallest breach of infection control, and her illness and death were the low point for us. Pierre lovingly tended to her throughout her illness, despite the obvious threat to his personal safety. He even dug her grave.

New patients were still being admitted to the emergency ward and, if their complaints were suggestive of Ebola, they were examined in one of two separate rooms. If Ebola seemed probable, they were directed to Pavilion 3.

With even the slightest hint of Ebola symptoms being enough to land you in the quarantine ward, I'm sure there were a handful of people who were healthy until they were misdirected and caught the disease there.

The hospital pharmacy could provide oral and parenteral drugs, including quinine, chloroquine, antibiotics, sedatives, and analgesics, but there was no water or electricity.

As a rule, needles had not been reused between patients, but these sharps had not disposed of properly, which meant that health care workers were at high risk for needle-stick injuries, especially in the diminished lighting of the ward. We gave instructions to limit injections and infusions and to encourage family members to provide maximal oral hydration to their relatives.

By May 20, Pavilion 3 was full, but enough nurses had volunteered for duty to allow the opening of an additional quarantine pavilion. As soon as patients were in their recovery phase, they were directed to a nearby convalescence pavilion, where the risk of contamination was much lower.

I worked with Dr. David Heymann of WHO Geneva, overall coordinator of the response, to set up surveillance systems. He had participated as an EIS officer in the original Yambuku outbreak and had kept a calm head amid all the waves of infection.

My most important task was to decipher the epidemiology and identify all the cases and their contacts. My secret ambition was to trace the chain of transmission back to "patient zero," the person who was the unlucky first target when this zoonotic disease jumped the species barrier from its animal host to us, and to prove that this outbreak was linked to a single infection. This meant going out with the teams to try to identify cases. With a student from Bandu medical school to translate, I trained Zairians to do the data collection and analysis.

The big questions were, Where did people die? How many were there? How old were they? We created a questionnaire with space for "Who do you think infected you?" and "Who were your contacts?"

As data started coming in, we divided cases between "probable" and "suspect" based on symptoms, with coded data for "Who do you think infected you?" that we could use to trace further back along the chain. We examined the data to see how many were health care workers and how many were not, as an indication of how well our prevention measures and improved procedures were working.

I was trying to use the data to help focus the search on the people where the infection rate was highest. Our goal was for the community to immediately report all deaths so the deceased could be buried safely, and to get all suspected persons with illness out of the home and into a clinical setting where they could get treatment and, equally important, not infect anybody else.

During the investigation of anybody who had died or was suspected of having Ebola, the team would trace and record the name of all their contacts while they were ill. If the person turned up positive for the infection, then all the contacts would be reassessed and followed for twenty-one days to see if they got sick. Contacts without symptoms did not pose a risk of spreading infection. However, the nature of the response is usually defined by how well these individuals are managed. This ranges from checking in on them periodically with instructions to call if they get ill, to quarantining a whole village for twenty-one days with armed guards to enforce the confinement. Needless to say, the decisions you make determine how much community cooperation you get. This was especially true during the early days, when those quarantined were not even provided with food rations.

Once we'd instituted basic controls and hygienic procedures among health care workers to stop the spread, the next challenge was a matter of cultural persuasion: sending out researchers on motorcycles, and later medical students on bikes, to convince local residents to stop hiding the sick, and then to radically alter their ways of handling their dead. We also established multiple reporting systems, including a rumor registry of possible cases and deaths, and reporting through the local radio system of the Kikwit Diocese. With no mass media available—not even newspapers—our communications effort could rely on nothing more sophisticated than posters and loudspeakers on corners. Through all this we had to tackle the community's magical thinking. The original outbreak in the hospital was thought to be have been from a curse by somebody who had not been invited to share a meal with his colleagues at work.

In Zaire, it is customary for family members to wash deceased loved ones in preparation for burial, with lots of touching and kissing, and the saving of hair and nail clippings. This is suicide with Ebola, when we can detect up to 10 billion units of viral genetic material in each milliliter of blood in fatal cases. Given that hard truth, local residents eventually came to accept the men in orange jumpsuits putting victims immediately into body bags, spraying them down with Lysol, then carrying them away on flatbed trucks. Foreigners drew greater outrage than these local volunteers, but still, their job was doubly dangerous—both from the threat of infection and from the threat of abuse by angry villagers.

We would often hear the names of victims being wailed into the night, and we knew the grief was combined with fear. The dread of a horrible disease was compounded by the fact that not even the doctors and nurses had been able to protect themselves. In fact, the health care system was the amplifying note. Dying alone in your hut isn't an outbreak. It's hospitals that aggregate infections and—unless there are the strictest of safeguards—pass them along.

In the evenings I would put on protective gear and look after patients in the wards, but providing medical care with sweat in your eyes and a fogged-up mask was tricky. This was especially true of taking blood at twilight, from a writhing patient, whom you were about to stick with a needle. But it was also easy enough to simply trip and land on your face.

In the midst of all of this, we still had to take care of our basic needs. The only place we could find to stay was the home of a local "businessman" whose business seemed to consist of dealing in black market goods and consuming massive quantities of alcohol. But that came to an abrupt end when he decided to be amorous in the middle of the night with a sleeping CDC colleague.

After the international team supplied hospital staff with protective clothing and disposable syringes, the number of new cases dropped. Actively finding cases, and disseminating health information to the local population, also contributed to lessening the spread of disease outside the hospital.

Eventually, from tracing back through suspect cases and many false leads, I found patient zero, the initial victim— Gaspar Menga. He was a forty-two-year-old charcoal worker admitted to Kikwit General Hospital on January 6, 1995. A

Seventh-Day Adventist, he had not eaten bush meat, nor, to the best of our knowledge, been in contact with another Ebola patient prior to becoming ill. But his charcoal plot was on the edge of a dense forest, and under the canopy. During his woodcutting forays and charcoal-burning pit diggings, he would have been exposed to a wide array of possible animal vectors including bats, insects, and rodents.

Patient zero directly infected, fatally, at least three members of his family, along with an additional ten members of his extended family. This took place over a period of nine weeks and in an area encompassing Kikwit and three surrounding villages.

This identification of patient zero provided a target for the new incoming animal reservoir teams. I also got to help as they collected ticks, rodents, bats, mosquitoes, and amphibians, trying to figure out where this virus had come from. The leading suspect was fruit bats. Overall we collected more than fourteen hundred samples for reservoir testing.

Ultimately, the outbreak affected 315 people, with a fatality rate of 81 percent. Nearly every case was traced back to an infected family member, friend, or health worker who had been in direct contact with another patient, or who had experienced a needle stab or undergone surgery. More than 70 percent of the early-generation cases were hospital personnel.

Overall, 166 cases were female and 149 were male. Thirty-two percent of these were health care workers and 21 percent were housewives who usually nursed a sick family member or performed the ritual cleansing and burial preparation practices for them. Transmission during this outbreak was mainly person to person through contact with bodily fluids and ritual cleansing of bodies before burial, a task usually performed by women.

The last identified case was a twenty-seven-year-old housewife from Nzinda, Kikwit, admitted to Kikwit II Maternity Hospital on June 24, 1995, for the management of a septic abortion. She was discharged on July 14 and died at home on July 16.

On August 24, 1995, the outbreak was declared over.

We had honed our epidemiological skills, increased our understanding of transmission and prevention strategies, and I'd had the opportunity to recognize and describe the concept of "superspreaders." Those are the people with large numbers of contacts who disproportionately drive epidemics. The archetype of this is Typhoid Mary, an Irish cook named Mary Mallon, thought to have infected fifty-one people and caused three deaths from typhoid fever in the New York area during the first decades of the twentieth century. The anomaly in her case was that she was completely asymptomatic.

During the year and a half after the Kikwit outbreak ended, international projects were initiated to support ongoing Ebola surveillance and to help maintain infection control practices at hospitals in the area. However, these efforts were interrupted by the civil war that has been going on ever since.

Mobutu was overthrown less than two years after the outbreak ended, but not before he and his clan had looted every bar of gold and piece of foreign currency that once sat in vaults, supposedly guaranteeing the "validity" of Zaire's currency. He died the same year of prostate cancer.

I returned a few months later to get bone marrow samples from survivors to develop new antibodies as a therapy, especially since the local clinicians had done a provocative trial suggesting great results from transfusing the blood of people who had survived the disease into those who were sick. The nuns were still there running the hospital. A reminder that love and the devotion to God trump Ebola every time.

4

A POX ON

BOTH YOUR HOUSES

*Now the Small-Pox arises when blood putrefies and fer-
ments, so that the superfluous vapors are thrown out of it
(forming blisters), and it is changed from the blood of in-
fants, which is like must, into the blood of young men, which
is like wine perfectly ripened.*

—Abu Bakr Mohammed ibn Zacariya al-Razi,
A Treatise on the Smallpox and Measles

We humans act like we own the planet, when really it's the
microbes and the insects that run things. One way they re-
mind us who's in charge is by transmitting disease, often with
the help of small animals, including rodents or bats. Seventy
to eighty percent of emerging infectious diseases are, in fact,
zoonotic. The rest, such as drug-resistant microbes, are completely of our own making.

This does not mean all microbes are bad. We owe them
many thanks for the fermenting of wine, beer, and cheese.
We've also harnessed them as biological production factories
and even as natural insecticides. I have a very healthy respect
for microbes. They are 3.5 billion years old, represent 90 percent of all life, can produce thirty generations in a day, and
have picked up the nifty trick of rapid genetic evolution by
swapping advantageous pieces of genetic material through

transposons and plasmids. In contrast, there is us: humans. Modern humans are about 200,000 years old, we produce a single generation in twenty-five years, and our genetic diversity is defined by localized mating patterns.

And even we are not really a single organism at all, but a hive collective inseparable from our human microbiome.

The human body contains 100 trillion cells, 90 percent of which are microbial cells in the gut and other orifices and on its surfaces. These "passengers" come from about ten thousand different microbe species that comprise the human ecosystem. The complex interaction with this microbiota plays an important role in keeping us healthy. At the same time, it is putatively associated with sexually transmitted infections, obesity, gastrointestinal diseases, diabetes, and rheumatoid arthritis. We already use "good" microbes or probiotics to treat a severe form of neonatal gastrointestinal infection and prevent diarrhea while we're taking antibiotics. Fecal transplants from healthy donors with good microbes are the treatment of choice for patients with a severe life-threatening colon infection. Called *Clostridium difficile,* this disease is associated with antibiotic use that disrupts the functioning of the good microbes in our guts. Finally, there is increasing data that early antibiotic use can lead to later obesity. Researchers now find that they can make obese mice slim by feeding them the bugs from a once obese sibling who became slim after the mouse equivalent of weight loss surgery. There are already provocative studies with fecal transplants from slim persons to those with obesity to test the link between obesity and an altered gut microbiota.

Sometimes microbes go rogue in the hunt for new ecologic niches, akin to us moving out to the countryside when the cities get too crowded. Since the advent of modern science, we've fought back fairly well. Smallpox, which most likely evolved from a rodent virus, was one of the greatest scourges of humankind and undoubtedly changed the course of human history, especially in the colonization of the New World where the natives were not immune. But, in 1980, a global effort declared that smallpox had been eradicated worldwide. So confident were we that we suspended smallpox vaccination programs. This was possible only because smallpox can't rely on animal hosts or reservoirs, but depends for its survival entirely on person-to-person transmission. If you interrupt the transfer to a new person by finding and isolating the very last human host for the disease, or protecting the uninfected with a vaccine, then you've wiped it out—gone forever. Unless you're keeping some of the virus alive in research labs, of course, which is another story. Unfortunately, with new advances in synthetic biology, the proverbial mad scientist could also readily reassemble it again from the published gene maps for nefarious purposes.

While the danger from native smallpox had been put to rest, there was concern that the ecological niche left vacant might be filled by a less deadly but still troubling disease called monkeypox.

In December 1996, while I was chief of CDC's Epidemiology Unit, Special Pathogens Branch, I took a call from my old friend from the Ebola outbreak in Zaire, Dr. David Heymann of the World Health Organization. He informed me of an outbreak of monkeypox in a cluster of twelve remote villages in the center of the Congo, and he asked for my help.

David had gotten $20,000 from the WHO director general for a three-week investigation, and he wanted me to head a team that included scientists from CDC and from the European Field Epidemiology program, which is the EIS equivalent in Europe.

Monkeypox got its name in 1958, when it was first identified in lab monkeys—crab-eating macaques—captured for use in neurological research. It's caused by a zoonotic virus within the same genus as smallpox, Orthopoxvirus, within the family poxviridae (home of the common wart virus). Despite the name, it is actually more prevalent in sun squirrels and other rodents, especially Gambian pouched rats. After a one- to two-week incubation period, it causes the skin of people infected with it to break out in deep-seated, firm dome-shaped lesions that can look like vesicles or pustules very similar to smallpox. Fortunately, it is quite rare.

Human monkeypox can be difficult to distinguish clinically from smallpox (to which it is closely related) and chickenpox (to which it is not).

You can test animals for monkeypox antibodies, tell-tale traces left behind when the immune system goes to work against a specific invader. If you find antibodies, you've probably found an animal host for the disease.

After the disease was first reported in humans in 1970 and led to an intense monitoring effort to see if the disease posed a risk to the smallpox eradication campaign. An earlier global yellow fever eradication campaign had been derailed, in part, because the disease was able to retreat into the jungle, sustain itself in animals, then resurface to infect humans. Over the next fifteen years there were only about four hundred cases of monkeypox in equatorial Central and West Africa, mostly in remote villages surrounded by tropical rain forests where people have more frequent contact with infected animals, including the consumption of bush meat. That local menu designation includes monkeys and other wild animals, but Africans eat rodents as well. Monkeypox has a death rate of about 10 percent (smallpox is much deadlier and closer to 30 percent), and a secondary human-to-human infection rate about the same. There is no safe and proven treatment.

The real question for us was, from this large new cluster, had we called it wrong? By discontinuing smallpox vaccination, had we opened the door to monkeypox infection? And were we now going to need to resume vaccination in Central Africa to prevent its spread? But smallpox vaccine is live virus, meant to provoke an immune response in people with healthy immune systems. The problem then was the prevalence of

HIV/AIDS (human immunodeficiency virus/acquired immunodeficiency syndrome) today—which meant that hundreds
of thousands of immunocompromised people would have no
defense against the live virus, and thus a return to mass immunization could be a disaster. It's always better to prevent
a disease than to treat it after you've got it, but at what cost?

The weight of this question and its history was not lost.
The largest and ongoing pandemic at the end of the twentieth century was HIV/AIDS, which too had once been a zoonotic disease and an emerging infection. Detailed forensics on
the virus genes suggested that it had originated in the 1920s
in Léopoldville (now Kinshasa) after successfully making the
species-jump from a related immunodeficiency virus of chimpanzees, likely from the handling of bloody bush meat. This
was a booming city of trade and commerce with rapid population growth and robust railways that had a million people
flowing through the city each year. The similarly booming sex
trade and likely reuse of syringes created a toxic mix to am-
plify the virus and spread it across the continent and farther,
via trade and travel routes. Despite potent descriptions of
"slim" disease the syndrome was not recognized as a distinct
illness in Africa for the next sixty years. This was coupled
with a flawed response in the United States due to the politics
of sex. The disease is now well established as a human pathogen, with 1.5 million deaths in 2013.

In February of 1997, I returned to the tropical paradise of
Kinshasa, which not surprisingly had not improved any
since I'd last visited a year and a half before. Chaos and corruption still worked as a tag team to keep everything nightmarish, and the civil war had only gotten worse.

WHO assured us that vehicles would be available once we
got into the bush, but first we needed permission from the

minister of health, whose entourage decided that we needed several of their own people on our team; we were not above the speculation that this was so they could earn the per diems. All of a sudden these distant cousins and assorted back scratchers were experts in virology and epidemiology. We were careful to not ask why, until that time they had worked as taxi drivers and clerks. We just hoped that once the negotiations were done, there would be enough room for the people who actually knew something, and not just for the shills.

Ultimately, we were fortunate to put together an excellent team that included people from the Ministry of Health, as well as Dr. Okitolonda Sespi from the School of Public Health at Kinshasa University. A big part of our job would be to take blood from a variety of rodents, trying to figure out which ones had monkeypox. We found an expat zoologist named Delfi Messinger to help us identify the animals.

But then we had to find a plane. The first one we looked at was held together with duct tape, which is somewhat figurative, but I know that it definitely, literally, had fuel leaking out of the wing. The pilot said, "Oh, don't worry. The moment we take off it will pressurize and there'll be no more leaking."

I said, "We're not getting in this," and nobody argued, and we kept looking, even though the delay was costing us time.

Eventually, we found a standard dual-propeller deathtrap and flew to Lodja, about five hundred miles east, and just south of the Sankuru Nature Preserve. This would be our jumping-off point, where we'd rent Land Cruisers and a big truck. This isn't a situation where you drop in at a Budget or Enterprise, put down your credit card, and make sure you get your frequent-user points. This is Do-It-Yourself Rent-a-Car. You track down someone in town who's got a Land Cruiser and say, "How much to use your truck for a week?" You have to put all the pieces together yourself, and if you veer off into a ravine, or rebels shoot it up with AK-47s, that's your problem. There's no insurance company that's going to bail you out after you pay the deductible.

Once we had secured transportation, and rations and supplies, we took off toward our ultimate destination at the epicenter of the Congo's monkeypox outbreak, a village in the Kayembe-Kumbi region called Akungula.

Monkeypox is the kind of exotic viral disease that keeps people like me challenged. The virus can spread not just through direct contact with an infected person's bodily fluids, like Ebola, but also from human to human through droplets in the air, like influenza. The incubation period is ten to fourteen days, and early symptoms include distinctive swelling of lymph nodes (different from smallpox), muscle pain, headache, fever, and a distinctive rash that typically progresses through stages of vesiculation, pustulation, umbilication, and crusting. In some patients, early lesions become ulcerated. The rash and lesions occur on the head, trunk, and extremities, and often even the palms of the hands and the soles of the feet.

But most of all, even if you've eliminated the monkeypox virus in humans, that isn't going to make it disappear. It can survive just fine without us, staying alive in its rodent reservoir. The virus will quietly spread from rat to rat or squirrel to squirrel, year after year out in the jungle, and you'll never know it except for the sporadic human infection. Then suddenly, out of the blue, you've got a new human epidemic on your hands. It can happen anytime, and you've got to be ready when it does.

What scared us about the situation in Akungula was not simply the number of human cases, but the fact that we were able to trace the cases way, way back, sometimes down a chain of eight or more infected persons. This suggested that monkeypox could spread from person to person as easily as a cold in a subway car. We already knew enough about its transmission to expect that people who came in contact with infected rodents would come down with the illness, especially young kids who'd never received the smallpox vaccination, which provides some cross-protection, and who developed their hunting skills by making snares and other simple traps to capture small animals. What we hadn't expected, and what had us really worried, was how easily the virus could continue to pass from person to person to person, no rodents required.

There were emerging cases throughout the Kayembe-Kumbi area, and the moment we got to Akungula, everybody started telling us what they'd seen and supposedly experienced. All this information had to be sifted through to try to understand what was really going on, and what we really needed to do.

We set up our portable lab in the compound and moved into the hut graciously provided by the chief of the village, Lomange Otshudi.

Starting out from the chief's hut each morning, we would break into small groups, each group taking a vehicle and heading for a village within a thirty- or forty-mile radius. Much of the time, the teams of epidemiologists had to hack their way through the jungle, creating their own roads.

When we arrived in a new region, we usually had the name of a local contact whom we could call on for help. In some larger cities, it might be a Catholic mission where the priest or the nuns could put us up. Instead of camping out somewhere, maybe sleeping in hammocks and eating cold rations, we'd have a hot shower, a regular bed to sleep in, and a nice breakfast complete with Nutella for our bread. It's surprising how luxurious even a spartan accommodation like this can seem, compared to sleeping on the ground, and how much it can cheer you up when you've been bouncing along rutted roads all day in the middle of nowhere. It's from those times that I understood the true meaning of "first-world problems." And the priest, nuns, and various acolytes living in chosen poverty always made me feel blessed and much closer to God.

In some rural areas, there would be a resident *infirmier*, or nurse, a local African who was typically the highest-ranking public health official in the vicinity, and very likely the only medical professional for miles around. They would deliver babies and distribute medicine, if the government could afford to provide any. They might work out of rudimentary health clinics with a handful of beds—you couldn't really call them hospitals, as they were mostly dreadfully underfunded and poorly equipped. Some of these were remnants of clinics the Belgians had built back in colonial times, when the Congo was the personal property of King Leopold.

In more enlightened times, villagers paid whatever they could afford for medical services, which might be nothing. People with money to spend were apt to get treatment at a real hospital in a bigger town.

Our procedure upon arriving in a new locale was to start by trying to look up any of these *infirmiers* and whatever served as the vestige of a local governance. For example, for the *Zone de Santé* of Kato Kwambe, we met with the supervisor, Omeshango Opanga, the *infirmier chef de santé*, or chief nurse, and the commissioner of that region, Mr. Omandala Odimo.

We also met Sister Jean, who was the nursing director at one of the local hospitals. You need to get the local people involved as you try to sort out what needs to happen and you establish the appropriate relationships in the community to get things done. This is not parachuting in from a plane to a village and saying, "Okay, I'm an American doctor. I'm taking over now." That never works. And why would it? Would you trust an alien with a green pointed head if he suddenly arrived at your local hospital and said, "I have all the answers, and I've come to save you?"

To do the work you really do need to engage with the local community and with the local governing structures to make sure you do the right thing. If you don't do that, the minute you leave, it's all over. Sadly, sometimes that happens even if you did, but we have to try. This is the true definition of global health: striving to improve the condition of people worldwide regardless of GPS (global positioning system) coordinates and an accident of birth.

And that's the big problem with most outbreaks—there's often no sustainability plan, not just for containing the disease itself, but for the basic public health functions, like surveillance.

At each village we would introduce ourselves, look for cases, take blood from people within households, check them for smallpox vaccination scars, and work on getting answers to the study questions. We did school surveys, and we looked at the vaccination history for smallpox over the defined area. This was so important to us because if the epidemiology of the disease had changed, and this was (a) more severe than it had been previously or was (b) being transmitted continuously by people without a need to go back to the rodent reservoir, then that might imply that we needed to resume smallpox vaccination in that area, despite the risk presented by the presence of HIV/AIDS. But that would be a tough call.

In most of these places we were the only outsiders to have shown up in years, and it took great skill from our local team members to earn the trust of the villagers, and then to get blood samples, which were scary and painful, especially for young kids.

For all the high-tech gadgets we now had to track and fight disease outbreaks, some of our most effective tools were almost comically simple. Going from one thatched-roof mud hut to another, looking for suspected cases of monkeypox, we carried old decks of smallpox cards. These were laminated, colored photos of a child with smallpox lesions, which could make the skin from head to toe look like pebble-grain leather. The cards had been used by doctors for years to help people around the world know what smallpox looked like. Given that the lesions were so similar, we figured the cards would be useful in helping people identify cases of monkeypox too.

For years, stacks of these cards had been gathering dust in a closet deep in the bowels of WHO, but we pulled them out and started taking them with us into the field. In villages where we stopped, we'd pass around the cards and ask, "Have you seen anyone who looks like this?"

When we found the telltale pustular rash, fever, and respiratory symptoms, we would take fluid from crusted scabs or vesicles, and swabs or puss from active cases. We counted facial scars, vaccination scars, and noted the age of the individual. The age distribution was mainly young people, although about a fifth were over fifteen years of age, which suggested that they had never been vaccinated for smallpox. It would have been good to know if any of these persons was infected with HIV, but we did not have appropriate approval from the ministry to test them.

Meanwhile, we offered a bounty for villagers to bring in small mammals such as squirrels, bats, monkeys, and rats.

In epidemiology, when we talk about chains of transmission—the paths a disease microbe travels from one host to another during an outbreak—one of the key questions is, will a point come when this chain becomes so long that it's impossible to break? That is, when do you have so many human hosts harboring a communicable disease that it no longer needs an animal reservoir at all? That's the point when you're no longer talking about an animal-borne disease. You're talking about a human disease.

The fancy scientific term is the "basic reproductive rate," which is a proxy for how infectious a disease is. If it is more than one, then people can sustain the disease indefinitely because each case is associated with at least one new person infected. Measles, for example, has the highest basic reproductive number of about fifteen, which is why you need to have extremely high vaccination rates to stop outbreaks. Influenza is about two to three, but it makes up for it with a very short incubation period, meaning the time from infection to illness. (This is the concept I was asked to explain to Kate Winslet and the writers of her film *Contagion*.) With any new disease, it's by calculating this number that you gain some sense of the magnitude of the problem.

In an outbreak like this, if you find that the average infected household has had fewer than one additional case of infection, then you conclude that the outbreak has peaked. But if the disease's reproductive rate is greater than one—if on average you're finding more than one additional sick person per household—that's a kind of tipping point. It means the disease is capable of sustaining itself in the community. It might even be gathering momentum.

So one of the crucial questions we needed answered was how many additional cases might be in that household. Then we would compile our results to get a big picture of what was going on.

If a virus's reproductive rate stays above one, it can persist in a population forever. This is every microbe's dream and every epidemiologist's nightmare. You have examples of those microbes that stick, you have examples of those that don't stick, and the critical factor that makes them stick. That's a critical issue for us as we think about the next global pandemic. Which ones get to say, "Hey, I made the jump. I never have to go back to the jungle again, slumming inside rodents." Many of our exclusive human diseases have successfully made that jump: measles, seasonal influenza, malaria, and HIV.

Overall, a disease like Ebola may have a basic reproductive rate less than one. But if the infected people are in a community or a hospital where there's effectively no infection control, then it can keep spreading for a long time before it burns itself out. Outbreaks always burn themselves out eventually, but the issue is, how long do you have to wait before that happens, and how much havoc will the community suffer in the meantime?

One of my companions in our Congo adventure was the amazing Joel Williams, of goat-eating notes fame from Oman. Trained as a veterinarian, he was a public health officer in the US Air Force who had a fellowship to study epidemics. He was one of the best epidemic intelligence officers I've ever worked with and a modern-day MacGyver—a TV secret agent from the eighties who could fashion whatever he needed using only a Swiss army knife and whatever junk was lying around.

All day long at the various villages where we stopped, locals would bring us wild animals they'd caught, and Joel would test them to see if they were carriers of monkeypox or any other diseases we were tracking. Essentially, Joel created a biosafety level 3 lab in the middle of the jungle. He traveled with a portable generator he'd bought in the local market in Kinshasa (which we joked was the one we brought from Atlanta but had never arrived with our luggage), a portable centrifuge, and all sorts of other equipment. It wasn't *Star Trek*, but you get the idea. Joel also created work space to dissect animals and put the various parts into canisters of liquid nitrogen. In his little jungle lab, he could do anything we needed him to do with the animals that people brought us. He could take blood samples, or he could professionally dissect the animals and extract whatever organ we needed to examine and send to Atlanta for testing. Joel and I would be up late at night, long after the teams returned from the village, using the light from a portable lantern to get all the animals processed before the next day.

But this research put us in a bit of an ethical quandary. We knew that the most common way people were getting infected was through direct contact with infected animals they were hunting and eating. So should we tell the local people to limit their contact with the animals they were used to hunting to avoid being contaminated? Obviously, we didn't want them to get infected, but at the same time we knew they were going to be hunting these animals anyway, and we really needed specimens. We struggled with this for a while because we could potentially be putting the trappers at risk of infection. In the end, we adopted the pragmatic view that the villagers were already trapping these animals for food and we were simply diverting them for research. We stressed limiting the handling of the animals till they were well cooked, and restricting contact with suspected cases to a single person, preferably the oldest member of the household who had either recovered from monkeypox or had a vaccination scar.

Of course, as we handled these animals, including their blood and body parts, we were concerned about not getting infected ourselves. We had medical scrubs, rubber gloves, and masks—although I think Joel was probably more conscientious than I was about steadfastly maintaining biosafety in the Congo's tropical heat. Anyway, we tried to be careful because we were an awfully long way from the nearest fully equipped hospital.

As part of his exceptional preparedness, Joel had all kinds of emergency gear that I would never have thought of bringing along. At one point, we noticed that a gigantic swarm of army ants had gathered outside our hut, and an attack seemed imminent. Joel told us, "If those ants get inside, we're done for." Then, out of the blue, he pulled out a huge plastic bottle of heavy-duty ant poison. We were all thinking, Where did that come from? The guy carries this stuff around in his luggage? He sprayed the liquid all around the perimeter of the hut, and the ant invasion never materialized. Joel knew how to keep animals under control. As I said, he was a vet.

Another benefit of traveling with a top-shelf public health officer was that he acted as our de facto restaurant inspector. Of course, I use the word "restaurant" metaphorically. There were never any places to eat—rural Congo is not exactly a tourist mecca. The buildings were mud huts with thatched roofs, and we usually slept on cots we carried with us, but whenever we were going to be in a village for a while, one of the first things we would do was to hire cooks. Our dining area was an open space in front of a hut with a single small table and some chairs. We'd sit there at the beginning and end of the day, and eat the meals our cooks had prepared.

As our food inspector, Joel observed the preparation for the evening meals and, at first, told us only what he felt we needed to know. Breakfast, we quickly noticed, was invariably leftovers from the night before. After a few days of this, Joel asked me, "Ali, have you noticed any refrigerators around here?"

No, now that he mentioned it, I hadn't. Well, what's a little intestinal distress, especially with ciprofloxacin as your best friend? If you don't think about it too hard, sometimes you can get through it okay.

I am a gigantic carnivore, but as a Muslim I observe certain food restrictions, one of which is that I try to eat only meat that is *halal*, meaning that it's been butchered in accordance with Muslim customs. (Think of it as the Muslim version of kosher.)

Now, it's pretty hard to be a choosey eater when you're roaming around the African interior like a character out of a Joseph Conrad novel. In rural Congo, far from the nearest restaurant with a multipage menu, I got pretty tired of eating nothing but local vegetables day after day. And despite all the rivers in the vicinity, there was not a lot in the way of fish for sale either. So one afternoon I decided, Fine, I'll buy live animals and take care of making them halal myself. I'll do the butchering.

The next morning, a villager brought me a live goat that I'd paid him for. I took a sharp knife, said, "*Allahu Akbar*" to give thanks, then sliced clean through the animal's windpipe and the carotid arteries in one swift motion to minimize suffering. Joel then did the obligatory inspection of the carcass to make sure the animal had been healthy. Mission accomplished. Everyone on the team, including the villagers we'd hire to do our cooking, was delighted—fresh meat! A few days later, I did the same with a brace of guinea hens that I'd bought. We all agreed it was a nice change to have meat in our diet again.

A few days after that, I noticed that my colleagues were more excited than usual. Even the goats tied up nearby seemed excited. I found out that a villager had just arrived with a live suckling pig, and my companions were waiting for me to butcher it. They were already fantasizing about all the bacon, ham, and pork chops that would be added to our week's menu. I had to tell them, "Look, you've got the process down, but you've completely missed the concept. Pork is simply not on the Muslim menu. Nobody—*nobody*—can make a pig halal." However, I was a good sport and paid for the pig anyway so the rest of our team could eat it.

Despite the fact that my job was all about how *not* to get infected, I admit that even I would be a little lax. Sometimes at night I didn't bother draping a mosquito net over my cot before climbing in. Insecticide-treated mosquito nets are the cheapest and most reliable way to protect yourself from the scourge of malaria, especially if, unlike us doctors, you don't have access to prophylactic antimalarial medication.

The thing about mosquito netting, when you think about it, is that the weave can stop insects a lot bigger than mosquitoes. And some of those things you really don't want in your bed. I recall waking up one morning to the sound of people banging around looking for fuel for the generator. I opened my eyes and saw a fat hairy spider the size of my hand crawling across the mosquito net a few inches from my head. Not a pleasant sight, but far better to find a tarantula on the net than inside the net. That was the end of my days of not always using a net.

Another member of our team in the Congo was the expat mammalogist Delfi Messinger, who was sort of an American version of Jane Goodall. She normally worked at a rescue center in the capital, Kinshasa, that specialized in wild bonobos. These are cousins of the chimps, but much gentler. If you think of a chimp colony as marine boot camp, with a rigid hierarchy enforced by muscle and intimidation, bonobo society is more like a hippie commune, where sex is the ever-present social lubricant that keeps everybody chill. She was quite a colorful character, an animal conservationist who'd lived in Africa for fourteen years. While a Peace Corp volunteer, she'd volunteered to help WHO with monkeypox once before. During a major uprising, when bullets were flying, she did not flee. Instead, to protect her rescued bonobos, she spray-painted "SIDA" in blood on the entrance of the compound where she worked. (SIDA is the French term for AIDS.)

The animals Delfi worked with had usually been abandoned by their mothers or injured by poachers, who hunt them for bush meat. She was a lovely woman, great with animals, but like Goodall, more identified with the animals than with the humans who made life increasingly difficult for her furry charges. I would try to pin her down about the genus and species of some local creature, and she would know what it was, but it was hard to get her attention long enough to get an answer. It wasn't that she didn't want to be helpful. It was more that she just didn't share our sense of urgency about the mission. She was accustomed to spending her days with bonobos, and bonobos are famously laid back.

The more serious problem we had to deal with was the First Congo War. We knew it had hit home for us when, as I mentioned in the introduction, a kid showed up on a motorbike saying that rebels fighting President Mobuto on behalf of Laurent Kabila, an ethnic Luba from Katanga Province, were less than a day away.

There have been tensions between various ethnic groups in eastern Zaire for centuries, especially between the agrarian tribes native to Zaire and the seminomadic Tutsi tribes that emigrated from Rwanda. Destabilization in eastern Zaire that resulted from the Rwandan genocide was the tipping point that caused numerous internal and external factors to align against the corrupt and inept government in Kinshasa.

Then, in the 1990s, a wave of democratization swept across Africa that put pressure for reform on Zairian president Mobutu Sésé Seko. He officially ended the one-party system he had maintained since 1967, but was ultimately unwilling to implement sufficient reform, alienating allies both at home and abroad. In fact, the Zairian state had all but ceased to exist, with most of the population relying on an informal economy for their subsistence. Making matters worse, the Zairian national army, Forces Armées Zaïroises (FAZ), was forced to prey on the population for survival.

Of those who fled Rwanda during the genocide, about 1.5 million settled in eastern Zaire. These refugees included those who fled the Hutu *génocidaires* as well as those who fled the Tutsi Rawandan Patriotic Front, fearing retaliation. Prominent among the latter group were the *génocidaires* themselves, including elements of the former Rwandan army, Forces Armées Rwandaises, and an independent Hutu extremist group known as Interahamwe. They were the guys closing in on us.

After we called the US embassy and they told us to evacuate, we sent villagers out to round up our team. Then we consolidated our samples into a single tank of liquid nitrogen and began the seventy-five-mile trek back through the jungle to the airstrip at Lodja, often floating our vehicles across rivers on pontoons.

The French documentary film crew whose plane was going to pick us up landed in a torrential rain, and as soon as it taxied up, panicked villages hoping to escape Laurent Kabila's rebels swarmed around it, until the security guards fired warning shots.

We were already pretty shaken up, and the weather was nightmarish, which meant that the takeoff from the landing strip was pretty rocky. I noticed that the guy next to me was extremely nervous. Another fellow across the aisle was muttering his prayers. Aside from concern about the plane crashing altogether, there was the matter of stuff that hadn't been tied down well. It was sliding across the plane, so concern that it might hurt somebody or the supplies, causing injury or busting out a door, was always there too.

I turned to my seatmate and told him, "You've lived a good life and if you have no regrets, then dying's not that big of a deal." I don't see myself as courageous, and I'm not foolhardy but, at the same time, if you're going to go out and help in these kinds of situations, you can't do the job if you're too concerned about your own safety. How do you tell others not to be scared if you're too scared to take action? Not fearing death has always given me clarity of thinking about what to do, because I don't have to deal with my anxiety before getting down to problem solving.

We made it out—barely. But the rebels overran the village a few days after we left and some of the people we'd worked with were killed. Far away or not, the sadness and outrage of finding that good hard-working people had lost their lives as pawns in a power struggle and over mere racism is always overwhelming.

Our work had been disrupted, but still we were able to demonstrate that there was no evidence for person-to-person transmission being sufficient to sustain the epidemic. The long chains of transmission were disturbing, but not surprising given the nature of the disease. Yes, the outbreak had been enabled by the cessation of smallpox vaccination, but we had proved that monkeypox's reproductive rate was still less than one, which meant it wasn't going to become the next global pandemic. It was a serious problem, but it was not the Problem From Hell.

The saving grace of smallpox is that there is no animal reservoir—if you knock it out in humans, that's it. There's also a very effective vaccine that can be combined with "ring vaccination," which means inoculating everyone likely to have come in contact with the infected individual. Then you can form an additional buffer of immunity if you want by also inoculating a second ring of people who may have been exposed to those in the first ring, meaning those directly exposed.

Monkeypox is a different matter. Not only can it recede into the jungle for any number of years before reappearing in humans, but it can be easily transported in the convenient carrying case known as a rodent. And these days, you can find the damnedest rodents in the damnedest places.

———————

Oddly enough, I did not leave monkeypox behind when I left the Congo. Seven years later, in May 2003, a three-year-old boy turned up in a clinic in Wisconsin with a fever (103°F) of unknown origin, swollen eyes, and a red vesicular skin rash. The child was hospitalized, and when doctors examined samples from his lesions under an electron microscope, they saw a brick-shaped virus, which is a flag for a pox virus. The doctors called the local health department, which called CDC. This was the first time monkeypox had ever been seen in the United States. Which had public health officials scratching their heads. How does a disease never before seen outside central Africa turn up in the American Midwest?

It turned out that the month before, a Texas importer had received a shipment of 762 African rodents from Accra, Ghana. The shipment included Gambian rats, rope squirrels, tree squirrels, brushtail porcupines, dormice, and striped mice. He then shipped these animals to distributors in six states, as well as Japan.

In Illinois, a distributor received the Gambian rats and dormice and housed them with two hundred prairie dogs. This distributor then shipped the prairie dogs to pet stores in Wisconsin, Illinois, Indiana, Missouri, Kansas, South Carolina, and Michigan. They developed lesions resembling smallpox, but for a long while no one noticed—imagine if this had been a deliberate smallpox attack on the United States. The only good news (for us at least but not the prairie dogs) was that we had identified the perfect animal model for monkeypox infections.

It turned out the Wisconsin boy was bitten by a prairie dog purchased from a local pet store.

When CDC got involved, a number of teams were heading out to different states, mostly in the Midwest, where they

would be trying to trace the disease in local rodent populations and follow up on the associated human cases. I asked to
lead the Indiana team, primarily because until then I had seen
monkeypox lesions only on young African kids. Seeing them
on Caucasian adults would be a first, and this was not just idle
curiosity. For a clinician like me, this could be useful diagnostic information.

I picked a top-flight deputy team leader, John Iskandar,
who had assisted me on my first outbreak with the contaminated ice on the cruise ship. The moment I got to Indiana, I did
something that would have drawn a reprimand at CDC headquarters. I said to John, "Okay, you're in charge," and then
I jumped in my rental car and—even though I was way too
senior to be doing this—drove around Indiana for several days
making house or hospital calls on every one of the patients
suspected of having monkeypox. You could say I was acting
irresponsibly, but I wanted to feel like an old-time epidemiologist again—a disease detective wearing out shoe leather,
looking for the facts, sifting for clues. It was also great to visit
patients who weren't going to die. In my line of business, I am
often the harbinger of death.

Along the way, I gained insight into the world of "pocket
pet" people in this country.

I visited one family that had close to a hundred pets, ranging
from mammals to snakes. I boned up especially on the world
of prairie dogs, and on the world of swap meets, which is often where you go to buy and trade exotic pets, and perhaps to
have the fur trimmed on the exotic pets you bought last time.

A lot of times, the people out walking prairie dogs as if
they were Chihuahuas were farm families living in trailers. It's
a little known fact among America's coastal elite, but it turns
out you can drag a giant vacuum cleaner out into the prairie,
stick the nozzle down a prairie-dog hole, and suck an animal
up out of the ground.

My deputy, meanwhile, was dealing with the bigger issues
of epidemiology surveillance, and he was doing it splendidly.

This included continued disease monitoring and a survey in a day care center, a school, and two local hospitals.

Of the 200 prairie dogs housed with the Gambian rats and dormice, 94 tested positive for monkeypox virus, including prairie dogs in pet stores in Wisconsin (44 cases), Indiana (24), Illinois (19), Ohio (4), Kansas (1), Missouri (1), and 1 case in New Jersey.

Between May 15 and June 20, 2003, a total of seventy-one people ranging in age from one to fifty-one were infected with monkeypox. Patients typically experienced fever, headaches, muscle aches, chills, and nonproductive coughs. This was followed one to ten days later by a generalized papular rash that developed first on the trunk, then limbs and head. The papules evolved through phases of vesiculation, pustulation, umbilication, and crusting. Every one of these patients reported direct or close contact with a recently acquired prairie dog.

CDC issued guidance on the use of smallpox vaccine, Cidofovir (an antiviral drug), and vaccinia immune globulin (an antibody preparation). Twenty-six residents in five states received the smallpox vaccination. Fortunately, no adverse reactions to the smallpox vaccine were reported.

The case fatality rate for monkeypox is usually between 1 and 10 percent. Although there was one sweet six-year-old with a severe brain inflammation from the virus infection, fortunately there were no fatalities during this US outbreak, which was most likely because this was the milder West African version of the disease than what I had seen in Zaire. But it was a valuable reminder, which is that we are increasingly not immune to a smallpox attack. The deliberate use of smallpox as a weapons is not farfetched due to synthetic biology. One of the great blights on our history is the giving of smallpox-infested blankets to Native Americans.

There's the urban myth of alligators in the sewers of New York, supposedly the result of owners flushing their exotic pets when they realize that a one-bedroom apartment on the

Upper West Side cannot accommodate a large, carnivorous reptile.

Our fear in the Midwest was the prospect of people hearing about monkeypox and releasing their prairie dogs into the wild. We knew that these critters had a fabulous ability to get infected. What we didn't know was what the infection rate was in any given population—what fraction of prairie dogs were carrying monkeypox? Of those that were, how rapidly could the disease they carried spread through a wild population before they themselves sickened and died? If people released their pet prairie dogs only after they showed signs of illness, did that make them more or less dangerous in the wild?

To be on the safe side, the Centers for Disease Control and Prevention banned the importation of all African rodents. The US Food and Drug Administration also issued orders banning the interstate shipment of prairie dogs and all African rodents.

The underlying truth here is that, in the age of air travel, a disease anywhere can very quickly become a disease everywhere.

5

A HIGHER FORM
OF KILLING

We had begun working on the biological warfare issue in 1993, after the World Trade Center bombing made it clear that terrorism could strike at home, and a defector from Russia had told us that his country had huge stocks of anthrax, smallpox, Ebola, and other pathogens, and had continued to produce them even after the demise of the Soviet Union.

—Bill Clinton, *My Life*

On October 15, 2001, I was coming back from a conference when I was detained at O'Hare International Airport by the FBI. Special Agent Don Duffy took one look at my brown skin and my passport with stamps from Saudi Arabia, Yemen, Egypt, Pakistan, and must have thought, Uh-oh.

I was taken to a little room off to the side, a sort of holding cell, by four heavily armed Chicago police officers who kept telling me to keep my hands out of my pockets. Officer Thomas, one of Chicago's finest, made sure I stayed put. Which I did, for several hours.

Agent Duffy asked me the same questions I'd already been asked, repeatedly: "What's your birth date? What's your age? Which countries have you visited? What was the purpose of your trip? Where do you work?"

I remember him, and various of his Chicago colleagues, scribbling notes I couldn't see as they tried to figure out what the hell to do with me.

It turned out my name had shown up on the new no-fly list that had been put together as a response to the attacks on the World Trade Center and the Pentagon just a few weeks before. It didn't matter to the police or the FBI that I was traveling with a US official (not my personal) passport. It didn't matter that I had a picture ID showing that I was a federal employee at the Centers for Disease Control and Prevention, or another that I was a senior commissioned officer in the uniformed services of the US Public Health Service (also with a photo). My various travel documents didn't impress them at all. What did impress them was that I had brown skin and a Muslim name.

So I sat in a chair in the windowless room while various officers from various agencies came and went, some just glancing in, some doing good cop–bad cop routines. Meanwhile, my flight to Atlanta was called, and it was boarded, and it took off without me, providing an opportunity to observe at close hand the nation's heightened security precautions in a post-9/11 world.

Eventually they let me go, but only after phoning CDC back in Atlanta and speaking to Ms. Harris, the night receptionist, and asking her if she knew a Dr. Ali Khan. Fortunately, she did. She's a lovely person with whom I'd always chatted as I came and went at all hours. But I've always wondered what would have happened if they'd called CDC number I'd given them and reached a fill-in receptionist who'd never heard of me. Would I have been hustled off to Gitmo? For that matter, what did they know about the woman they'd just spoken to? The phone number with the 404 area code could have been a direct line to Al Qaeda headquarters in some cave in Tora Bora, with a crafty Mata Hari standing by to answer. Asking the receptionist was not exactly a Cracker Jack–level of police work. And as for probable cause, my being detained was like an African American being stopped for DWB, "driving while black." In my case, the offense was FWM: "flying while Muslim." In the fifteen years (and counting) since, I've gotten used to the "Red Muslim" folder at immigration, and the room off to the side to await my judgment.

I was able to catch a later flight, but it was almost two in the morning by the time I made it home and crawled into bed, exhausted.

But I hadn't even fallen asleep before the phone rang. It was a fellow epidemiologist, Tracee Treadwell at CDC.

"Ali, we need you in Washington. There's been an anthrax attack on Capitol Hill, and you have to help sort it out."

So in little more time than it would take to put on a cape in a phone booth, I'd gone from suspected terrorist to freedom fighter, summoned to the front lines to save the nation from a biological attack.

The sun was barely over the horizon as the CDC Gulfstream lifted off the tarmac en route to Washington. The reason for urgency was a standard 3.5" × 6.5" envelope that had shown up in the office of Senate Majority Leader Tom Daschle the previous day. It was prestamped with thirty-six cents' postage, bore a Trenton, New Jersey, postmark, and was tightly sealed with plastic tape. The return address read:

4th Grade
Greendale School
Franklin Park NJ 08852

When an intern working for the senator opened the envelope, a small cloud of dust as fine as talcum powder had burst out. Some of it landed on her lap and on her shoes, and a bit more landed on the pant leg of an intern next to her. When she looked at the letter inside the envelope, she saw the words "anthrax" and "die now." She dropped it on the floor and ran from the room, presumably in a panic.

The full message, which I doubt she had read completely, said:

09-11-01
YOU CAN NOT STOP US
WE HAVE THIS ANTHRAX
YOU DIE NOW
ARE YOU AFRAID?
DEATH TO AMERICA
DEATH TO ISRAEL
ALLAH IS GREAT

Within minutes, first responders came running into the massive Hart Senate Office Building: six from the Capitol Police, six from the FBI, one from the SAA, six from the Hazardous Device Unit. The eventual tally was thirty-eight responders in all. The Capitol Police carried handheld devices that gleamed red—preliminary verification that this powder was anthrax. What they neglected to bring were Tyvek suits, which they should have been wearing, or at least some sort of respiratory protection, along with gloves and gowns that could have been stripped off and discarded.

This mistake was compounded by the fact that, while they ordered everyone out of the building and sealed it off, they left the building's cooling and ventilation system running for another forty-five minutes before Scott Stanley, an FBI agent with a PhD in biomedical sciences and extensive training in bioterrorism, got there and told the sergeant at arms to shut it down. As a result of that delay in containment, technicians in hazmat suits would be collecting specimens from carpeting, chairs, and ventilation ducts—even the stairwells—throughout the one-million-square-foot structure.

Stanley put the letter in a hard plastic container, and then physicians and technicians with the FBI began collecting nasal swabs from all staff members who had been on the fifth and sixth floors. They also went to work with the attending physician for the US Capitol to give affected staffers, as well as first responders, immediate doses of ciprofloxacin, the second-generation synthetic antibiotic that had been the gold standard since 1987. If we zap you with enough ciprofloxacin you're not going to die. However, "enough" means staying on it for sixty days, and the side effects may include a ruptured Achilles tendon. So before we went too far down that road, we needed to set limits by identifying those who'd been exposed at the Capitol Building.

The Daschle letter was the lead story on all three major television network newscasts on the evening of the fifteenth, but bioterrorism was already in the news. Three weeks earlier, similar envelopes containing anthrax spores, also processed in Trenton, had arrived at the offices of the *New York Post* and at the office of Tom Brokaw, at that time anchor of *NBC News*. One of Brokaw's assistants had opened the NBC letter on September 25.

Here again there was a photocopied message:

09-11-01
THIS IS NEXT
TAKE PENACILIN [*sic*] NOW
DEATH TO AMERICA
DEATH TO ISRAEL
ALLAH IS GREAT

Soon, Brokaw's assistant was complaining of redness on her chest that eventually turned black, as well as of a low-grade fever. Dr. Sherif Zaki (with that name, you wonder how long he was detained at airports), CDC chief pathologist, examined a tissue sample from her wound and confirmed cutaneous anthrax.

On September 29, the seven-month-old son of an *ABC News* producer had been brought to the studio by his babysitter. By now he had developed a bright-red sore on the back of his left arm.

October 1 was the day Tom Brokaw's assistant at NBC began taking ciprofloxacin. It was also the day an assistant to CBS anchor Dan Rather noticed that she had a mark on her face, which she thought might be from an insect bite. It was anthrax.

Even before these high-profile cases, two employees of the tabloid publisher American Media, in Boca Raton, Florida, had been diagnosed with anthrax. And even though the state had seen fewer than twenty cases of anthrax in the past hundred years, and even though most of those victims were in occupations where exposure was obvious, such as mill workers handling animal hides, and even though these unusual diagnoses in 2001 came less than a month after the attacks on New York and Washington, DC, they did not immediately trigger suspicions of terrorism. Instead, investigators focused on the fact that the first victim, Robert Stevens, a sixty-three-year-old photo editor, had gone hiking in North Carolina and taken a drink from a waterfall in a cave.

Stevens's doctors raised the alarm after noticing the distinctive shape and color of the anthrax bacteria from his brain linings. The deadliest form of anthrax, inhalational, tends to infect the brain linings, causing a characteristic finding on autopsy called a cardinal's cap. The local laboratory, with technicians recently trained by CDC as part of the Laboratory Response Network, confirmed the diagnosis of anthrax. This was a definitive diagnosis, but the specimens still had to go to CDC for a second verification. The FBI was engaged but terrorism was not suspected. Sometimes CDC is a little too conservative and intellectual. In medicine, they say, "When you hear hoofbeats, think horses, not zebras." We should have been thinking zebras.

That leisurely attitude changed, however, a few days later when forensic investigators discovered anthrax spores on the computer keyboard and other places at Stevens's office. They realized that Stevens had most likely received a contaminated letter without noticing the puff of spores that would kill him a few days later. They never found the letter, but a joint FBI–Postal Service investigative task force, named Amerithrax, was born. That initial diagnostic stumble was a harbinger of a response that always seemed slightly out of sync, and always trying to catch up with, the fluidity of the evolving situation and the pace of new information.

CDC epidemiologists began to comb through databases of suspicious infections elsewhere in the United States. And now, only a few weeks after the initial shock of 9/11, people around the country were starting to panic all over again.

On October 4, a few days before the environmental samples tested positive and Mr. Stevens's diagnosis was confirmed by the state lab, Health and Human Services Secretary Tommy Thompson held a news conference. In it, he said that while sporadic cases of anthrax did occur, this one might "be a result of the heightened level of disease monitoring being done by the public health and medical community." Three times Thompson emphasized, "The system works." Six times he said, "In fact this was an isolated case." Pressed by journalists, Thompson specifically ruled out terrorism and mentioned the swig of water from the stream inside the cave in North Carolina.

Robert Stevens died the next day. A second American Media employee, seventy-three-year-old mail sorter Ernesto Blanco, died the same week.

On October 12, senior Senate staffers met with the Senate sergeant at arms, Al Lenhardt, to discuss security concerns. The chairman of the Senate Judiciary Committee, Patrick Leahy, announced that he was no longer accepting deliveries of any US mail. What neither he nor anyone else knew at the time was that his very own anthrax letter, also mailed from Trenton, had already arrived and been sitting in his office, unopened, since October 9.

―――――――――

When I arrived in Washington at nine thirty on the morning of October 16, CDC had virtually no experience responding to biological terrorism. At that time I was CDC's chief science officer in parasitic diseases, but I hadn't been rushed to the scene because of my close acquaintance with parasites. The reason they wanted me was because I had cofounded the US Bioterrorism Preparedness and Response Program at CDC two years earlier, and I knew the people with expertise in the field. I also had experience managing outbreaks.

Before this time, if you had wanted to buy, say, bubonic plague, either over the counter or through the mail, the only thing you would have been asked was "VISA or MasterCard?" A microbiologist named Larry Wayne Harris—who was also a white supremacist, as it turned out—actually had ordered and received plague through the mail in 1995. Which underscored a more ominous threat than terrorists taking up biology: their most likely victims would be themselves—and that was biologists taking up terrorism.

Then again, it doesn't take a genius, or a chemist, like *Breaking Bad*'s Walter White to do serious damage with an agent like ricin, a highly lethal poison made from an extract of castor beans. All it takes is the beans and some acetone—and there is a history of disgruntled truckers, for instance, extracting it and mailing the lethal powder to judges who'd pissed them off.

However, when it comes to committing murder and mayhem on a massive scale, *Bacillus anthracis* is definitely the weapon of choice. Usually associated with cattle, or hides, or soil, anthrax can form dormant endospores that are able to survive in the harshest conditions, as indicated by the fact that anthrax spores have been found on every continent, including Antarctica. When these spores are inhaled, ingested, or come into contact with a skin lesion on a host, even after centuries lying dormant, they can reanimate and multiply rapidly. And they come in a size that's just right for penetrating deep into your lungs.

While anthrax does not spread directly from one infected animal or person to another, the spores can move around all too easily on clothing or shoes, or just on the wind. The body of an animal that had active anthrax at the time of death is highly infectious, and spores remain at burial sites for decades. Disturbed gravesites of infected animals have caused reinfection after more than seventy years.

It's this kind of hardiness that makes anthrax a natural agent to be weaponized. During World War II, the Germans were experimenting with organophosphorous nerve agents—tabun, sarin, and soman—and the Allies had to keep up. But anthrax is a living thing, and so the question remained, was this bug hardy enough to be delivered by way of an explosive device, as in a bomb or an artillery shell? To find out, the British Army's Royal Engineers, in 1942, conducted a notorious experiment on Gruinard Island, an isolated spot off the coast of Scotland. They staked out eighty sheep in a circle with an explosive shell in the center. The shell contained a strain of anthrax called vollum 14578. As hoped, the anthrax bacillus remained lethal. The shell exploded, the sheep died, and the island remained quarantined for the next forty years.

During those four decades, a movement called Operation Dark Harvest took hold, with activists, including some scientists, demanding that the government decontaminate the island. The group went to Gruinard (in hazmat suits, presumably) and collected three hundred pounds of contaminated soil, samples of which they threatened to leave "at appropriate points that will ensure the rapid loss of indifference of the government and the equally rapid education of the general public." One sealed package was left outside the Porton Down military science research facility in Wiltshire; another was left in Blackpool, where the ruling Conservative Party was holding its annual conference. A cleanup began, and in 1990, after almost half a century, the island was declared safe. Once again, the lesson is that disgruntled scientists can be dangerous. But this was a lesson gravely misapplied when it came to the anthrax letter attacks in DC.

During World War II, the United States established its own biological and chemical weapons facility in what had been home to the US Army Air Corps 2nd Bombardment Squadron, outside Frederick, Maryland. Once the flyboys deployed to England, also in 1942, Detrick Field became Fort Detrick, home of the US Army Biological Warfare Laboratories.

American scientists studied various agents, including anthrax, until 1969, when President Nixon announced that the nation would unilaterally end its biological weapons program. At the same time, the US Army set up USAMRIID, the US Army Medical Research Institute of Infectious Diseases, to do defensive research—developing vaccines and other countermeasures to protect US forces in the event of a biological attack.

Also during the Nixon era, the Soviet Union agreed to suspend biological weapons research, but the treaty they signed in 1972 provided no means for verification. Seven years later, outside the city of Sverdlovsk (formerly, and now again, Yekaterinburg), approximately a hundred people, as well as livestock grazing underneath the track of a plume of anthrax, died of anthrax. Soviet authorities blamed the deaths, along with butchers' subcutaneous exposure, on ingestion of tainted meat. But while that might cause the gastrointestinal and cutaneous form of anthrax, it would decidedly *not* cause the inhalational form that killed the townsfolk. The medical records were sequestered or destroyed.

In 1979, it became obvious that Sverdlovsk harbored a research facility. Built just after World War II, it had continued efforts begun by the wartime Japanese to grow anthrax concentrations impervious to antibiotics. In March of that year, a technician in Sverdlovsk removed a clogged exhaust filter from the anthrax drying machines and, though he left a note explaining why he had temporarily shut down the equipment, his supervisor recorded nothing in the logbook. When the next shift supervisor came in, he simply turned the machines back on.

Before the machines could be stopped and the filter replaced, as much as ten kilograms of anthrax wafted up into the sky oh so near—but happily missing—the city of 300,000, in what has been called the "biological Chernobyl." The incident was reported to military command, but local party bosses, including future president Boris Yeltsin, colluded to cover up the accident in blatant violation of the Biological Weapons Convention. Within a few days, workers in a ceramic plant across the road were dying.

The full, scary truth did not emerge until 1992, when Harvard molecular biologist Matthew Meselson took in a team of inspectors. Their most frightening determination was that, had the winds been blowing in the opposite direction, hundreds of thousands of people could have died.

During the time of Meselson's visit, the Soviet Union was disintegrating, and a Colonel Kanatzhan "Kanat" Alibekov, deputy director of Biopreparat, the Soviet biological weapons program, decided on a career change. He emigrated to the United States and became the subject of a terrifying *New Yorker* profile, after which he published (as Ken Alibek) a chilling book called *Biohazard,* detailing just what the Russkies had been up to at their research facilities hidden in the Ural Mountains, about nine hundred miles east of Moscow. It seems the folks in Sverdlovsk had come up with a particularly nasty agent called anthrax 836, destined for warheads that would sit atop the SS-18 ICBMs then targeted at American cities. In *Brave New World,* published in 1932, Aldous Huxley described "the explosion of anthrax bombs hardly louder than the popping of a paper bag." The Russians had finally caught up with Huxley's dystopian imagination. They'd also treated the Biological Weapons Convention like a loan document that you might sign without bothering to read.

By 1997, President Clinton had been thoroughly briefed on all the above, and Secretary of Defense William S. Cohen announced that vaccination against anthrax would become mandatory for most US service personnel. There is still controversy about the vaccine used, and whether or not it gave rise to Gulf War syndrome. That decision to vaccinate also gave rise to a multibillion-dollar industry producing—and destroying upon their expiration date—tons of prophylactic materials for dealing with anthrax, plague, and botulism, among other deadly agents.

But then President Clinton read *The Cobra Event,* Richard Preston's thriller about a biological attack on the United States, which very dramatically made the point that when it came to biological agents, America's bald eagle was a sitting duck.

Appropriately spooked, Clinton pressured Congress to appropriate money to establish the national public health biodefense program, which included $156 million for the US Bioterrorism Preparedness and Response Program at CDC, with Scott Lillibridge as the first director, and me as his deputy.

One of the first and most important things we did in this new program was try to determine exactly what we might be up against should anyone get the notion to attack us with living things. So we assembled people from universities, people from the intelligence community, and people from government, and we put together a three-tiered critical agent list. Naturally, every scientist wanted the toxin he or she specialized in to be on the A list: those with the most likely impact, and for which we needed dedicated antidotes and public health systems.

Despite the lobbying pressure, for critical agents A we settled on anthrax, smallpox, botulism, plague, tularemia (rabbit fever), and the viral hemorrhagic fevers caused by Ebola and the Lassa family of viruses. (I admit—those last two made the cut mostly because I was in special pathogens. Viral hemorrhagic fevers probably didn't need to be in category A.)

Category B included some other agents that had been used for bioterrorism in the past, such as rickettsia and Q fever. It also included bugs such as the salmonellas that could easily contaminate food and water supplies, as evidenced from numerous natural outbreaks.

The first significant biological attack in the United States was in 1984, when the Rajneeshee sect actually used salmonella in a trial run to contaminate salad bars in The Dalles, Oregon. They wanted to see if they could get enough people sick to stay at home during a local election. They managed to sicken over seven hundred people, though I'm not sure how many were registered voters. And there are examples too numerous to mention of disgruntled employees spiking the break-room donuts with pathogens. (Just a word to the wise.)

Category C was emerging pathogens: things we were keeping an eye on that could potentially become widespread. Some of the scariest zoonotic diseases of all, these were unlikely agents because so little was known about them, but they deserved attention as future contenders.

My routine FBI contact during the DC anthrax outbreak was Scott Decker, an agent I'd gotten to know while assembling the bioterrorism response program. Having these previous relationships turned out to be a crucial element in our effectiveness, enhancing our ability to rapidly exchange information and coordinate patient visits.

I remember, when CDC was first establishing the bioterrorism defense program, an early meeting with some of the heads of the National Security Council that included Ken Bernard, Richard Clarke, Sandy Berger, and Peggy Hamburg, then the assistant secretary for planning at the Department of Health and Human Services and their lead for bioterrorism. We talked about some of the things that make biology such a great option for terrorists, including multiple delivery systems and the ability to choose your scale from one individual to mass casualties, and from death to disabilities. There is good science and simple logistics that can allow you to produce these agents at low cost, and defending against them is difficult. They also don't damage the physical infrastructure. Essentially, you wipe out the people, and then, depending on the agent, walk into the deserted city with everything else good to go. Biological agents are also easy to conceal. Unless somebody specifically says "I did it," it's very difficult to attribute a biological attack to a specific country or terrorist group.

In June 2001, we'd already been discussing the asymmetrical nature of the threat, and the disproportionate number of deaths that bioterrorism can cause, compared to other means of causing havoc, when five months into a new administration and just four months before 9/11, Vice President Cheney instigated Operation Dark Winter, a senior-level bioterrorist attack simulation that scared the pants off everybody.

This tabletop exercise simulated a localized smallpox attack on Oklahoma City, with subsequent attacks in Georgia and in Pennsylvania.

It focused on evaluating the inadequacies of a national emergency response, which were (and still are) numerous. In other words, the simulation was designed to spiral out of control, creating a contingency in which the National Security Council would have to struggle to determine the origin of the attack, then try to contain the pathogen.

Because the United States was not able to keep pace with the disease's rate of spread, a new catastrophic contingency emerged in which massive civilian casualties overwhelmed America's emergency response capabilities, then exacerbated the notable weaknesses of the US health care infrastructure in its inability to handle such a threat. In the simulation, governors closed borders between states, which foreshadowed events fifteen years later when Governor Christie of New Jersey forged his own path for quarantine of Ebola responders returning from West Africa.

What the simulation conclusively demonstrated was that, when it came to something like an anthrax attack on Washington, we had no idea what we were doing.

———

When I arrived in Washington on the morning of October 16, the Capitol Building was strung with crime scene tape and crawling with FBI agents. There's always a lot of confusion at the beginning of a major disease outbreak, but here we had the added mayhem of a criminal investigation, compounded by the overlapping local and federal agencies trying to understand what was going on, compounded by the recent infusion of 9/11 World War III paranoia.

Our first meeting was with the sergeant at arms, and then with Sherry Adams, chief of the Emergency Health and Medical Services of the Health Department for DC. But as Dr. Adams made clear to us, her jurisdiction as a city employee didn't extend to the Capitol or to other federal buildings. This gave us our first inkling of the complicated bureaucracy we were going to have to negotiate to get anything done. We also met with Dr. John Eisold, the Capitol physician who played a critical role in tending to Congress and their staffers. We also met with the Federal Emergency Management Agency (FEMA) and with the Environmental Protection Agency (EPA).

Our overall CDC team leader was Dr. Rima Khabbaz from Viral Diseases (obviously another "real American" from solid and trustworthy Anglo-Saxon stock), an excellent senior manager and extremely critical thinker who had to deal with, among other things, the political maneuvering and the media.

I was the team's operational head, the guy down below in the engine room keeping things running.

We were treating the letters as an assault, and despite all the uncertainties, we had no choice but to make decisions—life or death decisions. That's a highly stressful position to be in, which is why you need to keep your mind as clear as you possibly can. But I had been awake for two full days, and I'm not sure I could have slept if I'd tried. I was too busy trying to figure out what in the world was going on.

The weapon used in the assault was a deadly disease, and amid the mayhem previously described, we had to calmly identify who had been exposed, who might yet be exposed, and who was already suffering the effects. We also needed to put safeguards in place, because anthrax spores could be anywhere.

And anthrax is a particularly deadly weapon. A teaspoon of powder in a letter-sized envelope can contain billions of spores, yet it only takes about five to fifty thousand to kill half of the people exposed. A dozen or so spores would be enough to do in some folks. What kills you isn't the anthrax bacillus itself, but the fact that as it multiplies it releases toxins that cause your blood pressure to drop and swelling to settle in.

You can become infected by inhaling the spores, or by getting them on your skin, where they cause black, painless lesions that people often mistake for spider bites. (The name anthrax actually derives from *anthraki*, the Greek word for "coal," as in "black as coal.") Or, as is often still the case in Africa, you can become infected by eating tainted meat. Oddly enough, recent victims in the United States are often traditional drummers. They get drumheads made from animal hides from Africa, the hides turn out to be infected, and banging on the drums releases the spores into the air. In Europe you can get infected from injecting infected heroin.

We determined that there had been 67 people working in the immediate vicinity of room 216 where the envelope with the "4th Grade, Greendale School" return address was opened, and 301 people overall on the fifth and sixth floors. The incubation period for anthrax, whether the spores have been inhaled or put in contact with the skin, is from one to seven days but can be as long as sixty days. Which is why you have to take prophylaxis for two months.

We had no idea how many people had been present in the building as a whole when the spores began to circulate, but thanks to the ventilation system that had not been shut off, our lab tests found thousands, if not millions, of spores in offices, corridors, and stairwells. We got swabs from furniture on every floor of the building, and we hustled them off for testing. But the priority was not the furniture, it was the people.

Which meant that we wanted cultures from everybody, which resulted in long lines waiting for nasal swabs. We did 150 tests on Monday, 1,350 tests on Tuesday, and 2,000 on Wednesday, then farmed out this flood of samples to the National Institutes of Health (NIH), to Walter Reed, to the Armed Forces Institute of Pathology, to Fort Detrick, and to Analytical Services, a lab near CDC in Norcross, Georgia. It ultimately added up to 7,000 human samples.

Meanwhile, we were setting up an epidemiology team, a clinical team, a surveillance team, an environmental health team, an intervention team, and a communications team to manage press conferences, write press releases, and generally interact with the public. We were briefly headquartered in the Capitol Building itself, but as our group expanded we moved to offices in the US Botanic Garden, which, conveniently, had been closed for renovations.

Our structure in the field and at headquarters was still rudimentary, because our Bioterrorism Preparedness and Response Program was still figuring out what an emergency operation center should look like. Most of our previous responses had been done on an ad hoc basis, but now we were evolving toward more of an incident command system that resembled how various fire and law enforcement agencies managed a fire.

This was a fixed organizational structure that would support finances, planning, operational and logistical activities, an incident manager reporting to the CDC director, and then the specific scientific unit.

By 1:00 a.m., October 16, the first lab tests came back positive for anthrax. In the end, almost everything tested from room 216 came back positive.

We immediately put 227 people on ciprofloxacin. The final tally for positive nasal swabs was 20 of 30 individuals in the vicinity of the mail in interconnecting offices; 2 people from an adjacent office; and 6 responders. But given the ability of anthrax spores to travel far and wide, we had to look beyond the immediate and the obvious.

Working with the local health jurisdictions, CDC quickly established enhanced passive disease "monitoring" in emergency rooms (we were careful to use that term instead of the more common "surveillance," because surveillance meant something different to our FBI colleagues). This meant that we went around asking, "You have anything that looks bad? Fever of unknown origin, maybe? Difficulty breathing?" Another colleague, Scott Harper, began looking for new and previous cases of meningitis (brain inflammation) or lung infections that could be anthrax. The presenting illness could look like various things, but then you would realize that the victim worked at the Capitol and—bingo.

Later, we would bring up people from the National Institute for Occupational Safety and Health to help with the environmental teams scouring the building, running multiple samples a day through the ventilation system. They found spores in seven of twenty-six buildings tested in the vicinity of Capitol Hill, and ultimately the EPA spent $27 million to scrub them down.

After this immediate triage, the more forensic phase of the investigation was based not on "follow the money," but "follow the mail." Relying on time stamps, and working with the US

Postal Service, the FBI traced the Daschle letter back through the mailroom pigeonholes and the unstrapping machines for unbundling mail, following each stage in its movement from Trenton on the ninth, to the Washington P Street facility on the twelfth, to the Dirksen Building mailroom of the Hart Senate Office Building, to room 216.

Meanwhile, reports were coming in from Bethesda Naval Hospital and from NIH that there were more and more positive cultures, with heavy, rapid growth in each—meaning a hell of a lot of spores. But some of the early tests had been done quick and dirty using Tetracore crime scene kits, so we sent these samples to CDC for confirmation. We also consulted with serious anthrax researchers back in Atlanta, especially Arnie Kaufman, to tell us what to do with all the information that was coming our way. Ironically, two years earlier, CDC had been all set to shut down the anthrax program, but it had gotten an eleventh-hour reprieve with the emergency bioterrorism funding.

I briefed the congressional staff and met with health officials from Maryland and Virginia. There was a lot of cell-phone calling back and forth—and by the way, cell phone reception in the Capitol is horrible.

By now we had taken 1,081 environmental samples from the Capitol. We were using high-efficiency particulate arrestance (HEPA) to vacuum out the Hart building and the Ford building where a machine to sort mail for the US House of Representatives had tested positive, and we replaced the air filters. We also removed all the mail. There were soon other environmental swab samples positive from the Dirksen building, where all the mail of the US Senate was handled, as well as from three offices in the Longworth House building.

On October 17, Speaker Dennis Hastert shut down the House of Representatives for five days. The Hart Senate Office Building was already closed. Mail delivery was halted at the White House, and the nine justices of the Supreme Court vacated their building for the first time since the structure was opened in 1935.

On October 18, the White House mail facility tested positive for anthrax, and tests confirmed another anthrax infection of the skin, this on the right middle finger of the newsroom assistant at the *New York Post*.

On October 19, a Washington police car was swabbed for anthrax and tested positive.

Overall, the laboratory response network laboratories tested more than 125,000 environmental specimens alone, which represented over a million individual laboratory tests.

On October 25, the Senate approved the USA Patriot Act.

By this time, we had ten EIS officers working with us, and CDC had similar teams working with the networks in New York, with the newspapers, and on the two cases in Florida. We were looking at the census of emergency rooms, looking for unexplained deaths. We were looking for sepsis, respiratory disease, gastrointestinal disease, unspecified infections, neurologic diseases, even rashes, because anthrax causes a black skin rash.

We were deep within the fog of war, combined with *CSI*, mixed with elements of *24*—that Kiefer Sutherland show where the clock was always ticking. If somebody got a real good snootful of the spores, the incubation period could be as little as two days. We were overwhelmed by conflicting demands and different bureaucrats and wondering who was in charge and who was being officious and who was obstructing and who was helping—and still having to act. If you take the wrong action in our line of work, people die.

BRENTWOOD

On October 19, fifty-six-year-old Leroy Richmond arrived at the emergency room of Inova Fairfax Hospital in Falls Church,

Virginia, with respiratory problems. The attending physician suspected pneumonia, and she was all set to send him home with some antibiotics, but he was tenacious and said something about where he worked: Brentwood, the postal facility that processes all mail heading to Capitol Hill.

The Virginia state officials were alerted to what was going on, and we sent Scott Harper over to investigate. He found Mr. Richmond sleeping comfortably and breathing room air. The patient had lost six or seven pounds in the last three days, and he'd had cramps. But he had no external lesions.

He had increased white cells, but a relatively normal chest X-ray. Luckily, his astute emergency room physician had given him a CT scan, which showed a widening of the mediastinum, the space between the lungs—a symptom associated with anthrax. The scan also showed a slightly increased liver, mediastinal lymphadenopathy (enlarged lymph nodes in the center of the chest), patchy lung infiltrates, and a unilateral effusion, which means fluid on one side of his lungs. The enlarged lymph nodes suggested the possibility that Leroy could have lymphoma. He did not initially have a fever, but he developed one later that evening, and his blood cultures were positive for anthrax the next day. He never had any growth on his nasal swab. The emergency room doctor put Richmond on intravenous ciprofloxacin; she later added rifampin and clindamycin.

The previous day, another Brentwood employee, fifty-five-year-old Thomas L. Morris Jr., had gone to Kaiser Permanante, presenting himself with specific concerns about anthrax but mild illness. But he was not so lucky. His general practitioner called the health department and was told that anthrax posed no danger for postal workers. The Kaiser doc sent the patient home and told him to take Tylenol for his cold symptoms and return if the symptoms got worse. Three days later, just hours after calling 911 with labored breathing and describing himself as a victim of anthrax poisoning, Morris died.

The day after the mayor announced the case of anthrax from Brentwood, another Brentwood employee, Joseph P. Curseen

Jr., drove himself to Southern Maryland Hospital Center in Clinton, Maryland. He had passed out at mass a day earlier, refused EMS help to finish taking communion, and gone to work that evening before arriving home early in the morning with complaints of upper abdominal pain, nausea, and diarrhea. His X-ray appeared normal, and he was diagnosed as having stomach flu, after which he was given fluids for suspected diarrhea and, after he stated that he was feeling well, sent home. No one asked where he worked. He died the next day.

We hit Brentwood in true *CSI* fashion, with swabs, wipes, and vacuum filtration. The 400,000-square-foot facility at 900 Brentwood Road in northeast Washington employs seventeen hundred people who process the mail for Congress and federal agencies. Meanwhile, a similar story was being played out in New Jersey with postal workers from the Trenton facility where state health authorities had seen their first case the day before; the facility closed and put the workers on prophylaxis.

The curious thing was that we had not seen any cases from the postal facilities, even though we knew that all the letters, even those arriving in Florida, had gone through the US Postal Service. This sustained the false perception that only those who opened the letters were at risk.

Here's what we discovered:

When you seal the back of an envelope, there's always open space where there's no glue at the edges of the flap. That's because envelopes go through sorting machines that flatten them for machine reading of the zip code. Brentwood's sorting machines process up to thirty thousand envelopes an hour, exerting thousands of pounds of pressure per square inch on each envelope. By pressing down so hard and so fast, these machines would have done a great job of causing the spores to poof out the sides.

These machines are also cleaned daily with highly pressurized air, and that maintenance alone could have shot spores as high as thirty feet into the air.

We ended up closing down the place for more than two years. When all was said and done, the anthrax contamination would cost almost $320 million to clean up.

By October 23, we realized that mail from Brentwood didn't just go to government agency mailrooms as we'd thought. Instead, it went to 352 other places, including ordinary post offices, corporate mailrooms, and a great many embassies. We developed a chart of how Brentwood related to the rest of the world, showing how all the mail went through the facility to and from various zip codes, in and out, and where it went via which couriers.

So now we deployed people in full protective equipment, in the middle of the night when they wouldn't freak people out, to start swabbing all the post offices in the city. We took 3,281 samples on Sunday, 1,500 samples on Monday, and 1,300 samples on Tuesday.

Meanwhile, the FBI was secretly swabbing mailboxes all over the Northeast, trying to find the exact box in which the perpetrator had deposited the letters.

Then there was another unwelcome development: several colonies of the anthrax bacillus were discovered in the P Street mail facility in Washington. We tested all five hundred mail-handlers who worked there. The question was, should we start all of them on a sixty-day regimen of antibiotics?

At just about that time, I was scheduled to be part of a videoconference arranged by the National Medical Association, a leading African American physician's group. Fortunately, the evening before the big stream, I had dinner with some of the organizers, one of whom had been an associate dean back when I was at Downstate Medical Center. Talking with this group the night before helped me avoid getting ambushed, because they made me realize just what a lousy job we'd done in

terms of communicating with the African American community. The black doctors started telling me about the issues as
they saw them, in particular their distrust and concern about
the allocation of prophylaxis.

Some opinion makers around Washington had begun to
suggest that we—CDC and the city's health department—were
focusing an inordinate amount of time and energy on protecting and treating the elected officials and their staffers on Capitol Hill. Were we being as conscientious in our attention to the
thousands of people working in the city's post offices? Given
that many postal workers in DC are African American, it was
an issue with clear racial overtones.

Some were going so far as to say that the rich white people
on Capitol Hill—and even their dogs—were getting ciprofloxacin, but that the poor had to settle for old doxycycline. In
truth, the two drugs are equivalent. (The dogs receiving medication were the law enforcement dogs sniffing for drugs and
explosives.) But mistrust can grow into a huge problem when
people fear that a disease outbreak could suddenly turn into a
deadly epidemic.

We were now getting positives from environmental swab
samples taken at postal facilities at the CIA, the Capitol Building, the Department of Justice, the Supreme Court, even the
White House. And given the events of 9/11, which had taken
place just a few weeks prior, we had to confront the possibility
that this was not only a nationwide attack, but an indication
of the "new normal." This was very stressful and anxiety pro-
voking for some responders. Many people in the midst of a
war—or if they think Armageddon is coming—would prefer
to be closer to their loved ones. We had at least one public
health person who asked to be sent back home to Atlanta to
be with his family.

———

The FBI had sent cerebrospinal fluid taken from Robert Stevens, the Florida photo editor, to the laboratory of Paul S. Keim, a plant geneticist in Flagstaff, Arizona, who had developed a DNA fingerprinting technique. In the early 1990s, Keim had worked on a project for the CIA in the town of Al Kakam, forty miles southwest of Baghdad, where United Nations inspectors had found hundreds of large paper bags thought to contain anthrax. The powder turned out to be *Bacillus thuringiensis,* or Bt, a similar bacterium, not lethal to humans and used for pest control. It had been treated with a drying agent called bentonite.

The FBI then took photographs from an electron microscope showing these bentonite-coated spores of anthrax from Iraq and sent them to Keim as well. The Iraqi samples did not match the samples found in the recent attacks. Instead, Keim determined that the anthrax that had been sent to Washington was Ames, a domestically produced strain widely used by bio defense researchers. John Ezzell, a PhD microbiologist at the US Army Medical Research Institute of Infectious Diseases (USAMRIID) in Frederick, Maryland, had previously determined that the strain taken from the offices of Tom Brokaw was Ames as well. And it turns out that Ames strain was used in only eighteen labs worldwide, fifteen of which were in the United States, with one each in the United Kingdom, Sweden, and Canada.

Even so, retired colonels now moonlighting as commentators, former commanders of USAMRIID, and the news media in general continued to opine about how this outbreak must have originated overseas.

Ezzell, in speaking to his superiors, had referred to how frightening it was to be seeing "weaponized anthrax." Technically, this would mean that the spores had been encoded with a chemical additive to prevent clumping and to facilitate their dispersal into the air. But that wasn't the case. This was Ames strain, pure and simple.

The initial impression of weaponization was likely because of accumulating data that these spores were spreading very effectively to other envelopes and were very "bouncy," meaning that they were capable of being reaerosolized when tested in the original contaminated office in the Hart building. The dogma had been that natural spores would be very "sticky" because of electrostatic charges. This was yet another outbreak where dogma, preconceived notions, and the standard playbook needed to be thrown out the window,

Unfortunately, although it was inaccurate, Ezzell's comment went viral, as it were, repeated endlessly at the Pentagon, at Health and Human Services, and at the White House. For those in the Bush administration who were itching for a war against Iraq, "weaponized" came trippingly on the tongue. Otherwise, the word "weaponized" was struck from the lexicon, and the populace was reassured that all the anthrax in government labs was accounted for.

The FBI set about collecting samples from each of the eighteen labs known to work with Ames to see if they could identify anything distinctive.

ABC News contributed to keeping the rumor alive by saying that the presence of bentonite in the anthrax was a trademark of Saddam Hussein's biological weapons program. The fact that the White House tried to downplay some of these assertions only seemed to egg them on. Meanwhile, Peter Jahrling, an exemplary virologist and scientist at USAMRIID, mistakenly began to describe the spores as having been treated with silicon, another chemical additive sometimes associated with Iraq. Again, studies would specifically rule out that possibility.

Spore samples were sent to the Sandia National Laboratories in New Mexico, where engineers analyzed them with specialized software and electron microscopes and identified the presence of silicon. Silicon, of course, is second only to oxygen as the most common element in the Earth's crust. Moreover, the silicon detected at Sandia was under the external surface of the spores, meaning that it had been incorporated naturally rather than as the result of some artificial treatment.

Dwight Adams, the director of the FBI laboratory, confirmed that the spores contained no additives, and that the anthrax was not antibiotics resistant. But *ABC News* and the *Wall Street Journal* editorial page kept referring to "weapons grade" anthrax, and that the spores had had their electrostatic charges eliminated in order to facilitate aerial spreading. The *Wall Street Journal* specifically tried to implicate Saddam Hussein, along with "bin Laden and his Al Qaeda network as a front or ally" (despite the fact that there was no relationship between the two at all). This was all in an effort to try to explain the fine nature of the powder in the Daschle letter, which was quite fluffy and bouncy. Previous dogma held that the spores would adhere to a surface from electrostatic charge.

For its part, the FBI went a long way down this dead-end path, even traveling to sites in Kandahar, Afghanistan, where Al Qaeda supposedly had tried to develop biological weapons, collecting more than four hundred samples, but still finding no evidence of Al Qaeda or Saddam Hussein's involvement in the attacks.

USAMRIID had as many as seventy staffers working in support of Amerithrax. But by the end of 2001, the FBI was asking these government weapons scientists to take lie detector tests. In the months ahead, the FBI would distribute subpoenas to each of the fifteen labs researching anthrax in the United States, requiring each scientist involved to submit a sample of his or her strain.

But the FBI already had the culprit in their sights, or so they thought. His name was Dr. Steven Hatfill, a virologist who from 1997 to 1999 had worked at USAMRIID doing research on Marburg virus and monkeypox. He had also worked at NIH. He had a medical degree from the University of Zimbabwe, but he'd claimed to have earned a PhD in microbiology, and to have been a member of a British medical society—neither of which was true. These prevarications, coupled with his propensity to speak cryptically and to wear long trench coats to create the aura of a secret agent, evidently triggered the Bureau's suspicions. This, despite the fact that Hatfill had never worked on anthrax and, in fact, had spent his entire career working on viral disorders. Once again: anthrax is a *bacterium*.

In 1999, Hatfill had gone to work for Science Applications International Corporation, a company that did contract work for the military and the CIA. While there, he gave PowerPoint presentations to local public safety officials urging greater preparedness against biological attack. He had also written an unpublished novel in which a wheelchair-bound man attacked Congress with plague bacteria.

A month after the letter attacks, molecular biologist Barbara Hatch Rosenberg, who taught environmental science and health at the State University of New York at Purchase and served as the chair of the Federation of American Scientists Working Group on Biological Weapons, told a Biological and Toxin Weapons Convention conference in Geneva that the anthrax used was derived almost certainly from a US defense laboratory. She promoted the theory that the anthrax mailings were an inside job, perpetrated by a scientist who "has the right skills, experience with anthrax, up-to-date anthrax vaccination, forensic training, and access to USAMRIID and its biological weapons [alluding to but not specifically calling out Hatfill] as part of a secret and illegal US bioweapons program." She was dead wrong, but the "inside job" theory was gaining traction.

Under the glare of television lights, the FBI searched Hatfill's apartment and found nothing of note. In his car, though, they found a hand-drawn map of a wooded area with several spring-fed ponds just a few miles northwest of Fort Detrick, which led to an extensive search, complete with bloodhounds, of the seven-thousand-acre Frederick Municipal Forest. All they found was a clear plastic box with large-diameter openings, which gave rise to a theory that Hatfill might have waded into the shallow water of the pond and put anthrax into the envelopes while using the box as a partially submerged, airtight chamber. A bit far-fetched.

But that night, *ABC World News* reported on the investigation as a major development. It was, in fact, *ABC News* that first publically identified the suspect as Hatfill, who had taken a $150,000-a-year job at Louisiana State University teaching public safety personnel how to respond to terrorism. The university quickly terminated his contract. And the piling on continued.

New York Times columnist Nicholas Kristof wrote five pieces about the investigation, noting that the suspect had up-to-date anthrax vaccination as well as the ability to make anthrax because of his working knowledge of biowarfare agents—both wrong. Before *ABC News* blew Hatfill's cover, Kristof alluded to him as a shadowy "Mr. Z" alleged to have used anthrax against black citizens of Zimbabwe. In later sworn testimony, Kristof admitted that much of his reporting was based on hearsay.

———

On November 5, I took a break from all this craziness and went home for a while. When I came back on the sixteenth, I met with the EPA to begin the challenge of cleaning up the Hart Building, long since closed and cordoned off, along with all the reports and red tape filed inside. Eventually, we put a gigantic tent over the whole building (shades of Walter White once again) and decontaminated it with chlorine dioxide. It would not reopen until January 22, 2002.

November 16 was the same day an FBI team sorting through 280 barrels of quarantined mail bound for Capitol Hill found the anthrax-laced letter addressed to Senator Leahy. It too had been postmarked in New Jersey on October 9, but was inadvertently rerouted to a State Department mail facility in Sterling, Virginia.

It was at this time that the postal service began using electron-beam technology to radiate mail. At first they overdid it, and for a while the mail showed up pretty crispy. But then they dialed it back, and also limited the treatment to mail going to government facilities.

By now we knew of twenty-two anthrax cases and five deaths. The cases were evenly divided between inhalation and cutaneous infections. Oddly, the victims included two people with no obvious connection to the targeted sites or to the mail routes. On October 31, Kathy Nguyen, a sixty-one-year-old Vietnamese immigrant and hospital stockroom worker in the Bronx, died of inhalation anthrax, but no trace of the bacterium was ever found in her workplace or in her apartment. There were three tense days in New York City, with discussions of swabbing the subways—a subway release seen as a potential source of exposure—and possibly putting the whole city on prophylaxis. The fact that we found no additional cases, and that despite aggressive monitoring, did nothing to reel us back from that precipice.

If that case was not unusual enough, Ottilie Lundgren, a ninety-four-year-old widow in Oxford, Connecticut, died of inhalation anthrax on November 21. Tests showed that the sorting machines at the Connecticut postal facility that processed bulk mail for Lundgren's carrier route were contaminated. If spores could fly out of an envelope onto another envelope, they could surely fly into somebody's lungs. And she might have been one of the few people who only needed one spore to get infected and die.

The FBI then went off on another tangent, using a technique called whole genome amplification to test a piece of dead skin found on the envelope addressed to Senator Leahy, an effort that would take about two years to complete. Ultimately, the skin was traced to a technician at the FBI lab who had accidentally contaminated the evidence as soon as it arrived.

The FBI was still trying to find anything that would differentiate the DNA from the bacterium that killed photo editor Robert Stevens from that of the original Ames strain of anthrax. (The name "Ames" is actually misleading. In 1981, army biologists at Fort Detrick were looking for new strains of anthrax to be investigated. Per the army's request, scientists at Texas A&M forwarded a sample scraped from the organs of a cow that had died on a ranch in Jim Hogg County, Texas. They sent it in a prepaid mailing label with the return address of the National Veterinary Services Laboratories in Ames, Iowa, and thus the Ames strain was born.)

The FBI asked USAMRIID to send some of the Stevens sample to Paul Keim's lab in Arizona, hoping to find some distinctive marker. Keim was able to extract DNA from the anthrax, but it turned out to be plain vanilla Ames. But Keim knew that, aside from the original dead cow from Texas, Ames had never been observed in the wild. His conclusion, which he shared with the FBI, was that the source of this infection came out of a laboratory.

In a separate line of inquiry, one scientist from USAMRIID noticed that some of the anthrax from Senator Daschle's office gave rise to irregular colonies called morphotypes, which had a yellowish color not associated with Ames. So here was the distinctive marker they were looking for.

But it took them almost four years to discover that the perpetrator they were looking for had been right under their noses all along. And it was not Robert Hatfill or, for that matter, Saddam Hussein.

In January, on the day we were supposed to reopen the Hart Senate Office Building, somebody broke through a temporary wall and found nine used hazmat suits in the base-ment near the loading dock. This is where workers during the initial investigation had stripped off the suits and air hosed themselves—a perfect way to aerosolize everything in the room!

So now we had to start over, taking nasal swabs and putting the forty-nine people there for the opening, including a police captain and several officers, on prophylaxis.

But if there were a larger lesson to be derived from this episode, it would be that Murphy's Law should never be un-derestimated.

Clearly, we still didn't know how to properly remediate buildings. Anthrax in a large area is a regional denial weapon. If you spread these spores in New York or Washington, you in-fect millions of people, but worse, you could make it unsafe for anyone to set foot there ever again. It's like the ancient custom of strewing salt over the soil of a defeated city, to make sure that it remains defeated, not unlike the fate of Gruinard Island.

As a postmortem, we met at the Capitol with some of the key people from the local area, including the city health com-missioner, to discuss what went right and what went wrong. From our partners in the locality we listened to complaint af-ter complaint about how we, the Feds, had not kept them in the loop. This was the big outbreak when people started to ask who the heck was in charge.

We were told that we needed regional integration of pub-lic health, and hospitals, and the population at large. We also needed to do more to recognize the diversity of the population and master the art of cross-cultural communication. In other words, we needed to become more human, and we needed to make friends before the fact.

But the biggest issue remained postexposure prophylaxis and vaccination. It had been done on the fly and not done very well, and the frustration was increased by the confusion over the use of ciprofloxacin versus doxycycline. We also left too much discretion to the individual, and different localities had different recommendations, which confused people and, frankly, pissed them off. If CDC, with fifteen thousand of the best scientific brains in the world, couldn't come out with a straightforward guideline for treating anthrax, how could an ordinary citizen know what to do?

In our sessions there were also more wonkish recommendations about horizontal coordination, identifying best practices, and setting up platform-independent communications. And here the overriding question was, where does federal responsibility begin and end?

There is markedly improved regional coordination in the Capitol now than there was in those days. We now have now much more clarity about who's in charge—namely the Department of Homeland Security, with the FBI in charge of any criminal investigations. But others might suggest that the White House is in charge. When it really hits the fan, decisions get pushed up to the national security advisor and the president.

Four years later, in 2005, we were still trying to sort out these issues when another disaster struck New Orleans, and it was Hurricane Katrina that brought about the sweeping transformations required. After that crisis we did a complete rethinking of emergency response in the United States.

And yet, it's not as if our systems are bulletproof.

It was not reassuring when, over a period of months in 2014 and 2015, military personnel at the supersophisticated, supersecret Dugway Proving Ground in Utah mistakenly shipped live anthrax samples, sometimes via FedEx, to twenty-four labs in eleven states and two foreign countries. Or when CDC shipped a culture of nonpathogenic avian influenza that was cross-contaminated with the highly pathogenic H5N1 strain of influenza to a BSL-3 select-agent laboratory operated by the United States Department of Agriculture.

This kind of thing can only happen when there is lack of accountability; that is, nobody gets fired when stupid things happen. Because these are not inherently stupid people. At least they have PhDs.

It's just that people do sloppy work when they think they can get away with it, and this is not a problem you can regulate yourself out of. The only way to avoid mistakes like this is to create a culture of safety, enforced by strict accountability.

The other enduring truth is that crazy people will always be with us, and that law enforcement needs to be intellectually and emotionally flexible and attuned in order to avoid biases and preconceived notions, and to withstand pressure from politicians with agendas.

Psychologists talk about two completely different ways in which the mind solves problems. System 1 thinking is quick and superficial, based on the rules of thumb and easy answers called heuristics, which include what's known as "prejudices" and "preconceived notions." System 2 is deeper and slower, more agile and reflective. From what I observed, I would say that the investigation of these anthrax attacks was based way too much on system 1 thinking.

Part of this was "the headquarters effect," which means busywork and checklists rather than taking time for real creativity and insight. Agents were encouraged to interview anyone and everyone, and to report back almost daily, which led to pointless intrusions into the lives of tangentially related people and engendered resentment within the scientific community. Most of all, it completely missed the big picture, which some would say was pretty obvious. It was as if no one ever took twenty minutes to sit back, look around, and connect the dots. This was, after all, the same FBI that had disregarded warnings that bin Laden had sent extremists to the United States to take flying lessons.

———————

Assigned to lead the anthrax investigation was thirty-two-year veteran Van Harp, the same agent who had led the flawed review of the FBI's disastrous 1992 standoff against survivalist Randy Weaver at Ruby Ridge.

Van Harp's choice to examine the envelope from Senator Daschle's office was a researcher at Fort Detrick named Bruce Ivins, who worked with highly purified Ames anthrax. But, of course, examining this specimen to determine the density of spores per gram in the same biosafety level 3 containment facility that he routinely used for other anthrax experiments compromised the FBI's sample.

Ivins had been with the US Army Medical Research Institute since 1980. He'd done his thesis on diphtheria toxin, and he'd worked on chlamydia and cholera. In 1991, with the outbreak of the Persian Gulf War, he began working with *Bacillus anthracis*. He was listed on the patent application as a coinventor of a next-generation anthrax vaccine known as recombinant protective antigen, or rPA. The old vaccine had been blamed for serious side effects, including immune system disorders, but congressional funding came and went with the budget cycles. Meaning that Ivins had hopes for a big score, but no certainty.

If anyone had bothered to look, they would have found myriad emails from Ivins expressing concern that federal support for anthrax research, including his next-generation vaccine, was losing ground. A curious investigator—even a rookie Hollywood screenwriter—would have noted as well his conspicuous enthusiasm for a perceived biological warfare threat. One of his bosses described his interest in the subject, and his general demeanor, as "squirrelly."

Ivins, in other words, had the classic motivation (not to mention the psychological profile) of a classic villain out of *Spider-Man*. Didn't the FBI ever watch movies?

By the spring of 2000, still hoping for a windfall, Ivins was testing his new rPA on rabbits, subjecting them to aerosolized anthrax.

As soon as the Stevens case from Florida hit the news, Ivins emailed an acquaintance at CDC, Arnie Kaufman, offering to help with the investigation. Kaufman would later describe Ivins as being "agitated" over the "mountain stream in North Carolina" theory. Kaufman said that Ivins seemed to take the case personally. Did he, perhaps, have a personal interest in keeping the theory of the case centered on terrorism?

Later, when the FBI searched the Frederick Municipal Forest for evidence against Hatfill, one of the locals who volunteered to help was Bruce Ivins. He was like the Woody Allen character Zelig, popping up everywhere.

Bruce Ivins had grown up in Ohio as a classic science geek, awkward but eager for approval, and very smart. He worked hard at being likable: he could juggle fruit and play the piano. But the fact is, Ivins had been hired for his supersensitive position as a bioweapons researcher with no evaluation of his psychological state, and with no knowledge that he'd been under intense psychiatric care. And not just for depression or marital troubles or feelings of inadequacy. Among other things, he had confided to his psychiatrist that he'd burglarized a sorority house, and that he'd been thinking about murdering one of his colleagues. As his shrink would later reveal to authorities, he fantasized about obtaining cyanide to poison a neighbor's dog and ammonium nitrate to make a bomb. He told members of his group therapy sessions that he'd been carrying a gun for years hoping a mugger would give him shit. He spoke of feelings of isolation and desolation, and he thought of himself as an avenging angel of death. His psychiatrist later described him as creepy, scary, spooky.

She put him on Valium (antianxiety) and Celexa (antidepression), and later Zyprexa, an antipsychotic drug for schizophrenia and/or bipolar disorder. Yet he still had around-the-clock access to Fort Detrick's biocontainment labs and the deadly pathogens stored there. On his annual army checkup he acknowledged having memory changes, trouble making decisions, hallucinations, and anxiety. He also said he was receiving outpatient psychiatric treatment for what he described as job-related stress.

Ivins had made his first known threat while still an undergraduate at the University of Cincinnati, telling a roommate who'd broken into his stuff, "I can drop something in your water." He also experienced rejection from a member of the Kappa Kappa Gamma (KKG) sorority, but rather than simply recalibrate his search image for the girl of his dreams, he became obsessed with KKG.

In the early 1980s, shortly after taking his job at Fort Detrick, Ivins drove for three hours to West Virginia University, broke into the KKG house, and stole the sorority's book of rituals. Earlier, while still a postdoc in North Carolina, he had met graduate student Nancy Haigwood, and upon learning that she was a member of KKG, stole a lab notebook she needed for her dissertation, then anonymously returned it a few days later in the main post office. After she got her degree and took a job as a virologist in Gaithersburg, Maryland, she discovered the initials "KKG" spray-painted on her fence, on the sidewalk in front of her house, and on the window of her fiancé's car. Instinctively, as she would later report, she knew it was Bruce.

Meanwhile, he was having creepy, overly intimate conversations with another female lab worker, stole her computer password, and read her email. As Ivins's own daughter would later reveal, he was inordinately taken up with the O. J. Simpson case, the Oklahoma City bombing, and the JonBenét Ramsey murder. He wrote numerous letters to various newspaper editors about the arrest of Ted Kaczynski, the Unabomber.

One of the letters Ivins wrote was to the editor of the *Frederick Post* defending sororities signed "Nancy Haigwood." Then he sent a copy of the same letter to a mother whose son had just died in a fraternity hazing accident. He subscribed to a bondage magazine and had it delivered to a post office box under the name of Nancy Haigwood's husband.

When the FBI sent out a mass mailing asking for help with the Amerithrax investigation from the thirty thousand members of the American Society for Microbiology, Nancy Haigwood called the FBI immediately and fingered Bruce Ivins. The Bureau took down her name, and they interviewed her, but it would take seven years for them to put her tip to use.

This mentally unstable stalker was the same Bruce Ivins who, on October 22, 1997, had received a thousand milliliters of purified Ames anthrax bacteria suspended in liquid from the army's Dugway Proving Ground in Utah. These he combined with Ames anthrax spores cultured at Fort Detrick for use in upcoming experiments. He stored the spores in his lab and listed the batch as "RMR-1029" on an army reference material receipt record.

By 2001, the military had commissioned the traditional anthrax vaccine to be produced by a company called BioPort (later Emergent BioSolutions), but it would take millions of federal dollars to get them ready to produce the vaccine. Meanwhile, development of Ivins's own vaccine was being blocked, and interest seemed to be shifting to other biowarfare pathogens such as smallpox, glanders (caused by *Burhholderia*), tularemia, and plague. For a man trying to sell a solution, a crisis could never have been more conveniently timed.

In August 2001, Ivins began spending night after night and weekends alone in his laboratory. He continued to maintain an erratic schedule of solitary work at all hours throughout the period during which the anthrax samples were created, packaged, and sent.

Later, it would be discovered that the mailbox in which the anthrax letters were dropped was at 10 Nassau Street in Princeton, immediately adjacent to an office of the KKG sorority. This was nearly two hundred miles from Fort Detrick, but the round trip could have been made in less than eight hours.

It was also discovered that the $0.34 federal Eagle envelopes used to send the anthrax spores had certain defects that identified them as being exclusive to a shipment on sale in only five post offices in Maryland and two in Virginia.

Ivins could never satisfactorily explain the string of late nights he spent alone in the high-containment facility at his lab immediately before the mailings. He also had no alibi for the periods of time when he could have driven to New Jersey to mail the letters.

Most damning, though, was that the anthrax-laced letter sent to Senator Daschle had carried the return address "4th Grade, Greendale School." Just before the attack, Bruce Ivins had begun contributing to the American Family Association, a Christian advocacy group involved in a federal lawsuit contesting corporal punishment of a fourth-grade student at Greendale Baptist Academy in Milwaukee.

Six months into the anthrax investigation, the army assigned a medical officer from outside Fort Detrick to conduct an investigation. It became known that Bruce Ivins had failed to report contamination of his office by anthrax spores into late 2001. Of the twenty-two offices that technicians had scoured for spores, the only one containing Ames strain anthrax belonged to Ivins. But neither Ivins nor anyone else was disciplined. The media did not pick up on it, and nobody followed up on any of the inconsistencies and implausible statements Ivins had made.

Around this time, all anthrax researchers were required to submit samples of the strain used in their labs. Ivins did so, logging in his sample as "RMR-1029." But he had placed his sample in the wrong kind of test tube and the Bureau rejected it. Shortly thereafter, Ivins submitted a second sample of Ames.

In May 2002, the outside investigator who worked for Fort Detrick delivered a 361-page report concluding that the available information pointed toward no clear answers.

Six months after that, FBI Inspector Richard L. Lambert took the place of Inspector Van Harp. At just about the same time, Congress voted to approve the Iraq War resolution.

In February 2003, Secretary of State Colin Powell held up a vial of white powder in a speech before the United Nations saying that less than a teaspoonful of dry anthrax in an envelope had shut down the US Senate. He made the association with Iraq—the fact that in the 1990s the Iraqis had possessed eighty-five hundred liters of liquid-form anthrax.

And although smallpox was eradicated worldwide in 1980 and resided in only two repositories, Iraq had never certified that it had no residual smallpox virus. Iraq had also worked on camelpox (a local disease), had a freeze-drier labeled "Smallpox" in Arabic during a UN weapons inspection in 1984 (to make vaccine, according to Iraqis), and could have bought some smallpox (variola) virus on the black market from a rogue Russian scientist with access to samples in the declared smallpox repository, or the clandestine biowarfare program. Those accumulated flimsy facts and speculations were enough for the US Defense Department to reintroduce smallpox vaccination for the military. CDC also "assisted" in this war effort by establishing a national smallpox vaccine campaign for health care workers (for an illness that you can prevent by vaccinating people up to a week *after* exposure). But early reports of serious adverse reactions associated with the smallpox vaccine—in the form of serious rashes, fevers, and cardiac arrests—ended the campaign that must not be named.

But no stockpiles were ever found in Iraq, and Saddam Hussein's mobile germ warfare labs turned out to be fictitious. Powell's statements did not jibe with the findings of the engineers at Sandia National Laboratories, who said that the anthrax used in the attacks had not been chemically treated. It had been known as early as the fall of 2001 that the anthrax came from the Ames strain, indicating that its most likely source was Fort Detrick, or one of the other very few centers in the US biodefense network that used Ames anthrax.

In March 2003, the Defense Department awarded Ivins its highest honor for nonuniformed personnel, the Decoration for

Exceptional Civilian Service. The award was for his efforts to revive the long-troubled anthrax vaccine.

Five days later, on March 19, 2003, President Bush launched the war in Iraq.

On December 5, 2003, the Brentwood postal facility reopened and was renamed in honor of Thomas L. Morris Jr. and Joseph P. Curseen Jr.

In March 2004, with encouragement from Vice President Dick Cheney, officials decided to purchase 75 million doses of a next-generation anthrax vaccine. This would provide a three-dose treatment regimen for 25 million people. These doses would be held in a civilian strategic national stockpile. It was also a way of keeping the manufacturer of such a vaccine going so that it could be ramped up as needed. As part of this effort, a company called VaxGen was awarded a contract worth $877 million, payable as soon as it began to deliver the 75 million doses of rPA, the vaccine that Ivins had patented.

As a codeveloper of the patent, Ivins received checks totaling more than $12,000.

Agent Lawrence Alexander joined the anthrax investigation in January 2004. By the end of the year he had concluded that Hatfill had nothing to do with the attacks. At long last, he began to focus the Bureau's attention on Bruce Ivins.

VaxGen had arranged for animal experiments to be carried out by a subcontractor, the Battelle Memorial Institute of Columbus, Ohio, and Ivins was summoned to the Pentagon to provide up-to-date information about the new product's effectiveness. It was noted that Ivins sent Battelle anthrax spores from the highly purified mixture he had labeled RMR-1029.

Alexander knew that Ivins had limitless access to RMR-1029, and that he was highly proficient in handling anthrax. He also suspected that Ivins had thrown the FBI a curve by submitting a bogus sample in April 2002. Alexander also had the evidence of Ivins's highly erratic email messages, concluding that he was not merely eccentric, as his colleagues had described him, but mentally unstable.

The FBI seized Ivins's flask of RMR-1029 in the summer of 2004. It appeared that when Ivins had provided a sample in response to a subpoena in 2002, the sample was bogus. When confronted with this suspicion, Ivan said that his senior lab technician had provided the sample, not him.

His account of submitting the sample of RMR-1029 did not add up. His inventory book left 220 milliliters of anthrax RMR-1029 unaccountably missing. His only explanation was that he was not good at math.

Shortly thereafter, Ivins began to throw away suspicious materials such as his list of Kappa Kappa Gamma chapter addresses.

In 2006, the government terminated the $877 million contract with VaxGen due to stability issues, ending Ivins's hopes for his next-generation vaccine.

That fall, Ivins bought a device that would detect bugs on his phones, as well as a tracking device so that he could see when his emails were received and opened and to whom they were forwarded.

In May 2007, Ivins was summoned before a grand jury in Washington, DC. He immediately hired a former state prosecutor as his lawyer.

The Amerithrax investigators had followed up on over a thousand samples of anthrax in four countries and determined that only eight samples, each evidently descended from Bruce Ivins's flask of RMR-1029, matched the anthrax found in the anthrax letters. The Institute for Genomic Research demonstrated that the genome signature matched the RMR-1029 anthrax to the letters.

In April 2008, almost seven years after the attacks, Ivins was detained by investigators while his home was searched. Amid his juggling gear they found a bag of materials that he used for cross-dressing. Later, they found bondage pictures on his computer, as well as a large cache of handguns, a bulletproof vest, and homemade body armor. He'd been using his basement as a firing range.

That spring, federal prosecutors drafted a formal prosecution memo, the first step toward seeking a grand jury indictment of Ivins for the five anthrax murders. The army had already taken away his lab privileges. Meanwhile, Ivins seemed to be deteriorating, drinking more and more heavily.

In June 2008, the Justice Department and the FBI agreed to pay Steven Hatfill a $5.82 million settlement. Hatfill also sued Kristof of the *New York Times* but lost, the court deciding in favor of the journalist on the theory that Hatfill, at that point in time, was a public figure.

———

Because of Ivins's bizarre behavior at group therapy and elsewhere, he was apprehended and taken to Frederick Memorial Hospital for psychiatric evaluation.

Shortly after he was released, he filled three prescriptions: the antidepressant Celexa, the antipsychotic Seroquel, and Depakote for mania and migraine headaches. He also picked up a package containing seventy tablets of Tylenol PM. He was later found at his home lying in a pool of urine, cold to the touch.

At the time of Ivins's death, Senator Leahy was still insisting that even if Ivins was guilty, he could not possibly have acted alone, asserting that others had to have been involved in the plot. And on August 5, 2008, Richard Spertzel, the retired USAMRIID deputy commander and UN bioweapons inspector, wrote an op-ed in the *Wall Street Journal* still insisting that the anthrax in the letters had been altered to be more lethal, and that it was too sophisticated a product to have been produced by a solitary scientist in a US lab.

Making biological weapons is still not simple for the would-be bioterrorist. While the apocalyptic cult Aum Shinrikyo had success with the Tokyo subway sarin attack in 1995, it was unable to create anthrax as a bioweapon despite significant resources. Unfortunately, however, every year since 9/11 it has gotten easier to produce anthrax as a biological weapon, and terrorists remain actively in pursuit of talented microbiologists with evil in their hearts.

6

MIGRATIONS

This is what the LORD, the God of the Hebrew, says: Let my people go, so they may worship me. If you refuse to let them go and continue to hold them back, the hand of the lord will bring a terrible plague on your livestock in the field—on your horses and donkeys and camels and on your cattle and sheep and goats.

—Exodus 9:1–3

It was November 2002, when a middle-aged couple dragged themselves to the Mount Sinai Beth Israel medical center in New York City, a city still on edge little more than a year after 9/11 and the anthrax mailings. They presented with headache, high fever, joint pain, and extreme exhaustion—so far, a typical day at the emergency room. But what got the doctors' attention were the couple's mysterious, painful, balloon-like swellings in the groin, also known as buboes, as in bubonic plague.

A few hours later, when the blood cultures grew the typical "safety pin" bacteria, doctors descended upon the couple with antibiotics, and news crews converged with their television lights. New York had not seen a case of bubonic plague in more than a century.

Suddenly, Beth Israel was at the center of a national emergency, and the FBI was all over the place trying to understand whether these two were terrorists who'd infected themselves, or nice people who'd been infected by terrorists. In 2001, when the anthrax letters hit the East Coast, bioterrorism was not the conclusion to which everyone jumped. This time it was. Once burned, twice shy.

Through CDC's bioterrorism program, we'd given plague training to first responders in New York, but the question now was whether we should activate the Emergency Operations Center, then start prophylaxing the hundreds of thousands of people who might have been deliberately exposed to the bacteria.

Bubonic plague enters through the skin, and once inside the body, the bacteria travels to lymph glands in the groin, neck, or armpit. When these microbes multiply they trigger an immune response that causes the characteristic swellings. If untreated, bubonic plague causes death in 50 to 60 percent of cases. Two other types of plague, if untreated, are almost always fatal. These are pneumonic plague, which comes from breathing in the bacteria, which then multiplies in the lungs to cause pneumonia, and septicemia plague, in which the infection enters the bloodstream, then often spreads to the brain to cause meningitis.

Happily, it took only about a day for public health authorities to put the fears of bioterrorism to rest. As it turned out, the couple, Lucinda Marker and John Tull, were vacationers from Santa Fe, New Mexico, and they'd taken ill in their hotel room. New Mexico usually accounts for about half the seven or so cases of plague in the United States each year.

The New York City health department conducted an investigation into how these people might have been exposed. This included a call to Dr. Paul Ettestad, the public health epidemiologist for the New Mexico Department of Health, who was surprised, given that they had not seen any cases of plague that year, and it was already late in the season. But somebody on his staff recognized the name of the couple and remembered that there had been an infected pack rat found on their five-acre property. It appeared that the rat had been carrying fleas that in turn carried *Yersinia pestis*, the bacterium that causes plague, and that the fleas had found their way to Marker and Tull.

Dr. Tom Frieden, who would later become the director of CDC, was the New York health commissioner at the time, and he credited the city's emergency room surveillance system with ruling out bioterrorism. Good information allows you to spot trends, and also to spot when there are no trends.

Lucinda Marker recovered easily, but John Tull, an athletic lawyer who volunteered for search and rescue teams in the Sangre de Christo Mountains near Santa Fe, developed septicemic plague, with the infection coursing throughout his body. His buboes were smaller than his partner's, suggesting that her lymph nodes might have been doing a better job of fending off the infection. His blood pressure fell to 78 over 50 (normal is 120 over 80), and his temperature hit 104.4°. His kidneys were failing, and there was so much blood clotting that his hands and feet turned black, one of the reasons why the plague in the Middle Ages was labeled the Black Death.

It may have been that his case was complicated by type 2 diabetes. Another theory was that Marker and Tull had been bitten by the same flea, but that he wound up with more than his fair share of the bacteria.

Either way, he was put in a medically induced coma for three months. Eventually, he had to undergo amputation of both legs below the knee.

Plague, like smallpox, has a long history that over the centuries has changed the course of political and cultural events. In the fourteenth century, the second plague pandemic traveled along the Silk Route from Asia into the Near East, Europe, and North Africa, wreaking so much havoc that it completely restructured European society. One of several, likely routes of infection into Europe was infected Italian sailors fleeing the siege of Caffa in the Crimea, where Mongols had flung dead plague cadavers over the walls to infect the populace, one of the earliest recorded instances of biological warfare. The infected rats needed no such help in spreading. Through successive waves of infection, the plague marched across the continent and killed at least 100 million people, or one-third of the population. All of a sudden, a huge percentage of the serfs who'd been the involuntary labor force of feudalism were dead, and as a result the ones who survived could demand more—a pittance and a half, maybe, rather than just a pittance—for their work. But a bit of free agency entered into the picture, which over the next few centuries gave rise to the middle class.

It was the world's third plague pandemic that reached the New World. It started in China in 1855 and spread via port cities such as Hong Kong to all populated continents, claiming at least 12 million lives in India and China alone. The rats with their fleas carrying the plague bacterium jumped ship in San Francisco, having come in on the steamship SS *Australia*, which in January 1900 arrived from Honolulu where an outbreak raged. The ship's cargo was offloaded near the outflow of the Chinatown sewers, just as the Chinese residents were getting ready to celebrate the Year of the Rat.

What followed was a public health disaster that prefigured the response to AIDS in the 1980s. It was run-of-the-mill racism propped up by the belief that the Chinese were more susceptible to disease due to their rice-based diet. So they were subject to two quarantines: the first with cordoning rope that permitted the whites to leave Chinatown, the second with barbed wire that protected white businesses and churches.

The governor of California actively denied the outbreak in an effort to protect the economy, and with another tactic that foreshadowed the 1980s HIV pandemic, blamed the federal government, as well as the Marine Health Service and the San Francisco Board of Health, for perpetuating the outbreak. The local newspapers were silent.

A new governor and a new federal health official led to a more aggressive approach focused on deratting and sanitation, and by 1904 the number of cases in the Chinatown outbreak declined.

But then came the 1906 earthquake and wholesale destruction throughout the Bay Area. During the rebuilding, another plague outbreak occurred, and this time it affected primarily white people. The response was immediate and vigorous, but even so, it was too little, too late. The lackluster response when the disease had been thought to affect mostly a despised minority was likely a factor in letting the fleas migrate to other rodents and then spread out all over the West.

The natural plague reservoir in rural China are giant gerbils, marmots, and ground squirrels. Black rats and their fleas spread the disease in cities and globally via shipping lanes. There's good reason docked ships have rat guards on mooring lines, and the US Public Health Service used to perform deratting operations on vessels entering the United States.

As for the American West, prairie dogs became the new reservoir of choice, though ground squirrels and pack rats also carry the disease, and recently cats have been implicated.

Prairie dogs serve as an "amplification host," carrying the disease into their burrows, then spreading it far and wide. There's actually a "plague line" that runs north and south along the hundredth meridian, passing through Central Texas. That's also the boundary, more or less, of the prairie dog population and one of many reasons why I don't recommend that you vacuum a prairie dog out of its burrow if you're looking for a pet.

Plague serves as a pretty good model for the multistage process that allows a zoonotic disease to find a new ecologic niche. The bacterium needs to be transported to a new place and introduced there into a new host, such as a prairie dog or mosquito. It's only when the disease is established in this new reservoir or vector that it becomes endemic in the ecosystem. Still, there's always an element of mystery, and certainly an element of serendipity, to the question of what sticks and what doesn't. When humans are the only host and disease is transmitted person to person it's simpler: all you need is for individuals to travel. Most of the great epidemics of the New World—smallpox, measles, polio, tuberculosis—are "gifts" brought across the Atlantic from the Old World. Plague differs only in that it came across the Pacific.

But it's a given on this planet that all life is opportunistic, and will spread wherever it can find a suitable habitat. And one thing we know is that the diseases we're subject to are never static, and we can't afford to believe that just because a disease is "over there," that we don't need to worry about it. In many cases, what's over there can come here, and novel diseases can establish themselves in novel environments, especially now as the climate changes and temperatures rise. This is how chikungunya and dengue have traveled up from the tropics and reestablished themselves in the United States via the *Aedes* mosquitoes in Florida.

WEST NILE

A few years before the plague scare in New York, I got a call from Marci Layton, a former Epidemic Intelligence Service officer and friend, then head of epidemiology for the New York City public health department.

"We have an unexplained cluster of illness. Neurologic symptoms, including paralysis, difficulty breathing, and in some cases, involvement of the nerves of the head. We're thinking maybe botulism, and we called CDC for antitoxin, but that doesn't add up. Can you help us?"

To combat emerging infections, you need astute clinicians willing to say, "You know what? This is different and I need to look into it. I need to call somebody and raise the alarm." Then, of course, you need to couple that with astute public health practitioners who take the astute clinician seriously when she calls.

Marci set the gold standard for being a practitioner who understood her community and understood epidemiology and public health well enough to spot the zebras amid the ordinary horses. She followed up on a call from a clinician in Queens who had two patients with paralysis. Follow-up showed a cluster of eight severe cases of encephalitis (brain inflammation), all within sixteen square miles in the northern reaches of the borough. She could have said "no big deal" and moved on, but if she'd said that, she would have failed to recognize one of the great epidemics of the last decade. This virus quickly migrated out from Crown Point, moving across the United States and up into Canada, then down into Mexico and South America.

We connected Marci's New York team with CDC's Division of Vector-Borne Diseases in Fort Collins, Colorado, where they promptly diagnosed St. Louis encephalitis (SLE), which turned out to be wrong. But at least they were in the right vicinity.

Like SLE, this was a mosquito-borne flavivirus, with birds serving as amplifying hosts. But SLE rarely causes severe neurologic human disease—a few cases a year from the United States is the norm—and not in New York City. And it doesn't cause disease in birds. Which was the giveaway.

Prior to and concurrent with the human outbreak, public health officials had noted lots of dead birds, especially crows, falling from the sky.

Birds don't go to the emergency room when they're sick, or have loved ones to bring them chicken soup if they don't feel up to leaving the nest. To avoid becoming lunch, they have to keep going until they keel over. Which they sometimes do in midflight. So, yes, they literally fall out of the sky.

A veterinarian at the Bronx Zoo noted the deaths of a couple of Chilean flamingoes, a cormorant, and a pheasant. She failed to get the attention of CDC, but the specimens from the animals and a crow were sent off to the US Department of Agriculture (USDA) labs in Ames, Iowa, where they were negative for the usual bird and encephalitis viruses. These samples were also sent to CDC at Fort Collins, and the correct diagnosis came back—a month after Marci's call.

So one of the long-term surveillance systems we set up in New York was actually dead-bird surveillance. When we picked up these avian casualties and assessed them, we found involvement of multiple organs, including evidence of encephalitis. We took specimens from these big-city birds, and from infected mosquitoes collected in Connecticut, and from human brain tissue taken from a fatal case of encephalitis, and subjected them all to genomic analyses using nucleic acid testing and genome sequencing. All the markers pointed to West Nile virus (WNV), a flavivirus within the Japanese encephalitis antigenic complex. As it turned out, this was the first time this Old World pathogen had been identified in the Western Hemisphere.

The disease gets its name from the West Nile district of Northern Uganda, where it was isolated from a febrile patient in 1937. Tests of the patient's serum resulted in the isolation of a virus with physical and pathologic properties similar to and sharing immunological relationships with those of two other flaviviruses: St. Louis encephalitis virus and Japanese B encephalitis virus. Mosquitoes of the *Culex* species appeared to be the primary vectors for both.

The first recognized epidemic of WNV occurred in Israel in 1951 in a small town outside of Haifa. Of the village's 303 inhabitants, 123 came down with the characteristic symptoms of fever, headache, muscle aches, anorexia, abdominal pain, rashes, and vomiting.

Serosurveys demonstrated that WNV was endemic along the Nile, with several large outbreaks in Egypt over the next three years. Older children and adults appeared to have higher seroprevalence, while younger children seemed to have more symptomatic illness, suggesting that WNV was mainly an infection of early childhood.

Animal studies suggested that the virus was infectious in a wide range of species, including birds, particularly crows, and nonhuman mammals, particularly horses and donkeys.

There was another outbreak in Israel in 1957, with severe neurologic manifestations among a group of elderly patients in a nursing home. In 1962 in France, and in South Africa in 1974, patients developed meningitis or encephalitis. Similar outbreaks occurred sporadically in Russia, Spain, South Africa, and India.

Then, in 1996, the epidemiology and clinical spectrum of WNV appeared to change when a large outbreak occurred in Bucharest, Romania. This was the first WNV outbreak to be centered in a predominantly urban area, and it was the first in which most of the cases involved infection of the central nervous system (CNS). It appears that the deteriorated urban infrastructure of Bucharest—unkempt areas conducive to mosquito breeding, the absence of protective screens on windows and doors, and an abundance of amplifying hosts in the form of domestic fowl—contributed to the epidemic.

The same high rates of central nervous system infection, as well as high mortality, continued during outbreaks in Morocco in 1996, in Tunisia in 1997, and large outbreaks in Italy and Israel in 1998. Generally, only 1 percent of infections caused neurologic disease, 70–80 percent had little to no symptoms, and the rest had a mild febrile illness.

As for the NY-99 strain detected in New York City, a similar avian epizootic among domestic geese had appeared in Israel during the previous two years. Then, in August of 1999, when the cases showed up in Queens, they had the same genomic sequences as cases occurring at the same moment in Israel.

During the summer of 2000, the foothold gained in New York led to the progressive spread of the virus throughout the

United States, with twenty-one human cases among ten counties in northeastern states.

A year later, the virus had expanded its range all the way to the West Coast, with sixty-six cases in forty-four states, the District of Columbia, and in five Canadian provinces.

So what caused it to stick? The right mosquito, and the right bird (generally passerine, or perching songbirds), combining to create the right enzootic cycle.

Besides being almost completely fatal to crows and their close relatives, the virus was also quite lethal to vultures and condors. So prior to its arrival in the western United States, the entire population of endangered condors, both in captivity and field released, was vaccinated with a new DNA vaccine to prevent an extinction-level event.

The following summer, North America had the largest outbreak of West Nile meningoencephalitis ever recorded anywhere: 4,156 cases, including 2,354 cases of meningoencephalitis and 284 deaths, with Louisiana, Mississippi, and the Chicago area hardest hit.

Most of the severe CNS disease continued to be in older individuals, but there were plenty of milder febrile illnesses in younger patients. We don't know what made the 2002 epidemic so intense, but in several areas of the country that summer the weather conditions were very similar to those in 1975, when a large epidemic of the related flavivirus, St. Louis encephalitis virus, had erupted. And we learned of new modes of person-to-person transmission, including from blood transfusions and organ transplantation.

So West Nile virus went from an oddity to an almost worldwide pandemic.

It's a cautionary tale for how disease can be translocated and transmitted anywhere. The degree of caution increases when we consider the fact that no one is quite sure exactly why this happens. Usually humans and many animals that get infected don't have enough virus in their blood to sustain the disease themselves. So either a fully infected mosquito made its way across from Israel to the United States and bit somebody, or conceivably an infected bird made the crossing. And then there's always the exotic pet trade, or a deliberate release.

Since 2002, keeping chickens in the suburbs, and even in the cities, has become a chic thing to do, the more "free range" the better. But it's good to remember that wild birds are the natural reservoir not only for West Nile, but for influenza viruses. The likelihood of infection is far higher in Asia, where free-range ducks and chickens can mingle not only with wild birds but also with backyard pigs and ducks. But even in the highly sanitized United States, you have to be vigilant to keep your hobby farm from becoming your own emerging pathogen farm.

EBOLA-RESTON, 1996

Outbreaks of Ebola continued to occur in the Democratic Republic of the Congo, occasionally undetected for a long period of time, either running its course unnoticed or spreading until it could no longer be ignored.

One time Ebola crossed my desk again was in 1996, with an outbreak of Reston virus in crab-eating macaque monkeys imported from the Philippines for research in a quarantine facility in Alice, Texas. These monkeys came from the same importer, Ferlite, that had been implicated in the original Reston, Virginia, outbreak—and why a Philippines Ebola virus is named after a US city. We suspected that the exporter had defied a ban that allowed shipping only captive-bred animals and had thrown in a feral animal from Mindanao to complete a six-pack of shipped animals. The thinking was that the disease was endemic in Mindanao, the second largest and southernmost major island of the Philippines, the source of the feral or wild monkeys. We were invited to do an investigation that did not turn up anything interesting to explain the source of infection from the animals shipped to the United States, except for a few positive dogs and animals. Mindanao was held by a separatist guerilla force, which limited ecologic studies. I did learn that macaques have humongous incisors, which are inches from you when you are sticking a needle in their groin to draw blood, and that Ebola is less scary than the herpes B virus that infects all of these monkeys and causes a fatal brain infection.

The puzzle of the Ebola-Reston was solved in 2008, when a number of pigs north of the capital city of Manila on the main island of Luzon started dying from a very severe form of porcine reproductive and respiratory virus (PRRV). The virus diagnosis was confirmed in the United States using a new gene chip that also, incidentally and unexpectedly, suggested that the pigs were coinfected with an Ebola virus. An ecology investigation around the farms identified Ebola-Reston in bats. The likely source for the infections of the research monkeys and the reason we had an Ebola virus all the way over in the Philippines was that there were the appropriately infected bats. And confirms that we should expect Ebola infections throughout the distribution of the bat reservoir.

POULTRY FLU, 2002

You couldn't prove it by me, but when birds get sick—at least this is true for chickens and turkeys—they show signs of depression. They also exhibit coughing and sneezing, watery eyes, and loss of appetite. Where they differ from humans is in edema of the head and, of course, in decreased egg production.

On March 6, 2002, while West Nile was ramping up for its big summer tour, a turkey-breeder flock—in Harrisonburg, Virginia, in Rockingham County, near the West Virginia border—was moved from one location to another for forced molting. Within the next few days, farmers began to see flu symptoms in the relocated birds, as well as in several other flocks owned by the same company.

Veterinarians took tracheal swabs that were sent to the National Veterinary Services Laboratories, Ames, Iowa, and on March 12 the lab confirmed a diagnosis of low-path H7N2: avian flu. Fortunately, while some bird flu causes disease in humans—an unusual H5N1 strain in Hong Kong infected both humans and birds in 1997—H7N2 affects only birds. Still, the ease with which flu can be transmitted from person to person, and thus the ease with which it could create a global pandemic, makes it a matter of perennial concern for disease detectives. All it would take to make H7N2 deadly to humans would be a shuffling of its genetic overcoat. But even without that kind of nightmare escalation, Virginia already faced a huge public health quandary in how to dispose of all the casualties. We're talking 5 million dead birds, and we're talking groundwater.

While waterfowl and shorebirds are the natural host species for avian influenza, these viruses have been circulating periodically among domestic poultry for decades. Poultry likely becomes infected from wild-bird feces contaminating the environment. However, since 1994, the live-bird market system has contributed to the spread, being implicated in several outbreaks in commercial poultry in the United States.

Once poultry are infected, they shed virus in both their respiratory and digestive tracts. This provides a highly efficient means of transmission via aerosols, contaminated feces, and indirect contact with contaminated equipment and materials.

This kind of flu comes in two pathotypes or varieties: low pathogenic and highly pathogenic. The highly pathogenic form is extremely contagious and lethal, causing sudden death in poultry, often without any warning signs, often with mortality of 100 percent. Low-pathogenic strains of avian influenza also can be highly contagious, but the infections are often subclinical, allowing the virus to spread undetected for lengthy periods of time. And even more worrisome, occasionally the low-path can evolve into a high-path form.

We think of Asia when we think of people getting infected by birds, but even here in the United States, chickens and turkeys may change hands up to five times—among retail markets, poultry auctions, wholesale dealers, farm flocks—before reaching the consumer. Every encounter also increases the opportunity for the spread of infection through the eggs, the egg trays, and other equipment.

In the Virginia outbreak, additional farms in Rockingham County began turning up positive, all within a two-mile radius of each other, and all connected by the same rendering truck that made a circuit to pick up the birds that died each day.

There was no direct link, but molecular fingerprinting showed that this strain was essentially identical to the strain that had been circulating in the live-bird markets in the northeastern United States for the past eight years.

On March 21, when the outbreak appeared on a turkey grow-out farm belonging to a different company and located thirty miles north of the index farm (meaning the site where the infection was thought to originate), it became obvious that this was not just a localized event. By March 28, twenty flocks had been identified as being positive for the virus.

Rockingham County is in the Shenandoah Valley in Northwest Virginia, situated between the Blue Ridge Mountains to the east and the Shenandoah Mountains to the west. The valley is twenty to thirty miles wide and stretches north to south for roughly a hundred miles.

Nine hundred and fifty of Virginia's more than 1,300 poultry farms are located in this one county, which leads the nation in turkey production with 213 farms, almost all of which are family owned, but with contracts with major poultry producers such as Pilgrim's Pride, Perdue Farms, and Tyson Foods. The number of birds in any given farm can range from 8,000 to 25,000 for chickens, and as high as 40,000 for turkeys.

At the time of the H7N2 outbreak, there were over 1,000 poultry farms and more than 56 million commercial turkeys and chickens in the valley. Of the 1,000 farms, there were approximately 400 with broilers and meat turkeys, 175 broiler breeder flocks, 50 turkey breeder flocks, and 3 table egg–layer flocks. If you wanted to know where to locate a worst-case poultry contagion, this would be the place.

The industry provides billions of dollars to the Virginia economy and employs more than twelve thousand people. The influenza epidemic of 1983 and 1984 cost Virginia farmers around 2 million birds.

In the spring of 2002, there was legitimate concern about the same kind of economic damage. But the overriding public health issue, aside from the question of what to do with all those dead birds, was how to bring good science to understanding this disease. How was it being transmitted from bird to bird and farm to farm? What did we need to do to stop that transmission?

By April 12, 2002, more than sixty flocks had been found to be positive, and Dr. William Sims, state veterinarian, canceled all public sales and poultry shows as well as visits to poultry farms. He also implemented a mandatory preslaughter testing policy.

Farmers of infected flocks were to be quarantined, and their respective poultry companies were responsible for destroying the birds within twenty-four hours. Still, the scope of the outbreak was already such that the Commonwealth of Virginia asked the USDA for assistance. This was the first time the federal government participated in the control of low-pathogen avian influenza in the United States.

On April 14, a joint task force was established, headquartered in Harrisonburg. When I showed up in the cramped conference room in the small one-story building, the state agencies in charge of agriculture and environmental quality were there as well as the health department and lots of federal agencies including the Agriculture and the Veterinary Corps. But, surprisingly, there were also representatives of the five big poultry companies.

This was unique in my experience: a case of the fox guarding the henhouse, almost literally. Which was troubling, because when you walk in the door to take on a public health mentality—in this case, the broader veterinary public health interest—you have to leave your business interest behind. The natural desire of an industry to protect its financial investment had to be weighed against the public health sector's need to stamp out the outbreak as fast as possible, and keep all the commercial partners as honest and transparent as possible.

In loving fashion, the person responsible for the epidemiology section greeted me with, "You're just another number cruncher on the sidelines. Hopefully, you won't ask me anything."

Virginia's Department of Agriculture used its emergency management structure to engage the Department of Health, Department of Transportation, and law enforcement. They also had the USDA looking at the blood antibodies of affected animals, nucleic acid testing, and virus isolation. The US Public Health Service came in to help support them with epidemiologists and with veterinary officers. And I was there because . . . Well, I'm guessing—whatever official reason they gave me—they needed a number cruncher or, more specifically, an expert on data systems and disease monitoring.

Law enforcement personnel were involved because one measure that had to be taken was to restrict traffic in and out of infected facilities. Somebody might be flinging dead birds in the nearest creek, or they might be trying to sneak chickens out from their farm to sell them to other farms. In the Public Health Service we don't have law enforcement standing. State troopers do.

To raise birds commercially, you have to mortgage yourself to the poultry industry. This is because of the up-front costs, and because of the business model the industry has developed to distance itself from responsibility for what they do. A chicken farm will have about a thousand chickens per hutch, and usually seven to eight thousand chickens per house. It costs farmers about $150,000 to build one of these houses, which are metal, climate-controlled structures. That's where mortgaging yourself comes in, literally. It's usually a fifteen-year note, which puts the financial risk of the operation squarely on the farmer's shoulders.

Once you've built the houses, the poultry company starts sending you chickens or turkeys, which remain company property. The drivers delivering the animals also work for the big poultry companies. Chickens mature in just six weeks, and then you ship them back to the poultry company for slaughter. You're paid based on weight, with a premium if your birds are healthier than average. A few weeks later, a new batch of chicks arrives. You have six or seven batches in a year, and if chickens are going to die, they're most likely going to do so in the first week.

By putting maximum responsibility on the farmers, the big poultry companies try to avoid losses, while also avoiding political heat. If there's an outbreak of avian flu, well, that's good old Farmer Jones at fault, not soulless agribusiness, even though it's very likely that the company's trucks may be spreading the disease between the farms. And if Farmer Jones's chickens die, there's still that mortgage payment due at the first of every month. (And, by the way, if you're worried about chicken waste destroying Chesapeake Bay or polluting nearby groundwater—talk to good old Farmer Jones.)

With chickens, they all come in and they all leave. When they leave, you have to clean the hutch, and then you start over. Turkeys are a little different—not all in and all out at once. Turkeys are typically on a farm for about four or five months, but some are let out earlier and new turkeys arrive, while other turkeys are given more time to stay put and fatten up.

Either way, when birds start to die, and when a contagion starts to spread, the birds need to be put down. But then what? That's where compensation, water table issues, and air quality issues come to the fore.

Governor Mark Warner, along with the Virginia congressional delegation, asked then US Secretary of Agriculture Ann Veneman to initiate a federal indemnification program for the birds being destroyed. But it wasn't as if the government had been somehow negligent, and that government negligence had led to the destruction of property. The birds simply needed to be destroyed because they were sick and infectious. And yet the USDA agreed to compensate the growers to the tune of some $37 million, representing the market value of flocks ordered destroyed, as well as the cost of disposal and cleaning up. I think the money was to buy cooperation, to get the growers to do the right thing with their flocks and protect the industry. I wonder if our global preparedness efforts would be better financed if governments always had to reimburse families, communities, and corporations affected by an outbreak.

In the Middle East, we had to worry about meat companies treating guest workers as being disposable. In Virginia, we had to worry about poultry companies hiding or disposing of dead birds any way they liked.

Of course it's legitimate to worry about farmers and the farm economy, but where do you find the balance between appropriately meeting the public health and economic needs of the community, and allowing an industry to hold the public hostage, saying in effect, "We can't do what's right until you give us money up front." The indemnity program was expensive cooperation, bought and paid for.

Our task force surveillance efforts started on May 22, and included once-a-week testing of dead birds from all premises, biweekly testing of all breeder flocks, and premovement testing.

One of our most successful techniques was called "barrel surveillance." Once a week, farms were required to place ten birds per house into a sealed barrel in their driveway, and then we'd come by, pick up these barrels, and take them off to collect tracheal swabs for laboratory testing. This gave us 100 percent coverage of all commercial poultry flocks without compromising on-farm biosecurity procedures.

My job was to keep a tally of all the birds that were dying in the turkey farms and chicken houses, compile the data, match it with the laboratory sample results, and get those results to the team. Piece of cake, right? The goal of this geek work was to understand what was going on from day to day. Where was this disease occurring? How did it spread? How should we change our prevention strategies to make things better?

To get a sense of how effective the prevention strategies were, and to offer suggestions for improvement, I rented a car and spent a few weeks driving around the Shenandoah Valley, making sure the barrel surveillance was working.

I chatted up the workers on the farms, offering advice on how they could protect themselves personally, as well as their flocks. I tried to make sure the data were being collected appropriately, but the reporting was mostly ad hoc, and the quality of the database we established from that reporting could have been better. There were eight primary forms being used: an investigation summary form, a herd exam form, a questionnaire for a case control study, a specimen submission form that included a sample form, a lab test form, a tracking list of where these birds came from, and a euthanasia disposal summary form. Then there was a cleaning and disinfection form, an infection control worksheet, a vaccination record, and appraisal assignment—all created just for the investigation.

Back at headquarters, my job was to put all those numbers together in a way that would make sense to the task force. We needed to understand actions prior to the outbreak that might have led to the spread of this disease, and how people were behaving now. I looked at what data were available to us using the GPS location of these farms, negatives and positives, what date the farm was positive, how long there were infected birds on the farm, what company was the source of the animals, whether it was turkeys or chickens, the age of the birds, the density of the flock, and the number of chicken houses on the farm. Also, how were people and trucks moving within and between farms? This was important because we believed that the trucks might be getting contaminated during their travels. And just as important, how did they get rid of their dead or dying birds?

A requirement was put in place that if you buried dead birds on your property then that fact, as well as the precise location, had to be registered on your deed. You also had to install long-term monitoring wells to make sure you weren't contaminating the water. This, needless to say, pissed off the industry.

Simple composting was deemed unworkable because during the roughly eight weeks it took to do that, you would have tied up the whole farm. So they tried offsite incineration, with sealed, leak-proof trucks picking up birds and euthanizing them enroute with carbon dioxide. (You don't need carbon monoxide: you only need to deprive them of oxygen and they die.) But burning was way too expensive, and then there was the issue of smoke, as well as the god-awful smell.

In the end, the best method of disposal made use of these wonderful things called agricultural bags, and then offsite burial in mega landfills. You put the dead birds inside the bags, and then they compost more discretely. Its very labor intensive, but you have to do it. You also have to make sure that people are spraying vehicles with disinfectant as they come on and off the farms.

The last positive case in Virginia was identified on July 2, four months after the first diagnosis, and the final quarantine of positive premises was lifted on October 9. A total of 197 flocks, representing approximately 20 percent of the thousand area commercial poultry farms, had been infected.

Approximately 4.7 million birds, or 8.4 percent of the estimated 56 million birds at risk, were destroyed to control the outbreak. The outbreak was estimated to have cost the industry $120 million.

Fortunately, during all this there was only one poultry worker who got sick, and then with only a mild respiratory infection. They found some antibodies in him, but they could never find virus, so there was no way to prove that he got infected from the birds or if he'd been infected previously.

But this was hardly the end of our worries with avian flu.

In 2003, in my capacity as CDC's acting associate director for Global Health, I was asked to try to field CDC teams to assess how prepared the Europeans would be for dealing with an outbreak of H5N1. We went over to try to figure out how to improve surveillance, disease detection, and laboratory systems.

They were on edge because, for the first time since the Hong Kong outbreak in 1997, we were seeing human disease associated with this strain of avian influenza and a very high case fatality if humans were unfortunate enough to get infected. Three people in one family had been visiting Fujian Province in mainland China and two died.

It was unclear exactly what was going on because of discrepancies in the reporting, but by midyear, there were outbreaks of the disease in poultry throughout Asia, even though they were not recognized as such. In December, animals in a Thai zoo died after eating infected chicken carcasses. Shortly thereafter, the infection was detected in three flocks in the Republic of Korea. I learned all about bird flyways and how bird migration patterns were responsible for intercontinental transmission.

H5N1 is a fast-mutating, highly pathogenic strain of avian virus that continues to evolve, with changes in antigenicity and internal gene constellations, and with an expanding host range that includes swans, magpies, ducks, geese, pigeons, and eagles, as well as chickens and turkeys on farms. This antigenic drift has rapidly resulted in highly pathogenic variants with little cross-protection.

The Asian H5N1 virus was first detected in Guangdong Province, China, in 1996 when it killed some geese, but it created little attention until it spread to humans through the poultry markets in Hong Kong the next year, killing six of eighteen people infected.

For the next eight years the virus was confined largely to Southeast Asia. By 2005, it would be affecting thirty-three out of sixty-four cities and provinces in Vietnam, where it led to the killing of nearly 1.2 million domesticated birds. Total avian mortality, including wild birds, was believed to have been around 140 million.

Then huge die-offs spread out from Qinghai Lake in central China, and followed the path of wild birds to Kazakhstan, Mongolia, and Russia, and from there to Turkey, Romania, Croatia, and Kuwait.

This avian outbreak became so notorious that it had not one but two *Time* magazine covers in 2004 and 2005, and led to marked improvements in global influenza preparedness. It also spawned difficult discussions of sharing of viruses within the global community and how to assure that any advances in medical countermeasures such as new vaccines made it back to the original infected populations.

By 2006, the disease was a panzoonotic (meaning a pandemic among animals), prevalent in India and North Africa as well, with the highest numbers of bird deaths recorded in Cambodia, China, Laos, Nigeria, Thailand, Egypt, Sudan, South Korea, Vietnam, and Indonesia. In Indonesia, there was a human outbreak of fifty-five cases including eight members of a single family in Sumatra who died. The World Health Organization reported this as being perhaps the first recorded instance of limited human-to-human transmission.

In 2008, a twenty-two-year-old man died in central Hunan Province, China. In February, a schoolteacher from northern Vietnam died, as well as three more people in China. The following month a woman died in Egypt. That summer the virus was found among birds in a poultry stall in Hong Kong, and a new regulation was instituted requiring that all live chickens not sold by 8:00 p.m. be killed.

In 2014, a resident of Alberta, Canada, died of H5N1 after returning from Beijing. This was the first known death from the disease in North America.

Since 2003, the H5N1 avian influenza has infected 638 people and killed 379 of them. The vast majority of cases were in Egypt, Indonesia, and Vietnam.

Disturbingly, in 2011, in closely related experiments, researchers at the University of Wisconsin and at Erasmus University genetically engineered this deadly virus to make it more infectious for humans and more transmissible by aerosols. While these experiments had a worthy goal—they were designed to identify the critical gene markers among these zoonotic viruses that can be a prelude to a human pandemic—the risks to human health were obvious. At the very least, the experiments should have been better regulated and reviewed before the scientists published in the medical literature their road map for creating a more dangerous virus that could kill half the global population.

In 2015, a different high-path H5N2 created what's become known as the poultry apocalypse in the American Midwest, causing the price of eggs to skyrocket everywhere. This outbreak originated as a single H5N8 virus in Asia, then swapped genes with North American flu viruses, then quickly spread among wild birds along migratory pathways. Chicken and turkey producers from Arkansas to North Dakota and Minnesota were affected, calling into question the entire concept of industrial farming. Security was stepped up by major players such as Tyson Foods and Cargill, including ten-foot-high perimeter fences, mandatory showers for workers coming and going from the facilities, and the washing of trucks. In Minnesota, the National Guard was called in to help.

In all, 48 million birds in fifteen states were destroyed, including nearly 30 million in Iowa, the nation's largest egg producer. The price tag for disposal was $1 billion—a tab picked up by US taxpayers. Which tells you why I am in the prevention business. It's a lot cheaper to fix the barn door before all the horses have wandered away.

But that H5N2 virus was not only responsible for the slaughter of millions of chickens and turkeys in the Midwest, it went on to cause disease in France, the largest poultry producer in Europe.

RIFT VALLEY FEVER

Rift Valley fever (RVF) is another mosquito-borne disease that appeared to be locked into a specific geographic area for centuries, then migrated.

When the Bible talks about the fifth plague of Egypt that occurs every few years based on climate conditions, that's Rift Valley fever. It causes abortions and death among livestock, and the sight of numerous dead animals in the fields and by the roadside does look biblically apocalyptic. Less often, it causes brain inflammation, eye inflammation and blindness, and hemorrhagic fever among shepherds.

In East Africa, in 1998, I had the honor and pleasure of working with the Masai people—tall, proud warriors of southern Kenya and northern Tanzania who drink cow blood (which is not such a good idea when the blood is contaminated with RVF). We roamed the Serengeti drawing blood from animals and people to study the extent of the disease. When Masai children gathered around to watch, we told them the blood tubes we were taking back to the United States were for midnight snacks.

Restricted for centuries to Sub-Saharan Africa, Rift Valley then jumped to Egypt in Northern Africa in 1977–78, with an estimated 200,000 people infected.

In 2000, the virus jumped again and found suitable vectors on the Tihamah, the southern part of the Red Sea coastal plain of Arabia, which extends to Yemen. That outbreak was initially misdiagnosed as yellow fever and we were in the midst of the usual set of animal health and human health politics. However, after a few months of assistance and aggressive prevention measures, we worked with WHO and the ministry of health to bring the outbreak under control. My parting gift from the minister of health was a lucite beheading sword!

Other examples of mosquito-borne diseases that have dramatically increased their range in the twenty-first century to include the Americas are dengue, chikungunya (causes an arthritis with fever), and Zika (a mild fever illness that in pregnant women can cause microcephaly, an abnormally small head with severe implications for the child's development).

Rodents, birds, bats, mosquitoes, and ticks, among others, can all carry disease to new places. It is a great boon to a microbe if you have a mobile reservoir or vector. But microbes can also hitch a ride in humans to a new location and set up shop among the local insects or other animals to emerge in a new area. And none of this requires a passport. That's why protecting everybody from many of these emerging diseases requires a planetwide approach. Even if all politics is local, all public health efforts need to be global.

7

— DIRECT FROM —
THE METROPOLE HOTEL

So many green streams and blue hills, but to what avail?
This tiny creature left even Hua To powerless!
Hundreds of villages choked with weeds, men wasted away;
Thousands of homes deserted, ghosts chanted mournfully.
Motionless, by earth I travel eighty thousand li a day,
Surveying the sky I see a myriad Milky Ways from afar.
Should the cowherd ask tidings of the God of Plague,
Say the same griefs flow down the stream of time.

—Mao Tse-tung, "Farewell to the God of Plague"

Outbreak investigations are like solving jigsaw puzzles. Or maybe ten of them mixed together. Some of the pieces fit in multiple places. Some pieces are missing. The puzzle you need to solve may be an image you've never seen before. And people may have died and will continue to get sick and die till you are done. Good luck—the clock is ticking.

The official narrative for the severe acute respiratory syndrome (SARS) outbreak that swept through Asia and grazed North America traces the first reported case to Guangdong Province, China. This was mid-November 2002, and the patient, a farmer, was treated in the First People's Hospital of Foshan, and then promptly died.

166 THE NEXT PANDEMIC

The first suggestion that the farmer's death might have been tied to some larger trend appeared later that month when Canada's Global Public Health Intelligence Network (GPHIN), an Internet-monitoring system that's part of the World Health Organization's Global Outbreak and Alert Response Network, picked up reports of an "unusual respiratory illness outbreak" from newspaper accounts in Guangdong. GPHIN sent their analysis on to WHO, but in Chinese, with only a small portion translated. An English-language version didn't appear until late January and, even so, the "unusual" outbreak was simply catalogued as one of the many such alerts every day in this country of 1.3 billion people.

Not that the Chinese authorities were exactly forthcoming. According to their law on prevention and treatment of infectious diseases, any such disease should be classified as a state secret until it is "announced by the Ministry of Health or organs authorized by the Ministry." Thus a virtual news blackout persisted. The bigger misstep was their failing to comprehend the magnitude of the outbreak and conduct a thorough investigation.

It was not until February 10 that the People's Republic came clean, reporting to the World Health Organization that there were 305 cases (including 105 health care workers) and 5 deaths of atypical pneumonia—all presumably from the same vaguely defined mystery illness. Then again, no one knew for sure, because no one could pin down exactly what they were dealing with.

Early in February, reports about a "deadly flu" had been sent via SMS (short message service) on mobile phones in Guangzhou. Trying to quell panic, the local media acknowledged the disease and listed what were said to be "preventive measures," such as using vinegar fumes to disinfect the air. Citizens made a run on local pharmacies and cleared the shelves of antibiotics, flu medication, and vinegar.

Later that month, officials said that the outbreak in Guangzhou had peaked, but that turned out to be wishful thinking. The disease was probably something humdrum, like mycoplasma, they said, a usually minor bacterial infection. They would soon be reporting another 806 infections and 34 deaths. Only in retrospect would this outbreak be connected with the coming storm.

On February 19, a cluster of avian influenza H5N1 was reported in Hong Kong. The virus was isolated from a nine-year-old hospitalized boy whose father and sister had just died of unknown causes. These cases were noteworthy because they represented an infection with a zoonotic virus but were unrelated to the larger outbreak. It did lead the public health community to assume, at least for a while, that they were in the midst of a new influenza pandemic.

Then, on February 21, Liu Jianlun, a sixty-four-year-old Chinese doctor who'd treated cases in Guangdong, arrived in Hong Kong to attend his nephew's wedding. He checked into room 911 of the Metropole Hotel. Although he'd had symptomatic respiratory problems for more than a week, he felt well enough to travel, shop, and sightsee with his brother-in-law. On February 22, he sought urgent care at the Kwong Wah Hospital and was admitted to the intensive care unit. He told his doctors that he was likely infected with whatever he'd been treating in Guandong and that he was not going to survive.

That next day, a forty-seven-year-old Chinese American businessman, Johnny Chen, a resident of Shanghai who'd stayed across the hall from Dr. Liu on the ninth floor of the Metropole, traveled on to Shanghai and Macao, then caught a plane bound for Vietnam. On February 26, he became ill and was admitted to the French Hospital of Hanoi. Dr. Carlo Urbani, an infectious diseases specialist working for WHO, attended Mr. Chen. He was also the first to recognize that this was not influenza or simple pneumonia, but something new. He reported the unusual respiratory disease to WHO, and urged Vietnamese officials to begin screening airline passengers.

In Hong Kong, other people, many of them health care workers, began to show up at the Prince of Wales Hospital with signs of the same symptoms: respiratory distress with fever and abnormal chest X-rays. Their lungs were filled with fluid, which meant that the alveoli—the little pockets where oxygen exchange actually happens—couldn't take in air.

Making matters worse, this was not a disease like Ebola for which the infection was obvious from the get-go, nor did it require some sort of intimate contact for it to spread. Even though these victims were incubating and shedding the virus, their symptoms remained under the radar while they went about their business, checking into hotels like Liu Jianlun, or hopping on international flights like Johnny Chen. As a result, clusters of people began to appear all over Asia with fever, dry cough, and muscle aches, and low platelet counts and low white-blood-cell counts that would progress to double-sided pneumonia.

The severity of the symptoms, as well as the infection of hospital staff, alarmed global health authorities fearful of another emergent pneumonia epidemic. But it still wasn't clear if these cases even had anything to do with each other.

By this time there were fifty-three patients in four hospitals in Hong Kong, thirty-seven with pneumonia. These people were being treated with the antiviral ribavirin and steroids, but secondary transmissions were still taking place among health care workers, family members, and other hospital visitors. Rumors began to circulate of cases popping up in Singapore and Taiwan, and even as far away as Toronto, Canada.

A week later, on ventilator support, Johnny Chen was medically evacuated to Hong Kong. During his treatment in Hanoi, seven hospital workers who'd cared for him developed symptoms. At least thirty-eight health care workers were infected.

On March 1, the fifty-three-year-old brother-in-law of Dr. Liu was admitted to Hong Kong's Kwong Wah Hospital. That same day, a businessman who'd traveled to both Hong Kong and Guangdong Province returned home to Taiwan, bringing the outbreak with him.

Dr. Liu, the index patient who'd first brought the outbreak from Guandong to Hong Kong, died on March 4, the same day that a twenty-seven-year-old man who'd also stayed on the ninth floor of the Metropole during Dr. Liu's visit was admitted to Prince of Wales Hospital. At least ninety-nine hospital workers (including seventeen medical students) were infected while treating him.

It appears that, even after all this, no one was using the basic precautions—wearing a mask, repeated hand washing—meant to protect medical workers.

On March 11, Dr. Carlo Urbani, the WHO infectious disease specialist who first identified this disease agent as something novel, traveled to Bangkok to attend a medical conference. He fell ill, and upon arrival in Bangkok he told a waiting friend not to touch him, but to call an ambulance to take him to a hospital. He was admitted and isolated in an intensive care unit where he was attended by CDC's Dr. Scott Dowell, head of the local Emerging Infections Program. Dr. Dowell collected critical samples—a nasopharyngeal swab, blood, and sera—and sent them to CDC headquarters.

On March 12, WHO issued a global alert. In time there would be reports of similar outbreaks in Toronto, Ottawa, San Francisco, Ulaanbaatar, Manila, and Singapore, as well as throughout China—in Jilin, Hebei, Hubei, Shaanxi, Jiangsu, Shanxi, Tianjin, and Inner Mongolia.

That same day, back in Atlanta, CDC issued its own health alert, and Nancy Cox, chief of CDC's influenza group, asked to speak to me. She'd been approached by officials from Hong Kong and from WHO because of the earlier isolation of H5N1 associated with two deaths in Hong Kong. It's also true that, when doctors see patients presenting with a communicable disease that includes fever and severe respiratory illness, they often just think influenza. Dr. Cox had been one of my earliest mentors and knew my reputation for digging into the epidemiology of exotic cases.

Dr. Cox briefed me about Dr. Liu and the other reported cases and clusters, and it was certainly not too far-fetched to suspect a link among them. But without a laboratory diagnosis, all we had to go on was very sick people with rapid respiratory failure, who had traveled to the Far East, and who might or might not now be dead.

Johnny Chen, the man who'd stayed across the hall from Dr. Liu then been treated by Dr. Urbani in Hanoi, died on March 13. Two weeks later, in Bangkok, Dr. Urbani died. Seven other guests from the ninth floor, and sixteen from the Metropole Hotel as a whole, became infected. Before all was said and done, about 80 percent of the Hong Kong cases could be traced back to Dr. Liu, making him the consummate example of the kind of superspreader I'd described earlier in the context of Ebola.

On March 14, a cluster of thirteen passengers became infected during Air China Flight 112 from Hong Kong to Beijing. From this time forward, there would be so many outbreaks on planes and so many infected crew members that it threatened to shut down air travel. The next day, Dr. David Heymann of WHO went so far as to issue a rare travel advisory, which galvanized a global response and put individual countries on notice that they needed to be transparent about what was going on within their borders. Swimming against the tide at WHO, which is a member organization, this was the most courageous and critical public health decision of the outbreak and likely prevented the disease from establishing itself in the broader community outside of hospitals.

Dr. Heymann also gave the mysterious illness a name— severe acute respiratory syndrome (SARS)—based on its symptoms, and declared it "a worldwide health threat."

Two days later, we got a report from the French Hospital of Hanoi: thirty-one patients, three on ventilators, one dead. Hanoi's Bach Mai Hospital had twelve patients, none on ventilators, one dead. The outbreak in the second hospital seemed different from what we were seeing elsewhere, in that a number of the infected people showed improvement after being treated with antibiotics and steroids. But it was not unusual in the chaos of an outbreak with so many unknowns to hear about all sorts of unexplained illness and deaths that even remotely seemed similar.

At CDC, we always have to keep asking ourselves, why do some people die of a disease and others recover? How can we even know if several cases are all the same disease? And who are these people who become superspreaders? Why them and not others?

Clinical characteristics tell you only so much, so until we have lab results we can never be sure what we're seeing. Fever, headache, flu-like symptoms—those symptoms apply to thousands of people around the world every day. Then again, most of them don't abruptly die or transmit the disease to their caretakers.

On March 16, back in Atlanta, we had a meeting in the Emergency Operation Center with Dr. Julie Gerberding, director of CDC at that time. This mystery disease was hitting closer to home. One health care worker in Canada was ill with fever and cough, but still had a normal chest X-ray. And then we had another suspected patient who'd been hospitalized after traveling to Hong Kong and Malaysia. This patient was not in Asia but in Virginia Beach, Virginia.

This is often the point at which widespread panic sets in—when an outbreak appears to have reached the United States. It's not that Americans don't care what happens in other countries and are only concerned about our own health. It's more the calculation that if an illness can get past our many protective public health measures, it must be really bad.

But the fact is, our infection control practices are not superior to those in other excellent hospitals in Hong Kong, China, Vietnam, Singapore, or Canada. The United States was just fortunate to not have a superspreader be admitted. We still have individual infections from contamination within the health care environment, from health care workers reusing contaminated drugs, or from multiuse of endoscopes that have not been properly cleaned, which leaves us every bit as vulnerable as the most primitive hospitals in Africa. Health care acquired infections of the bloodstream or urinary tract, of surgical wounds, and of the lungs may be a lot less dramatic than SARS or Ebola, but they're no less deadly.

Fortunately, this one report of a probable case in Virginia led to only twelve phone calls, which was good news, because it meant that things hadn't gone completely crazy yet.

The next morning we met with the city, county, and state health departments in Virginia, but this was a national-level response, and we needed to put together a team to assist with the local investigation. So what was the roster going to look like? Who were going to be the leaders? We needed to develop a line listing of all cases and contacts, publish definitions to help physicians identify suspect cases, develop a laboratory test once the agent was found, and then distribute it to all the states through the Laboratory Response Network. CDC would start pushing out dozens of guidance documents to cover potential treatment, prevention control practices in hospitals, and airport screening processes. For all that, the hard work was still at the local and state levels. That was where CDC guidance turned into nuanced policies and practices to protect local communities.

On March 17, an international network of eleven leading laboratories was established to determine the cause of the outbreaks and to develop potential treatments. CDC held its first briefing and said that fourteen suspected cases were now being investigated in the United States.

The next day, we had a lab conference call that brought us up to date on a physician who had been the source of a global alert. He had treated a patient in Singapore, traveled to the United States for a conference where he got ill, but was cleared for travel anyway. He then flew to Germany, where he was put in isolation. They had his samples in Marburg, and they'd done some electron microscopy, and they were thinking maybe it was a parainfluenza, a virus family really close to influenza, but not quite.

We had the specimen from Dr. Urbani that Scott Dowell had sent from Bangkok, and one of the throat swabs was positive for picornavirus, which causes gastrointestinal infections. We continued looking for rhinovirus, henipaviruses, paramyxovirus, chlamydia, mycoplasma, legionella, respiratory syncytial virus, herpes virus, influenzas, rickettsias, hemorrhagic fevers, Epstein-Barr virus, you name it. The only factor we could use to in any way narrow the search was to focus on patients who had died. Which at this point wasn't very helpful.

By that evening our lab had ruled out Epstein-Barr virus and a host of other infections, but then twenty new specimens arrived from Toronto, so we went through the process again.

On March 20, WHO reported that several hospitals in Vietnam and Hong Kong were operating with half the usual staff, because so many workers were staying home for fear of getting infected. WHO raised the concern that substandard care of those already ill might be contributing to the spread.

By this point, it had come to light that four Taiwanese who were believed to have contracted the disease on board the March 15 Air China Flight 112 had developed symptoms during their stay in Beijing, but then returned to Taiwan. Hong Kong authorities were now tracing all passengers and crew who'd traveled on the same flights, either the March 21 Air China Flight 111 from Beijing to Hong Kong, or Cathay Pacific Flight 510 from Hong Kong to Taipei.

Our lab crew thought they had a viral particle they could try to pull out from the samples, and they addressed it with polymerase chain reaction (PCR), a technology from molecular biology that amplifies a single copy or a few copies of a piece of DNA across several orders of magnitude, generating thousands to millions of copies of a particular DNA sequence. It's not a culture—it's a copy machine.

In culturing, you put in some cells and you wait for them to grow. With PCR, you just keep copying it again, and again, and again until you have enough that you can either see it as a band on a gel, or you can put in a probe and look at it. When you copy these things, the reagents you use have to be very close to the thing you're trying to copy. They're called "degenerate primers," or bad reagents, that latch on to the target entity and replicate it.

In trying to sort through the vast amount of data, much of which might be completely irrelevant, we created a scale to grade the patients and their likelihood of being a case. We established five clinical benchmarks, assuming that anyone with all five would be a definite. But then we had a couple that scored a five but didn't become cases. So we were still fumbling in the dark, and the worst thing you can do is to make an assumption, because you can be wrong: thinking that you're onto something sends you down a trail, which means you ignore other trails. And, yes, it is as confusing as it sounds. And all this amid the worst-case scenario—a deadly disease that's transmitted rapidly and efficiently, spreading worldwide.

Death is a pretty severe outcome, and as a result the media picks up on mysterious deaths in hospitals fairly quickly. It's noticing the less dramatic outcomes that's harder. That's why we in the disease detective business spend so much time monitoring social media and web traffic to try to uncover as quickly as possible the first hints of a new outbreak. This is one of the key ideas behind the Global Public Health Intelligence Network, ProMed, HealthMap, and Operation Dragon Fire.

You have to use every tool available to you until you can dispatch teams to get more and better information. That's why CDC has public health staff stationed all over the United States to work with the local health departments, as well as in key regions around the world. In the US, where information is fairly transparent, they can look for early warning signs in hospitals and pharmacies and doctor's' offices. It is much trickier overseas, especially in those regions in which local officials do their best to conceal the facts, or don't have systems in place.

You need to gather every bit of information you can, from whomever you can get it. In a sense, you're depending on the journalistic abilities of the medical staff where the patients are being treated, as well as good record keeping and good record sharing. That's what allows the aha! moment to happen. You say, "Oh, that guy's daughter caught it, and this other patient worked on the same floor of the same building as she did. I don't think that's a coincidence. It looks like transmission." Otherwise, there's only so much that CDC and WHO and other agencies can do. Which is why we've developed a near-religious obsession with data.

We were clearly dealing with a lung infection that led to fluid on the lung, and to pneumonia. When the lung leaks fluid, you need to measure the diffusion capacity, which is the extent to which oxygen passes from the air sacs of the lungs into the blood.

When you look at a chest X-ray, you have these two big black profiles on the left and right. When the air pockets within your lungs start filling up with pus, the two big black profiles are no longer black because the air pockets, the alveoli, are full of puss, and subsequent X-rays get whiter. Now if there's viral pneumonia, for the most part at the beginning, instead of the infection being at the level of the alveoli, the problem is in the surrounding cells. All that space becomes infected with cells and puss and the X-ray looks more mottled. In the end, though, it all progresses to acute respiratory distress syndrome and the alveoli and the surrounding cells look the same.

Back in Atlanta, where I was leading the epidemiology response, I was putting together all these pieces of information trying to give people a complete composite picture. This led to the first report from CDC tying the wider outbreak to the Metropole Hotel, and recognizing the role of Dr. Liu as a superspreader. Although I was forbidden from using the term for fear of panic, and because of associations with our earlier work with Ebola, it is now an established term.

We drew up a diagram, using data gathered by lots of hard-working disease detectives around the world. Then we mapped the index cases from each country, then drew a line to the place were each was thought to have become infected. All the lines converged on Hong Kong and, more specifically, the Hotel Metropole Hotel! This was a case in which a picture was indeed worth a thousand words.

It was at this juncture that we had a secret meeting with Jim Hughes, then director of the National Center for Infectious Diseases, and he asked the question a lot of us had been thinking: "Could this be bioterrorism?"

This was still only a year and a half after the anthrax attacks in Washington and New York, and just when the United States was launching its second invasion of Iraq. For months the Bush administration had been churning up fears and accusing Saddam Hussein of having weapons of mass destruction, including bioweapons. At the time, and with the same threats in mind, CDC was also giving a weekly account of the number of civilian health care and public health workers that had been vaccinated against smallpox, along with the number of side effects.

From a terrorist's perspective, the Hong Kong outbreak seemed like the perfect execution of a doomsday scenario. You have infected people leaving a popular international hotel and boarding planes for international destinations far and wide. Microbes can now spread to anyplace on the planet in less than seventy-two hours—a span of time shorter than the incubation period of almost all diseases. That's how you can show up looking healthy and feeling fine when you reach your destination, never knowing that you've brought a deadly contagion with you. Governments have airport screening for weapons and occasionally for sick persons, but they don't screen for microbes in you or in the environment. And they don't screen at all at hotels and shopping malls.

At this point, we still didn't know if the disease causing this outbreak had ever been seen before. It wasn't like another outbreak of Ebola where you knew what you were up against. Instead, it was the fog of war applied to public health.

On March 27, Hong Kong announced the temporary closing of all educational institutions. The Ministry of Education of Singapore also announced that all primary schools, secondary schools, and junior colleges were to be shut.

That same day, CDC deployed twelve people to five countries to help investigate the pandemic.

The first WHO teleconference was held on March 28, which included public health officials from all over the world, including China. There were 792 cases in Guangdong, 10 in Beijing, and a few in Shanghai, and 25 percent of cases throughout China were health care workers.

We were getting status updates about Vietnam—stable situation, ninety cases, twenty-three discharges—but also the suggestion of asymptomatic transmission, meaning that people were getting infected with a very typical illness but we weren't sure by whom, or if their infection was even related to this outbreak. Still, roughly 50 percent of people exposed were getting infected, which was really pretty bad.

By now Hong Kong had 11 deaths out of 370 cases. Of those, 149 were health care workers, with transmission to family members, visitors in the hospital, and other contacts. The Rolling Stones canceled two concerts scheduled for the city.

On March 30, Hong Kong authorities quarantined Estate E of the massive Amoy Gardens apartment complex. There were more than two hundred cases reported in that one building alone. The residents were later transferred to the quarantined

Lei Yue Mun Holiday Camp and Lady MacLehose Holiday Village, because Amoy was deemed a health hazard. Most of the cases were tied to apartment units with a northwestern orientation that shared the same sewage pipe. According to government officials, the virus had been brought onto the estate by an infected kidney patient who visited after being discharged from Prince of Wales Hospital. He infected his elder brother, who lived in a flat on the seventh floor. The virus spread through the plumbing, apparently through dried up U-shaped P-traps, and was blown by a maritime breeze to the ventilation unit of the estate's balcony and stairwells. The balconies were now closed and guarded by police. It had been confirmed that the virus could spread via droplets, but the situation in Hong Kong raised the possibility that it could be spread through the air. Regardless, the standard playbook for prevention measures was not working.

We were fortunate that Margaret Chan, who would go on to become the embattled WHO director during the Ebola crisis twelve years later, was the health commissioner for Hong Kong at the time. She readily agreed to call in additional infection-disease experts. That was certainly welcome after the foot dragging that had happened on the mainland when the first cases had cropped up in the fall. Ultimately, both the Chinese minister of health and the mayor of Beijing were sacked for their mishandling of the outbreak.

On April 1, the US government recalled all nonessential personnel from the consulates in Hong Kong and Guangzhou. WHO, as well as the US government, advised US citizens not to travel to the region.

On April 2, Chinese medical officials turned over a new leaf and began more accurate reporting of the status of the outbreak. Guangdong Province reported 361 new infections and nine new deaths, with cases also in Beijing and Shanghai. Chinese officials allowed international officials to investigate. Even so, the team was severely restricted in what it could do.

They were not given access to Guangdong until eight days after their arrival, and it was not until April 9 that they were allowed to inspect military hospitals in Beijing.

On April 6, a case was found in Manila: a Philippine national who had just returned from Hong Kong.

On April 9, James Salisbury, an American Mormon who taught at Shenzhen Polytechnic, died at Hong Kong's North District Hospital. He'd been diagnosed with "pneumonia" about a month before. His son Michael, six years old at the time, also contracted the disease but survived. This proved to be a high-profile death and led to more transparency from Chinese officials.

On April 11, the World Health Organization issued an updated global health alert, confirming once again that the disease was being spread by global air travel. Cathy Pacific, the global airline, almost went under as a result.

———

The day before that alert, I left Atlanta and spent twenty-four hours flying to Singapore to serve as a WHO consultant. This invite was facilitated by a great local public health champion, Dr. Ling Ai Ee, head and senior consultant for the virology laboratory, Department of Pathology, Singapore General Hospital.

I immediately started into meetings—no sleep, no shower—and was hit with a barrage of new information about what had been going on in Singapore and questions about what was going on globally. I'd been looking at the macro; the people in Singapore had been looking at the micro. The question was, as it always is, what could we learn from each other?

Singapore is an odd place, an independent nation with not much to build a country on. No common ethnicity, language, or culture, and not much land. And yet 5.6 million people live there—a tightly packed, sometimes volatile mix of Chinese,

Malays, and Indians, obsessed, so their critics say, with the five Cs: cash, condo, car, credit card, country club. I often refer to it as the nicest mall in the world.

Singapore's comfort and complacency result from having made the transition from third-world country to economic powerhouse in record time, based on excellent governance. The nation made the leap in a single generation thanks to the leadership of Dr. Lee Kuan Yew, but the price it has paid is the suppression of certain freedoms. Since 1959, when it slipped out from under British rule, it's prospered through what's called "soft" authoritarianism, which has made news with national campaigns to make people flush the toilet, stop spitting, and never chew gum, as well as public canings for offenders. It tried to offset a falling birthrate by setting up a national matchmaking agency, aiming particularly at affluent Chinese. Their longtime prime minister filed many libel suits to stop criticism, even from foreign press. So it was not the kind of place to take warmly to bad publicity, especially not a deadly outbreak that had already turned Singapore's bustling business district into a ghost town.

I met with WHO people and local health department folks, drinking from the fire hose, scribbling down notes as I tried to take it all in, hoping that I might be able to make sense of it later. When an outbreak's over, you get a nice linear thread of what happened, but when you're in the middle of it—and certainly when you first arrive on the scene—there's no thread at all.

Singapore was appropriately terrified, and because nobody was coming to the island, the price of a room at the Singapore Ritz had dropped down to the US government rate, so for once I could indulge myself and stay in a really nice hotel. Which didn't make it any less terrifying to be there, given that our first set of patients had been infected in a really nice hotel.

As a very wealthy meritocracy, Singapore has an excellent public health system, and the medical people I was dealing with were mainly ethnic Chinese who had been trained in elite universities around the world. They spoke English better than I did.

They explained to me how the first patient at Singapore General had been admitted on March 10, with gram-negative sepsis, which means a blood infection. But he'd previously been at Tan Tock Seng Hospital, where he became infected, picked up complications, then went to Singapore General. With a history of coronary artery disease and diabetes, he was admitted to the coronary care unit, where he promptly infected everyone else.

This high-profile cluster alerted the authorities to their outbreak and the trace-back investigation led to another smoldering outbreak at Tang Tock Seng Hospital that had been missed. It was triggered by three Singapore-based flight attendants who'd stayed at the Hotel Metropole for a "free-and-easy" holiday in Hong Kong. All three of them were hospitalized with atypical pneumonia, and one of them became the next superspreader and original source for almost all the infections to hit Singapore.

What local officials were beginning to realize was that this wasn't the outbreak they'd been expecting. The anticipated pattern would have been a case coming from the mainland with fever, cough, and a rapidly changing, rapidly deteriorating chest X-ray. That patient would live or die and, in the meantime, infect a few health care workers, and then all would be successfully contained.

What was happening instead was that they were already having an outbreak throughout the health care system. The spreaders weren't just infecting their caregivers but other patients, and even visitors to the hospital.

That's why I was there: the disease had gone off plan. The problem was, okay, how do we tackle it now?

A large part of sanity is about filtering—if you don't filter out the irrelevant details, you're heading toward schizophrenia. You've got a thousand voices throwing a thousand bits of data or puzzle pieces at you. Some are meaningless, some are salient, but you don't know which is which.

We needed to establish benchmarks and definitions that would allow us to know who to monitor, so we created three groups. There were observation cases, and then suspect cases that we put into two subgroups: likely or unlikely—cases were "suspect but unlikely' if they just had a fever, "suspect and likely" if they had contact and clinical history.

By a different metric we had six imported cases, including three other people from the Metropole Hotel, and two unrelated groups of two, where there was an old transmission. And then there was the mystery of the superspreaders. A typical case would transmit to one other patient, but the superspreaders could transmit to dozens.

With all the health care workers who were sick or dying, people who should have sought medical attention were now afraid to go to a hospital at all. Clearly, this virus moved with frightening ease from one person to another. At least one cab driver had been infected during the brief time he was transporting a patient. And we had to shut down a market when it appeared that a number of cases were being transmitted there. Which was the bleakest point in the outbreak—when we had to consider the possibility that we could have free-for-all transmission throughout the community.

The health department found me office space in their headquarters, where I worked with Suok Kai Chow, Singapore's director of epidemiology and disease control. He's a brilliant man, very thoughtful, and he stayed unruffled throughout all of this.

Which, unfortunately, was not a universal response.

A gastroenterologist at Singapore General Hospital had become ill, and now all the nurses on the ward were freaking out. Could they have been exposed? They started looking through the records to determine which day the gastroenterologist developed his fever and who had been with him.

This doctor had performed endoscopies upon two people, both of whom had been treated previously at Tan Tock Seng. It took a couple of days before staff at Singapore General said, "Wait, we need to put these people in isolation, they came from Tan Tock Seng and they might have SARS."

Later, four members of the radiology staff at Tan Tock Seng tested positive. Then a cluster showed up in the virology department, which included a staff nurse. So another panic set in. My god! The radiologists had contact with 5,758 patients! Where are all those people now? How can anyone possibly track them all down?

It was a whack-a-mole process, so the approach we took was to isolate health care staff and medical officers and medical students and keep an eye on all of them. To make this simpler, the task force decided to funnel all suspect cases, except for pregnant mothers about to deliver, to one facility.

We were in the midst of a deadly disease outbreak, trying to figure how and why it was spreading so fast, and we were under a lot of pressure to come up with answers. But the health care staff held up better than in other places, most likely due to better communication. In Taiwan, there was a mass resignation of doctors and nurses. At one point hundreds of patients, staff, and visitors were forcefully barricaded inside a hospital, which was low on gowns and masks, and with nobody in charge. The Taiwanese health minister had to resign over his handling of the outbreak.

On April 12, Dr. Marco Marra and colleagues at the Michael Smith Genome Sciences Centre in British Columbia, working with virologists at CDC, announced that they had broken the genetic code of the infectious agent. Based on the shape and particle size, they said it was a coronavirus: four out of four samples on the electron microscope were twenty-four nanometers, and the virus was circular. Coronaviruses usually cause diseases in pigs and chickens. They're also associated with a simple cold-like illness in humans. But there were also still some conflicting reports that SARS was due to a metapneumo-virus. However, scientists at Erasmus University in Rotterdam, the Netherlands, injected the samples into macaque monkeys and confirmed that it was indeed a new subfamily of corona-virus that was the causative agent. Cold comfort, but at least now we knew what we were dealing with.

On the sixteenth, WHO issued a press release stating that this new coronavirus was responsible for the SARS pandemic. We would no longer have to guess at who was a case. We would be able to make a specific laboratory diagnosis and re-fine our prevention strategy based on the confirmed cases and their transmission patterns.

In the hospital, we reverted to 1980s-style medicine, by which I mean that you didn't automatically have four or six members of the medical staff check in repeatedly with every pa-tient. It was better for all concerned to limit the staff's exposure.

We created six hospital response teams that included doc-tor, communicable disease person, environmental health offi-cers, and a computer program called Link to look for common contacts for multiple people. In addition, we had eight contact-tracking teams.

We were putting out new advisories, hygiene and sanitary precautions for persons diagnosed with SARS, advisories to hospitals on the discharging of suspect cases. We had to be sure that those being released were not going to go back home and spread the disease. The same was true of the dead, which led us to implement the use of double body bags en route to the crematorium. As we'd seen in our dealings with Ebola, it was hard to convince people to bury their loved ones in the equivalent of heavy-duty Ziploc freezer bags. But full-scale terror was persuasive, which led to resigned acceptance. The willingness of the bereaved to adapt helped tremendously in putting a stop to the outbreak.

On my second day I visited the American embassy, trying to educate our diplomatic staff about the period of infectivity, the attack rates on people, and the length of the incubation period. They asked me about my own risk of infection.

The fact is, I spent very little time on the wards, but given that this was a disease where you could be infected and infecting others before you knew you were ill, it was always a crap shoot. I always submitted to every monitoring procedure, both to serve as an example and to protect others. Beyond that, I kept busy enough to forget the fact that I might contract a deadly disease and die. It would hardly advance the cause of public health if I spent my nights rocking in a corner making epidemiology models of my own risk profile. However, after learning about the cases of the cab driver and those in the market, I called my wife and told her to drop everything and lay in a three-month supply of food, water, and other necessities in case SARS gained a foothold in the United States. That's how scary I found this disease.

But fear is much less useful than keeping an open mind. Even as you start putting pieces together and find a path that looks promising, you have to keep asking yourself, what are we overlooking? What are the other interpretations? What else might be going on here?

It's equally important years later to keep an open mind when you're seeing a third or fourth or fifth outbreak of what seems to you now like a familiar disease. You're telling the younger people, "Step aside, I know how to handle this," and you may be dead wrong. Worst case, you can wind up dead.

Ultimately, we reverted to a medical tool that had been out of fashion for five hundred years: the quarantine. Back in the days of the plague, isolating the sick had been state-of-the-art medical practice, but now much of the medical community discounted it. It seemed so low-tech and inefficient, not to mention disruptive.

But today you can place Internet-connected video cameras in the homes of the people you need to isolate. You monitor them by calling them at random times, three times a day. The person needs to be home to pick up and turn on the camera and say hi. That's it.

The Singapore government made it work, and they made good use of epidemiological data to very narrowly define the really high risk, and thus limit the imposition of controls. They also made sure there were wraparound services for those quarantined so that they didn't starve, and so they could still pay their bills. (In Toronto, a very public-spirited community did voluntary quarantine work, a system in which thousands of people isolated themselves for as much as ten days without coercion or enforcement.)

But a lot of this depends on local norms. When you educate the public about the risk of contagion and the importance of quarantining, usually they get on board. Singapore made it work in part by shaming quarantined individuals who were caught at the local pub. But they also relied on Singaporean's sense of civic duty. In a typically blunt Singapore style, during a May Day address Deputy Minister Lee Hsien Loong warned people against quack cures such as drinking alcohol, smoking(!), or abstaining from pork. After rumors shut down a mall, he used the country's Telecommunications Act to impose a fine of ten thousand Singapore dollars and three years' jail time for spreading rumors via social media.

———

In late May, we got a hint of how SARS might have begun. Samples of wild animals sold as food in the local market in Guangdong showed that the SARS coronavirus could be isolated from masked palm civets, even though the animals did not always show clinical signs. As a result, more than ten thousand masked palm civets were killed. Later, the virus was also found in raccoon dogs, ferret badgers, and domestic cats.

Later still, in 2005, two studies identified a number of SARS-like coronaviruses in Chinese bats, which may have originally infected animals held in Chinese live animal markets.

If any of this sounds vaguely familiar, down to the striking health care workers but unfortunately lacking Marion Cotillard, it may be because director Steven Soderbergh drew heavily on the SARS outbreak for his movie *Contagion*.

CONTAINMENT

On April 24, the Hong Kong government announced a HK$11.8 billion relief package designed to assist Hong Kong's battered tourism, entertainment, retail, and catering sectors, although they would not be removed from WHO's list of "affected areas" till June.

That same week the death toll in Beijing continued to rise, and authorities throughout the Chinese mainland were still closing down theaters, discos, and other entertainment venues. Some government ministries and large state banks were working with minimal staff levels. But, in time, even they got their outbreak under control. Not just health care workers, but the Chinese authorities in Beijing, including the most senior political leaders, shouldered the load and provided abundant resources. The outbreak led to the building of many new hospitals, and to the transformation of their public health and disease-monitoring systems. The Chinese have now become a global model for transparency during infectious disease outbreaks, and important new players in global responses.

On April 28, the World Health Organization declared the outbreak in Vietnam to be over as no new cases were reported for twenty days. They'd shut down the French Hospital, and now the problem was how to clean it up so that it could reopen.

On April 30, WHO lifted the SARS travel warning for Toronto. Three weeks later, at the WHO annual meeting in Geneva, Hong Kong pushed for its own tourist warning to be lifted. WHO officials refused at first, but after a recount of the number of SARS patients in hospital, they relented. There were no newly infected patients being reported in the city for the

Summary of Provable SARS Cases with Onset of Illness from November 1, 2002 to July 31, 2003

Areas	Cumulative Number of Cases			Median Age (range)	Number of Deaths[a]	Case Fatality Ratio (%)
	Female	Male	Total			
Australia	4	2	6	15 (1-45)	0	0
Canada	151	100	251	49 (1-98)	43	17
China	2674	2607	5327[b]	Not available	349	7
China, Hong Kong Special Administrative Region	977	778	1755	40 (0-100)	299	17
China, Macao Special Administrative Region	0	1	1	28	0	0
China, Taiwan	218	128	346[c]	42 (0-93)	37	11
France	1	6	7	49 (26 - 61)	1	14
Germany	4	5	9	44 (4-73)	0	0
India	0	3	3	25 (25-30)	0	0
Indonesia	0	2	2	56 (47-65)	0	0
Italy	1	3	4	30.5 (25-54)	0	0
Kuwait	1	0	1	50	0	0
Malaysia	1	4	5	30 (26-84)	2	40
Mongolia	8	1	9	32 (17-63)	0	0
New Zealand	1	0	1	67	0	0
Philippines	8	6	14	41 (29-73)	2	14
Republic of Ireland	0	1	1	56	0	0
Republic of Korea	0	3	3	40 (20-80)	0	0
Romania	0	1	1	52	0	0
Russian Federation	0	1	1	25	0	0
Singapore	161	77	238	35 (1-90)	33	14
South Africa	0	1	1	62	1	100
Spain	0	1	1	33	0	0
Sweden	3	2	5	43 (33-55)	0	0
Switzerland	0	1	1	35	0	0
Thailand	5	4	9	42 (2-79)	2	22
United Kingdom	2	2	4	59 (28-74)	0	0
United States	13	14	27	36 (0-83)	0	0
Vietnam	39	24	63	43 (20-76)	5	8
Total			8096		774	9.6

[a]Includes only cases whose death is attributed to SARS. [b]Case classification by sex is unknown for 46 cases. [c]Since 11 July 2003, 325 cases have been discarded in Taiwan, China. Laboratory information was insufficient or incomplete for 135 discarded cases, of which 101 died. [d]Includes HCWs who acquired illness in other areas. [e]Due to differences in case definitions, the United States has reported probable cases of SARS with onsets of illness after 5 July 2003.

Source: http://www.who.int/csr/sars/country/table2004_04_21/en/

Chain of Transmission among Guests at Metropole Hotel (Hotel M), Hong Kong, 2003

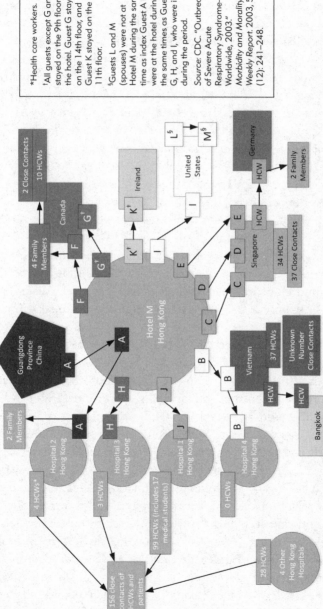

*Health care workers.

†All guests except G and K stayed on the 9th floor of the hotel. Guest G stayed on the 14th floor, and Guest K stayed on the 11th floor.

§Guests L and M (spouses) were not at Hotel M during the same time as index Guest A but were at the hotel during the same times as Guests G, H, and I, who were ill during the period.

Source: CDC. "Outbreak of Severe Acute Respiratory Syndrome— Worldwide, 2003." Morbidity and Morality Weekly Report. 2003, 52 (12); 241–248.

first time since the outbreak had hit the city in March. At the same time, though, a new cluster of about twenty suspected patients turned up in Toronto, and more than five thousand Canadians were still being quarantined.

On May 31, Singapore was removed from WHO's list of infected areas, and I was making plans to fly home to Atlanta. However, I had numerous reminders of the city-state for a few years due to letters I received—and even a visit to Atlanta—from a woman who read about my work and thought I was a messenger she had seen in her dreams. But there was nothing supernatural at play in ending the outbreak in Singapore. Instead, it was the result of the best outbreak management I had ever experienced.

On June 23, Hong Kong was removed from the WHO list, leaving only Toronto, Beijing, and Taiwan.

On July 5, WHO dropped Taiwan from the list—no new cases had been reported for twenty days, although around two hundred people were still hospitalized with the disease.

On July 9, 2003, WHO declared the outbreak contained. Even so, four cases were reported in China six months later, though these infections appeared to have been contracted directly from civets kept in cages at a market and a restaurant. Also, three later infections resulted from laboratory accidents and misadventures in China, Singapore, and Taiwan.

It would be May 19, 2004, a year and a quarter after the first reports, before WHO would declare China free of SARS. Ultimately, the pandemic would result in 8,096 cases and 774 deaths in thirty-seven different countries, with an estimated global cost of $40 billion. The final tally for the United States was 36 probable cases, including one health care worker and a family member presumptively infected by one of the sick travelers returning from Asia. A total of 8 cases were confirmed.

Fast-forward a decade to 2015, and an outbreak of MERS (Middle East respiratory syndrome, a cousin to SARS, and the result of a related coronavirus) killed 38 and infected 187 people in South Korea after a traveler returned from multiple Middle East countries including Saudi Arabia, then set up a chain of infections in two dozen health care facilities. The South Korean government was criticized for repeating most of the mistakes from SARS, including the failure to immediately inform and educate the populace, and a laxity toward quarantine. At the time of this writing, MERS has spread to sixteen countries from the Middle East.

Most cases are in Saudi Arabia with a link back to infected dromedary camels (in turn likely initially infected by bats). But 40 percent of patients are not linked to either camels or health care infections and labeled primary. Has MERS now established itself in the desert kingdom as a community cause of pneumonia and a continuing threat to health care facilities and visiting tourists? Will infected dromedary camels in Africa lead to outbreaks on that continent? Was SARS the rare genie that was put back in the bottle, and now MERS represents an even bigger global threat? The answers will not be subtle.

8

AFTER THE DELUGE

Brownie, you're doing a heck of a job.

—President George W. Bush to FEMA director Michael Brown
while touring hurricane-ravaged Mississippi

"Do good work."

Those were CDC director Julie Gerberding's parting words as she climbed aboard CDC Gulfstream to fly back to Atlanta.

It was September 2005, about a week after Hurricane Katrina had ripped through New Orleans, and the director was leaving four of us on the tarmac of Louis Armstrong International Airport. Her admonition was the full extent of our instructions, and just about the full extent of our resources. Like thousands of other people in the region at that moment, we had no transportation, shelter, or food.

Dr. Gerberding had flown down to show the flag at a press event with Secretary of Health and Human Services Mike Leavitt. Those of us who were staying—Dave Daigle, our communications guy; Terrance Manning, an environmental engineer, or at least a guy I mistook as an environmental engineer; Dr. Carol Rubin, a veterinarian and seasoned disaster expert with our Environmental Health Center Group; and me, the team lead—had come to help bolster a public health infrastructure that had been all but wiped out by wind and rising water.

But first we had to figure out how to get into town.

Fortunately, the head of our security office back at CDC had a connection with the Georgia National Guard, a Major Guidry, who diverted two local Humvees and four soldiers led by Captain David Smith and deployed them to New Orleans to assist in the response and to serve as our security and transportation team. It was late at night before they showed up, but we were ecstatic to be moving again after being stuck at the airport for what seemed like forever.

We wanted to get a sense of what was going on, but our first objective was to find someplace to stay, and to figure out where we could get something to eat. We had to travel two hours out of the city to find rooms. But the next morning, on just a few hours' sleep, we were back in our Humvees, winding our way into New Orleans along roads lined with debris and corpses.

Our first stop was the city health department, but city and county workers had been washed out of their homes like everyone else, and the place was deserted. So we made our way to the Garden District, where things were in better shape. The St. Louis Cathedral and the mansions near Audubon Park had been battered by wind but not flooded. It would take us a while to figure out the correlation between the socioeconomic level in this town and height above sea level.

Within the Garden District we found Kindred Hospital, a long-term care facility that had been evacuated and abandoned. There were the remnants of a US Army Reserve unit in there, but they seemed to be mostly just hanging out and drinking and eating whatever they could find. I asked them if they could help us get the place functional again. They disappeared shortly thereafter.

The hospital looked to have been pretty much forgotten and abandoned, and there were reports of looting and violence. When the National Guard unit accompanying us heard gunfire, we huddled into the Humvees and left. But, by the next day, CDC had negotiated with the hospital's corporate head-quarters, and we were allowed to officially commandeer the facility. Then our logistics experts showed up from CDC head-quarters to install wireless connections and make the building fully functional as a base of operations.

Using Kindred Hospital as our base camp—temporarily renamed the Federal Medical Resource Center—we sent teams to all the local communities, hospitals, and makeshift clinics to gather information. How many people were left in each community? Who was being treated for what? How could we provide necessary services? What messages did we need to send out to the community?

In public health, data is a continuous cycle, like blood flowing to the heart from all of your sensory systems, then being pumped back out in the form of communications and messages for action. Restoring anything resembling lifeblood to New Orleans in the wake of this storm was going to take some doing.

Hurricane Katrina was the costliest natural disaster in US history, and the seventh most intense Atlantic hurricane ever recorded. Only a few weeks after the devastation, Katrina would be followed by Hurricanes Rita and Wilma. The three storms together, and the subsequent flooding, killed between 1,110 and 1,800 people. Total property damage was estimated at $108 billion, more than double the damage wrought by Hurricane Andrew in 1992.

The Gulf Coast, of course, has a long history of hurricanes. The granddaddy of them all, the so-called Galveston flood of 1900, brought winds of up to 120 miles an hour (before the measuring device blew away) that threw up a sixteen-foot storm surge, leaving a death toll of between six and twelve thousand. The destruction was so vast that a realistic body count was impossible.

There have been many doozies since—Carla, Camille, Andrew—and in recent decades they did not arrive unannounced. Katrina's arrival had been heralded by coast-to-coast news alerts and much speculation about the damage to come, especially if New Orleans suffered a direct hit. Both the National Hurricane Center and the National Weather Service later won praise for providing timely and accurate information about the severity and the precise tracking of the approaching storm.

Katrina formed over the Bahamas during the last week of August 2005, then swept across southern Florida as a Category 1 hurricane, dropping a foot and a half of rain and leaving half a million people without power. There were twisted mobile homes, peeled-back roofs, and a handful of deaths from flooding and other damage, but it was not a catastrophe as these things go. Floridians are accustomed to hunkering down, and with help from the Federal Emergency Management Agency (FEMA) in the form of water trucks, ice, and medical supplies, they came through okay.

But then the storm headed northwest, its winds picking up strength from the warm waters of the Gulf of Mexico to become a full-bore Category 5 hurricane, with sustained winds topping 150 miles an hour—twice the speed of an ordinary Category 1. If it hit land with this level of intensity, it would disintegrate small buildings and pepper any that survived with shrapnel. Jeff Hingle, the sheriff of Plaquemines Parish, warned that if Katrina was still a Category 5 when it made landfall, the levees would never hold. And even if the water didn't smash the barriers, it would surely overtop them.

Outside the city, the executives of Louisiana's nine coastal parishes, or counties, ordered the mandatory evacuation of all residents. People were ordered to flee the area and seek higher ground well to the north. Even Louisiana's Society for the Prevention of Cruelty to Animals was foresighted enough to send its unclaimed pets to Houston with days to spare, as Douglas Brinkley detailed in *The Great Deluge,* his definitive history of Katrina and its aftermath. Unfortunately, the city's poorest human residents had no similar champion with the political will, resources, and planning to look after them.

Most of the evacuation orders were in force by Saturday, August 27, nearly two full days before the hurricane struck. Also on Saturday, managers of the Waterford 3 nuclear power plant west of New Orleans shut down the facility as part of their own emergency plan, with diesel generators continuing to provide just enough power to safeguard the reactor.

In light of all this, the city's assurances that its low-lying neighborhoods wouldn't be flooded, or worst case, that they could be pumped out quickly, seemed at best wishful thinking. At worst, it was unspeakable negligence.

At a closed-door meeting at city hall that Saturday, Mayor C. Ray Nagin appeared inexplicably confident that the storm would change course and miss the city. Just the year before, and after a flurry of televised reports about that disaster in the making, Hurricane Ivan had swerved east and bypassed the city. But as they say in the financial industry, past performance is no reason to bet the farm.

Nagin had the power to issue a mandatory evacuation order to the city's residents, but at a press conference that day he said he needed to talk to his lawyers first. According to the *Times-Picayune*, the local paper, Nagin was worried that hotels and other local businesses could sue him if their customers vanished and the storm proved a dud. After all, tourism in New Orleans is a $5 billion a year industry.

Then at 5:00 p.m. on Saturday, the mayor appeared with Louisiana governor Kathleen Blanco. Both Democrats, the two politicians still made an awkward pair. Blanco, a former schoolteacher, had taken over the governorship only the year before. During the campaign, Nagin had jumped party lines to endorse her rival, Republican Bobby Jindal. The resulting bad blood did not bode well for the ability of the mayor and the governor to work together in a crisis.

Out of that conference came an evacuation order for the city, of sorts. It was voluntary, meaning that the authorities "strongly advised" people to leave the city. If they didn't want to, however, they didn't have to. Some people took that to mean that the storm was no big deal. But that same afternoon, the National Hurricane Center suggested the possibility that Katrina could slam into the city within forty-eight hours with full Category 5 ferocity.

There was still time to make a getaway, provided that residents had the knowledge and the means to do so. Unfortunately, not even a mandatory evacuation order has the power to magically transport a population out of harm's way. One in four families in New Orleans, one of the poorest cities in the nation, earned less than $15,000 a year. Official announcements, including evacuation orders, were issued largely as televised news, yet a large number of city dwellers didn't have televisions. And people who can't afford televisions tend not to be able to afford cars.

Over the weekend, traffic streamed out of the city, and by Sunday the highways were so clogged that the eighty-mile drive to Baton Rouge took seven hours or more. But at least the people in the traffic jam were leaving. Twenty percent of the population stayed behind, and they were predominantly from the poorest sections of the city, which just happened to be the districts occupying the lowest ground.

Mayor Nagin and other municipal authorities seemed oblivious to the fact that more than 100,000 of the adult residents of their city did not have motor vehicles, or the $50 required for a bus ticket, or any way to bring along their pets, which many refused to leave behind. Making matters worse, buses—the lifeline for those without cars—had stopped running.

The municipal police force might have been able to assist the poor in getting out of town, but dozens of officers had already fled the city with their families, ignoring their obligations as public-safety officials.

By 3:00 a.m. Sunday, August 28, the hurricane's leading edge was some three hundred miles off shore, and the storm system was moving north at ten miles an hour. Aircraft flying reconnaissance over the Gulf of Mexico from Keesler Air Force Base's Hurricane Hunters unit outside Biloxi, Mississippi, reported that Katrina was now an immense five hundred miles in diameter—its top wind speed an unimaginable two hundred miles an hour. This was one of the most ferocious storms ever measured in the United States.

At 10:00 a.m. that Sunday, with landfall less than twenty-four hours away, reality at last got through to Mayor Nagin, and he issued a mandatory evacuation order, New Orleans's first. But it was woefully too little, woefully too late.

Also on Sunday, Michael Brown at FEMA's Washington headquarters hosted a videoconference that included President Bush, Secretary of Homeland Security Michael Chertoff, and emergency management officials from all the Gulf Coast states. If the participants spoke at all, they said they were ready to provide help if asked. The president asked no questions and left the call early. The possibility that the huge storm surge would smash through New Orleans's levees and drown much of the city for weeks was never broached.

At 3:00 a.m. Monday morning, August 29, a weather buoy in the Gulf of Mexico some fifty miles east of the Mississippi River registered waves forty feet high. Shortly thereafter, a surge of water broke through a concrete floodwall along the Seventeenth Street Canal in the northern part of New Orleans.

The Seventeenth Street Canal channeled water through the city from Lake Pontchartrain just above. The hole that appeared early that Monday morning started out small but widened as the hours passed. At this point, it was obvious that the lowest, most vulnerable areas of the city would be flooded.

Luckily, by the time Katrina made landfall later that morning, it was no longer a Category 5, but it was still a robust Category 3, with sustained winds averaging between 110 and 130 miles an hour. South of the city, in the fishing village of Buras in Plaquemines Parish, winds were measured at 161 miles an hour. Tim Jones of the *Chicago Tribune* later reported that the devastation looked like "a climatological war zone." Buras was utterly destroyed—housing, livestock, wildlife. Fortunately, its entire population evacuated in time, and no one died.

Not surprisingly, though it appeared to surprise all those in charge, with the slow-moving storm dumping heavy rains on inadequate levees, the Mississippi rose to new heights, until the extensive system of earthworks, which had allowed the city to exist, completely failed. The big river rushed back in to reclaim the lowlands it had been denied for decades.

The failure of New Orleans's antiquated levee system is widely considered to be the worst civil-engineering disaster in the nation's history. The system was managed by the US Army Corps of Engineers, which designed and built it following passage of the Flood Control Act of 1965. When Katrina struck, the corps had thirteen hundred employees in its New Orleans office alone. Though the agency was targeted by lawsuits following the collapse, an earlier act of Congress, the Flood Control Act of 1928, absolved it of financial liability.

Even on a good day, New Orleans's flood-control system was an aging, jury-rigged network of canals, floodwalls, pumps, and locks, and to anchor the walls the corps had apparently used steel pilings that were too short.

New Orleans is a saucer, and the levees, which typically rise ten or fifteen feet, are its rim. The precarious nature of New Orleans's reality, and the queasy feeling of unease it creates, can be reinforced by standing on top of a levee, where you can see that the river on one side is a whole lot higher than the streets on the other. When New Orleans was built it was all, barely, above sea level. At some time in the next century, the city will be well offshore in the Gulf of Mexico.

Water can surge into the city from the gulf to the south and from Lake Pontchartrain to the north. Some residential areas resembled shallow lakes after every heavy downpour. In severe storms, water spilled out of the levees often enough that the city maintained an elaborate network of twenty-two pumping stations to remove the water. Of course, the system worked on the assumption that, once water was pumped back up over the levees, it wouldn't all come rushing back through holes and cracks.

This system dated back to 1719, when Louisiana was the jewel in the crown of the French colonial empire and Jean-Baptiste Le Moyne, Sieur de Bienville, ordered the building-up and reinforcing of riverbanks in order to found a city. Even so, three years later, a hurricane made a direct hit and flooded New Orleans with water eight to ten feet deep. When the waters receded, levee building recommenced. More than one historian later observed that Le Moyne would have done far better simply building his city eighty miles upriver at Baton Rouge. But hubris, like *laissez les bons temps rouler* ("let the good times roll"), is baked into the character of the Big Easy.

Long before Thomas Jefferson bought Louisiana from France in 1803, the city fathers had decreed that a little engineering was all they needed to stay dry and bustling. Additional miles of levees were created on both sides of the river, but as silting elevated the river bottom, the water level rose with it, and the levees had to be raised periodically to keep pace. Meanwhile, like so many places along the Gulf Coast, New Orleans continued to subside, or sink, an average of three feet over the past century. The reasons ranged from the constant pumping of rain-flooded streets to the destruction of distant wetlands and barrier islands.

Optimism was not supported by the evidence. In 1849, an uptown levee collapsed, causing a violent surge of storm water. Two hundred city blocks were flooded, and much of the city remained underwater for more than a month.

In 1927, the Great Mississippi Flood devastated the entire Mississippi River Delta as far north as Arkansas. The levees were breached in more than a hundred places, leading to

countless deaths and as many as 200,000 people left home-
less. Many of those who suffered the most that year were African Americans living in St. Bernard Parish, just south of the
city, where engineers actually dynamited a levee in order to
lower the floodwaters threatening the richer neighborhoods
upstream. Small wonder that many African Americans in the
area today do not accept the idea that the boards that manage
the levees do so impartially.

Along with the high drama of big storms, the delta has also
suffered the slow but steady degradation of coastal marshes.
These wetlands not only sustain the marine life that enlivens
Louisiana's rich cuisine, but they also act as a buffer to protect the coastline when storms hit. Yet over the past century,
close to a million acres of marshland has been lost to erosion,
a situation made worse by dredging and channel building by
oil companies laying pipelines and servicing off-shore rigs. A
widely cited statistic is that the state loses the equivalent of a
football field's worth of land to the Gulf of Mexico every thirty-
eight minutes.

New Orleans is, on average, six feet lower than the river's
surface, and four-fifths of the city and many of the surrounding parishes were damaged by flooding. Some sections, nota-
bly parts of the Ninth Ward, are eleven feet below the river.
The majority of the deaths in the city occurred right after the
levees broke, and the people who drowned, many of them
elderly, were disproportionately located in low-lying, low-
income areas. In some of these districts, floodwaters lingered
for weeks before the murky, polluted, trash-filled water was
pumped out.

Housing in the low areas traditionally was occupied by
African Americans, who constituted two-thirds of the city's
pre-Katrina population. In the Lower Ninth Ward, most residents—three out of five—owned their own homes, but the
streets their houses were on were unpaved. Open drainage canals ran along some of them, as though they were village roads
in Asia or Africa. By contrast, the mansions of St. Charles

Avenue and the Garden District, and housing in Lakeview, Mid-City, the Warehouse District, and most of the French Quarter, sat on higher ground. Residents there were mostly white.

Some of the most pitiable deaths were those of people who died in the hot, airless attics of their homes, where they had climbed to escape the water rising from the lower floors. A few managed to smash escape holes in their attic ceilings and were rescued. Some scribbled "HELP" on their rooftops.

———

Those in charge of emergency preparedness in New Orleans shot themselves in both feet before Katrina ever arrived. As the storm approached, the Louisiana National Guard, rather than strategically distributing its boats and high-water vehicles at different sites around the city, consolidated all of its transportation assets at Jackson Barracks on St. Claude Avenue in the Ninth Ward, a former army post and now the Guard's headquarters, which dates back to the 1830s. When the levees broke, Jackson Barracks—being in the Ninth Ward—was inundated, and this essential rescue equipment was out of commission.

The fire department in this flood-prone city had a total of five boats to use in case of high water. Of these, only three were in operating condition when Katrina arrived, which meant that stranded citizens in need of rescue were out of luck.

The city did have a "mobile command center"—a retrofitted tractor-trailer stuffed with communications equipment—but no one thought to position it outside the flood zone. A "mobile" center isn't mobile if you never move it, and it's not of much use when it's under water.

With similar shortsightedness, the command center for all emergency services—the New Orleans police, state police, fire officials, National Guard, and Coast Guard, among others—was located at city hall. It made no difference that the emergency office was high on the building's ninth floor. When that building flooded catastrophically, there was no power, no personnel, and no communications, which made it a command center in name only. Small wonder that Mayor Nagin had jumped ship early on, setting up his own personal command center on an upper floor of the city's high-rise Hyatt Regency Hotel.

The only local agency that seemed to have a clue when it came to disaster planning was the Department of Wildlife and Fisheries. At the governor's direction, it had distributed its more than two hundred boats to various spots along the coast to be available for search-and-rescue missions as necessary.

And it wasn't as if the scale of the disaster that struck New Orleans was so unimaginable. Less than a year before Katrina hit, the October 2004 issue of *National Geographic* offered a detailed scenario of a major hurricane hitting New Orleans straight on, with catastrophic flooding that left whole neighborhoods submerged. It asked readers to visualize the French Quarter with water up to its wrought-iron balconies.

A few months earlier, hundreds of officials from an alphabet soup of government agencies had taken part in a what-if simulation organized by FEMA. What if a Category 3 hurricane struck New Orleans head on? The weeklong simulation used meticulous computer models devised by scientists at Louisiana State University. The best-guess scenario coming out of the university was ten feet of standing water across the city; as many as half a million people stranded, unable or unwilling to get out; 30 million cubic yards of soggy, putrid debris; disinterred coffins floating through the streets; and packs of wild dogs roaming anywhere there was dry ground. The simulation put the death toll in the city proper at 24,250, with another 37,040 dead in surrounding areas.

And yet, when *National Geographic*'s scenario pretty much came to pass on August 29, 2005, there was not so much as a single Red Cross–certified emergency shelter in any of the city's schools or civic buildings. Reason being: the organization had refused to approve any shelters because the city as a whole was too close to sea level, which is to say, in their estimation there was no such thing as a safe location anywhere in the city.

There was at least, as we learned later, an evacuation plan. Sort of. It was one and a half pages of a fourteen-page booklet that supposedly laid out the city's "comprehensive" emergency management program. It referred to officially designated "evacuation zones," which were supposedly flood-proof staging areas where residents would gather to be transported out of the city. But no evacuation zones were ever actually specified. Curiously, these were left to be developed "pending further study."

During the middle of the response, communications were horrific even back to CDC. I remember seeing a hand-scribbled note on a Dunkin' Donuts napkin that had been faxed to our Emergency Operations Center:

To: DEOC/CDC
From: ESF8, NOLA
Please send to the LSU, BR, Peter Maravich Arena ASAP
 IV Fluids
 Blood tubes
 Tylenol tabs
 IV catheters
 Z-PAK
 Motrin 800 mg
 Pillows
 Sheets—Disposable

That's called operating on the fly. It's also the basis for my quip, when I was director of the preparedness program, that we deploy the Strategic National Stockpile with no more than a request on the back of a napkin.

After the anthrax outbreak of 2001, Phil Navin, a retired colonel in the US Army and head of our Emergency Operations Center, worked with Dr. Rich Besser, CDC's future acting director and ABC's chief health and medical editor, to completely revamp the whole CDC internal reporting structure for disasters. Rich was in his second day on the job as CDC's chief of the Coordinating Office for Terrorism, Preparedness and Emergency Response when Katrina hit. For a while, there was chaos in our operations, and everybody wanted me to be talking to them. But under Rich's guidance, things got much better, as CDC fielded its largest response up to that time, across the Gulf Coast and shelters across the United States.

As terrible as the planning for Katrina was, the response afterward was even worse, taken to a tragic level by the nature of the disaster, by lack of information, and by bickering at the local, state, and federal levels that led to governmental paralysis.

Most fundamentally, communication between the mayor and the governor was terrible. Communication between the governor and the president wasn't much better. There was lots of lip service about how we were all working together. "Everything's great," you heard, but in fact there was no coordination and no collaboration. Meanwhile, we kept hearing that Mayor Nagin was off in Las Vegas, or on a weekend trip to Dallas, when he should have been in New Orleans trying to keep his city alive.

Much of the normal communications infrastructure was down, so to find out what was going on in a neighborhood you had to go there on foot, which was often hazardous if not impossible. Days passed before authorities realized how utterly devastated some of the low-lying neighborhoods, such as the Lower Ninth Ward, were.

Even inhabitants of the city who still had working telephones found that the storm had knocked out much of the state's 911 system, so a New Orleans radio station, WWL, fielded emergency calls instead. People in the Lower Ninth Ward telephoned repeatedly to ask for rescue boats. When the radio station couldn't help, at least listeners tuning in might recognize the voice of a caller as that of a loved one.

The major public health concern during a hurricane or other natural disaster is generally the risk of infectious diseases and not from the dead. Unlike Ebola corpses, decaying bodies of victims from natural disasters, although they are disturbing and deserve respectful handling, pose little disease risk. The other big issue is respiratory and diarrheal disease among clusters of people, especially in shelters, which puts the focus on good sanitation and hand washing. Fortunately, the United States is generally spared the typhoid and cholera endemic in other countries, as well as the measles outbreaks that often occur in relief camps. Tetanus is also a rare consideration as well as leptospirosis, a disease of rodent urine reported after floods. During Katrina, we did see a small cluster of two dozen cases of vibrio (an environmental pathogen) infection of wounds from floodwaters in Louisiana and Mississippi, some diarrheal illness in shelters, and a cluster of respiratory infections among Department of Defense responders. But, all in all, the most serious infectious health concern we saw was mold in flood-damaged homes.

As in New York after 9/11, fire and rescue people from all over the country, not to mention ordinary citizens, came to New Orleans to help, but the Emergency Response System really had no way to manage all those volunteers. And people just showing up at the Emergency Operations Center and saying, "Hi, I want to help" didn't help. It actually created a problem in that somebody then had to sort the helpers and figure out what to do with them. There were also "undocumented volunteers," as in people walking in and saying, "Hi, I'm a doctor." Okay, fine. But how could we be sure?

In a disaster, we much prefer to get volunteers through the Red Cross or the Salvation Army, because that means these volunteer organizations have already done the credentialing.

Ironically, the "environmental health engineer" we brought with us from Atlanta turned out to be from engineering services, which explained why I shouldn't have asked him to map water sources and do a risk assessment of potential contamination. But we all liked him even more as he turned out to be very full of positive energy and very useful, especially in bringing back information from the utility providers.

Before the storm, the mayor had advised that anyone without the means to evacuate should head to the New Orleans Superdome as a refuge of last resort. This was the city's one centralized emergency shelter, and it had been used for such purposes during two previous hurricanes. But even Michael Brown thought this was a bad idea. The mayor boldly announced that evacuees should wait at the Superdome for buses that would pick them up and carry them to safety. The only catch was that he never made arrangements for any buses to do the transporting. The only things the Superdome had going for it was an easy-to-spot location and vast interior space. It had never been furbished with adequate supplies, and no one talked about the fact that its base was twelve feet below sea level.

Even so, nearly ten thousand people took refuge at the enclosed stadium, camping out on the playing field, many of them stuck there for a week, but it was hardly an ideal sanctuary. During the hurricane, violent winds had torn large holes in the dome, and rain and fetid air poured in. There were no lights, no concession stands, no air conditioning. The huge interior was sweltering, dim, and crowded.

Arriving at the dome a week after the storm and seeing all the people waiting for rescue that failed to come, we were dismayed that there was still no power or food. Why had the federal government failed to take charge and moved people to a better location where they could be cared for? And why was it left to CNN to point out what was going on inside?

Without a doubt, there were a handful of deaths and crimes in the Superdome, as well as deaths in homes where people weren't taken care of, but the blame should fall squarely on the shoulders of the politicians, their cronies, and their political infighting. Their culpability should not be diminished by media images of a few locals looting TVs.

It was a huge systemic failure that led to the breaching of the levees, but the pain and suffering that followed was due largely to a failure of leadership and compassion. Astoundingly, Mayor Ray Nagin was reelected in 2006. Then again, the voting took place at a time when two-thirds of New Orleans residents were still displaced by the storm. Even more astoundingly, he went on to found a consulting company that focused on emergency preparedness. It struck me that, like so many third-world leaders who fleece their people, he never faced any consequences for the suffering he caused. In 2014, at least, he was convicted on twenty charges of wire fraud, bribery, and money laundering, unrelated to Katrina, and sentenced to ten years in federal prison.

The police superintendent, Eddie Compass, whose department displayed both ineptness and callousness during the crisis, was forced to resign. In *The Great Deluge,* historian David Brinkley tells how it became sport for police officers in Houston to photograph New Orleans patrol cars "way" off duty in the Texas city 350 miles away. Brinkley also recounts the rumor (which Compass denies) that the superintendent himself had stopped taking calls and disappeared just as the storm approached.

Also pushed out was the widely reviled FEMA director Michael Brown, a lawyer whose primary qualification for his incredibly complex job was having been judges and stewards commissioner for the International Arabian Horse Association.

I found the FEMA folks to be pretty disturbed about all the politics that had gotten them into the unwanted limelight. Despite the incompetence at the top, those down in the trenches were top-notch. In Jackson Square in the French Quarter, they brought in NGOs to feed the emergency-response workers, including me. In our first days in New Orleans, we contented ourselves with military-style MREs (meals ready to eat), but once FEMA got things organized, we were lining up like everybody else at the tents in Jackson Square, and it was definitely an improvement.

FEMA's biggest gaffe was not being prepositioned. They knew the storm was coming, and they shouldn't have waited for the governor to declare a state of emergency to begin doing what they do. They should have had school buses, ambulances, and McDonald's Happy Meals ready to go. As for relocating those with no way to evacuate, the city had 360 idle city buses on the day of the storm. With fifty passengers per bus, they could have ferried eighteen thousand people with one trip per bus convoy, had anyone thought to organize them into convoys.

Katrina was a collective failure by city, state, and federal officials (none of whom seemed to know what the others were doing). Adding to the pain and suffering, public-safety officials had no list of the names and addresses of people with special needs, even though New Orleans had an unusually high proportion of elderly and infirm residents.

I found out later that on Saturday the twenty-eighth, just as the storm was bearing down, FEMA director Michael Brown was, like Mayor Nagin, merely "monitoring the situation," working on the federalization of the response that was ultimately rejected by the governor.

When Governor Kathleen Blanco did ask for federal help, it was without much sense of urgency. She'd declared a statewide state of emergency on Friday, and on Saturday she formally requested that President Bush declare a federal emergency. Her request was not only late but also halfhearted and nonspecific—little more than a sloppily filled out legal form. Definitely not an emphatic plea for help from Washington. When those in charge don't communicate with each other, the people suffer.

The US government, including FEMA, would never make these mistakes again; a rare instance where lessons did not need to be relearned. And a stark reminder that citizens see their government's primary responsibility as being to keep them safe.

After Katrina, federal preparedness and response was completely restructured with a new national preparedness system that included national frameworks for protection, prevention, mitigation, response, and recovery; a new national preparedness goal; and, most importantly, a fresh focus on a whole community approach to getting ready and responding better. The outcome of this work was on display in 2012 during Hurricane Sandy.

Communication with the public is no less important. One thing I had learned during the Ebola outbreak in Kikwit was that rumors could shut down a response. So we had a public health officer, Scott Harper, who was dedicated entirely to rumor control.

According to one story going around, a rescue dog had gone into the water, taken sick, and died. This played into a larger narrative about "toxic soup," inspired in part by a report from the 2004 Louisiana State University simulation of a Category 3 storm, which suggested that if floodwaters covered the city for weeks on end, the sludge would soon come to resemble a "HazMat gumbo."

Indeed, there are thirty-one different EPA-designated Superfund sites—glow-in-the-dark toxic-waste dumps for which the federal government has assumed cleanup responsibility—littering this most flood-prone of cities, which novelist James Lee Burke once called "an outdoor mental asylum located on top of a giant sponge."

I did an interview on CNN walking through New Orleans streets showing people that the yuk in the floodwater was nothing worse than the washed-out Drano and toilet-cleaning supplies from under the city's sinks. You wouldn't want to drink it, but wading through it wasn't going to kill you. The most serious environmental hazard we found unleashed by the storm was mold.

No matter how baseless, horror stories from the rumor mill were hard on the morale of Katrina's first responders, many of whom didn't trust the authorities to begin with. They'd seen too many official screwups, and now they were thinking, Oh my God, one of our rescue dogs is dying. If I'm going to die, I don't want to go like this! And they expected us as public health professionals to have the straight scoop. We tried, but we could never find the source of the rumor of the dog, or an autopsy report, or anything else we could use to refute it. But we had to try. We had to take these things seriously.

Then there was the story about how the nonhuman primates used in research had gotten out of the Tulane animal facility and were running amok through New Orleans spreading Ebola. A variant was that frozen Ebola virus in the laboratory freezers had thawed and escaped into the population. Here again, we had to track down enough facts to put the hysteria to rest, and these two were easy. The Tulane animal facility isn't even in New Orleans, and if frozen and then heated up, viruses die.

Dave Daigle, our communications lead, had been a tank commander in the army, and he knew the city from his days as an undergrad at Loyola. He was fabulous in working with the media despite the lack of normal communications mechanisms. Given his military background, he also served as my executive officer and partner in crime.

When we ran across a box of previously looted, now abandoned, highly inappropriate tourist T-shirts on Bourbon Street, I asked him to liberate them. I couldn't, because I was wearing my uniform from the Public Health Service. I'd felt sheepish about not wearing it, especially after watching so many Coast Guard and National Guard helicopters and state wildlife boats on the news, pulling New Orleanians from their rooftops or directly from the polluted floodwaters. Seeing these men and women in uniform made me realize that I'd never fully embraced or understood the significance of my own uniform.

The US Public Health Service was founded in 1798 to provide care for mariners, and later to enforce quarantine against infectious diseases. The Uniformed Service Corp is all officers: six thousand doctors, nurses, pharmacists, dentists, scientists, veterinarians, and other health professionals. Nominally, we report to the surgeon general of the United States, but our supervisors are in individual US government agencies such as CDC, Bureau of Prisons, NIH, or the Indian Health Service. I'd inadvertently become an officer when I was mailed the application forms with my acceptance into the Epidemic Intelligence Service program at CDC. For all essential purposes, it was an alternative payment system to my colleagues who joined CDC as civilians. The only difference was that I was supposed to wear a uniform on Wednesdays. The culture was already beginning to change after the anthrax attacks as we saw ourselves in service to the nation as first responders to health emergencies. Once I got to New Orleans, I wore my uniform with pride every day until I retired as an assistant Surgeon General.

We tried to work with the New Orleans incident management and command system, but it took a while for them to set it up. We tried to go there every day, or every other day.

During the crisis, we became the de facto health department for workaday issues as well. Medical records were in disarray, the charity hospital was under water, yet women were still having babies that needed to be screened and inoculated, and tuberculosis patients still needed to be treated, and those with HIV/AIDS still needed to be located and provided with clinical services. Dr. Nicki Pesik led the teams to handle all of these with aplomb.

We also had teams stationed in all the emergency rooms and many of the makeshift clinics to actively collect data on every patient and track the number and type of injuries and illnesses. This led us to issue warnings not to start a generator inside your house (carbon monoxide poisoning), and not to go up on a roof with a chainsaw (dangers too numerous to mention). Then we had rescue workers who weren't wearing protective equipment, so we had the National Institute for Occupational Health and Safety come in to make sure these people (some of whom were of the "I'm here to help" variety) didn't get themselves, or anybody else, killed.

Dr. Jonathan Fielding, director of the Los Angeles County Health Department, who had arrived with a Los Angeles team to help, made the great suggestion that we put together a web page that people could look at once a day to give a snapshot of what was going on in the city.

So we created the New Orleans Dashboard, which explained the highlights of public health issues very quickly.

Meanwhile, we were still bouncing around in our search for lodging. We stayed at the hotel attached to the Ochsner Medical Center for a while, but then we got kicked out. Which is when we resorted to the extreme measure of sleeping aboard the USS *Harry S. Truman,* a *Nimitz*-class aircraft carrier. I stayed only one night on the ship because it was like sleeping in a coffin, with the bottom of the bunk above you about six inches from your face.

Then we went to the Omni Hotel. It didn't have potable water, but they had some electricity back up again. So we drank the bottled water, and that was our most stable location for a while until we had to evacuate due to Hurricane Rita.

We repaired to Baton Rouge for a while, rented a house for a few days, then went back to New Orleans. Hurricane Wilma was not that bad, and we just sheltered in place for that one.

Getting outside the city allowed us to see the huge discrepancy between all the devastation and the people still huddled in the Superdome—and the fact that elsewhere things seemed pretty normal. In the suburbs, McDonald's was open. Arby's was open. But those places might as well have been a thousand miles away. And I must admit that I was not immune to that trench mentality. At the beginning of the outbreak a reporter asked if she could bring me anything as she traveled to New Orleans for an interview regarding the public health response. I asked for clean underwear.

Which made you wonder . . . How is it that in our super rich society, we couldn't move those poor people in the Superdome someplace better? Every kind of service was being provided just down the road. Which just goes to show the role of money as the admission ticket to our society. With a car and a credit card, you're good to go. Without those basics, you're living in a different country, with a different set of rules.

The ugliness of that divide appeared a couple of days after the levees broke, when some black citizens famously tried to cross over to the west bank of the Mississippi—to self-evacuate—but were stopped at the bridge by police in riot gear who prevented them from entering the suburban town of Gretna. In terms of the breakdown of civil society, and the violation of civil rights based on class and color, this was perhaps the low point. Here in America, it looked like humanitarian concern was limited to "people who look like me."

By the time I left, the CDC team had grown to sixty or seventy people on the ground. We were working six and a half days a week, and I had to force people to take breaks to avoid burnout. We had a few stressed individuals who had to be sent back early. As a boost to morale, I also declared that on Saturdays Kindred Hospital was no longer a federal facility. On those days I would bring in beer and pizza for everybody. Every day, during my morning meeting, I would also give away one of our liberated and very inappropriate tourist T-shirts to recognize somebody who had done a really good job.

All in all, we felt good. When the mayor was asked, "Is it safe to come back into the city?" he said, "We're monitoring the population every day and from the Public Health Department—we'll be able to know if people are safe."

That was us he was talking about. We'd accomplished our mission. We'd done "good work."

By the time I was ready to leave, Bourbon Street was beginning to show signs of life. Some buildings had power and others had generators at night. The day before I left, we went to eat at the place across from our hotel, and all of a sudden the waitresses took off their shirts and started dancing on the counter while customers began stuffing paper bills into their panties.

I turned to my buddy and said, "Okay. New Orleans is coming back."

9

SIERRA LEONE

All I maintain is that on this earth there are pestilences and there are victims, and it's up to us, so far as possible, not to join forces with the pestilences.

—Albert Camus, *The Plague*

At the hut where we were to board the water taxi, a young man handed me a bright-orange life preserver, but it didn't have straps or buckles. Welcome to Africa, I thought. Good to be back. This time it was Ebola, and I'd come to Sierra Leone in February of 2015 as a short-term consultant for the World Health Organization.

It was almost dark as we set off down the coast from the airport to Cockle Bay and the Aberdeen area of Freetown where, supposedly, I was booked into a place called the Sierra Lighthouse.

In the lobby, waiting to check in, I ran into Dr. Carol Rao, an old CDC friend from China, who'd come to the hotel for a dinner for a parting colleague because the restaurant, overlooking a beautiful bay, served up gigantic tropical lobsters for $20—a bargain for Westerners, but probably a month's income for the guy who drove the water taxi.

The Lighthouse was two star, which meant running water and electricity, but no elevator, and an air conditioner in the wall that didn't work. I was on the fourth floor, and there was so little water pressure that it was hard to take a shower. But I was doing better than several of my colleagues who'd showed up at the place they were booked and been told their reservations had been lost. They ended up staying at the Radisson Blu, which was two to three times more expensive. This was February, and they were going to have a Super Bowl party that night, which added to the cognitive dissonance I already felt, talking about lobster dinners in a low-income but beautiful country in the midst of an Ebola outbreak that had the whole world freaking out. Nothing like rooting for the Patriots or the Seahawks while being reminded to not mix alcohol with the mefloquine you're taking as prophylaxis for malaria.

En route to Africa I'd passed through Geneva, which was my standard operating procedure when working on behalf of the WHO. I always stay at a hotel in the Paquis on the edge of the red-light district where the World Health Organization gets me a discounted rate. I have breakfast at the same coffee shop on Rue de Lausanne, then take the No. 8 bus that goes past the central train station, Gare de Cornavin, all the way to the WHO, known in this part of the world as OMS, for Organisation Mondiale de la Santé.

For three days the officials there brought me up to date on suspected conditions in Sierra Leone, giving me instructions of a sort, but it was never quite clear what I was being asked to do. The idea seemed to be "You're the expert; we're sending you in—good luck. Go help them with whatever they need." And I must admit that this is my favorite set of directions.

When I arrived in Freetown in the later afternoon it was nearly 100 degrees. I saw some Chinese putting on masks and gloves as we left the plane. In the airport Ebola posters were plastered everywhere, and I had to ignore the compulsion to wash my hands. Local health workers took your temperature as you proceeded into the terminal, and then you started filling out forms about where you'd traveled.

There was customs, then immigration, and then a thermal scanner, and then baggage claim, where I was met by a young man from WHO whose job was to round up the assorted consultants. He grabbed my passport and asked for $40 in US currency for the water taxi.

We made our way outside into the heat and across a dirt road where we picked up the shuttle that took us to the hut by the dock where they passed out the "decorative" life preservers. They wouldn't keep you afloat, but if something bad happened, the flash of orange bobbing in the water might help them know where to start looking for the bodies.

After an uneventful night in the room with no air conditioning, a car arrived to take me to the WHO office in town, which was about a half hour drive from the Aberdeen district. A lovely young woman named Isatu welcomed me and gave me a long checklist of meetings I would need to attend: the security briefing, the human resources briefing, and what I needed to do to get my medical clearance from the doctor. We listened to some lectures about safety and health, and about where to pick up cell phones—I'd been assigned a mobile with a local number. The vagueness and uncertainty of my mission was still fairly surreal, but I assumed that at a certain point somebody would say, "Here, let me tell you what you're supposed to do."

My next task was to go get a badge, and it was on the minivan to the UN Development Programme office where I was to have my picture taken that I ran into Dr. Eilish Cleary. She was the chief medical officer in New Brunswick, Canada, she'd worked in Sierra Leone twenty years before, and she'd already been here for a couple of months on this outbreak as head of the surveillance cluster in Port Loko.

"What do you do?" she asked me.

I said, "Well, usually I'm an epidemiologist, but I'm not sure. I think I'm supposed to work with Matt Craven." He was the former McKinsey consultant I'd heard was in charge of operations.

She said, "No. You're an epidemiologist. You're supposed to work with me."

So that's how I found my contact—by accident, on a mini-van. Welcome to Africa, again.

We met again the next morning, by which time Dr. Cleary had been able to review my CV. "All right," she said. "Given your experience, you're supposed to go to these four districts: Kono, Koinadugu, Bombali, and Tonkilili. All in the northeast."

Then she laid out what she wanted me to do. In the newly created position of a regional epidemiologist, I would go from district to district to provide technical support. That meant looking for any change in the rate of transmission, determining how to stop any increases, and then thinking about how to roll out the Integrative Disease Surveillance and Response framework, or IDSR. This was a new system being implemented so that we could go from the emergency response to a more sustainable system of disease monitoring within the community.

It was during this briefing with Dr. Cleary that I heard about the two Cuban physicians who'd died of malaria. The first one had neglected to take prophylaxis and the disease was never recognized. The second's malaria was recognized, but he'd died so abruptly that he couldn't get care. It was a good reminder to stay up with our mefloquine, and that malaria posed a greater risk to the response teams than Ebola.

The outbreak of the dreaded viral hemorrhagic fever had begun in the early spring of 2014. It had originated and smoldered in neighboring Guinea for a few months, so Sierra was late to be infected, but then it surpassed its neighbors in the number of cases and deaths. As of January 2016, it was still the only country with active cases. This was not unexpected given that Sierra Leone, on the coast of West Africa, is a low-income country still recovering from the effects of a decade-long, brutal civil war.

This tropical nation of 6 million people would have been much better served with an all-out preparedness effort the moment the first case was reported in Guinea. An objective indication of the state of the health system was that the country had an average life expectancy of forty-six years (eighty-six in Japan for comparison), and infant mortality of 107.2 deaths per 1,000 live births (1.6 in Iceland for comparison). That infant mortality is an unmitigated tragedy, with 10 percent of all children dying in the first year after birth.

Sierra Leone's rudimentary health infrastructure was easily overwhelmed by the novelty and highly communicable nature of Ebola. Practitioners had to cope with superspreader events; cultural practices that promoted close contact with the sick and dead; densely populated urban and periurban slums; resistance of the populace to identifying cases and contacts; and select counterproductive national response decisions such as large-scale quarantines, punitive bylaws, and poor early messages.

By summer, the country's leaders had realized that they were not getting the results they wanted from the public health–centered approach they'd been taking. This was in no small part because the ministry of health didn't have the medical intelligence to comprehend the full scope of the problem. So the president created a large, new coordinating structure, the National Ebola Response Center, or NERC, led by, of all people, the minister of defense.

The NERC was replicated in all the districts and called the DERC, the District Ebola Response Center, each run by a district coordinator, each designated by the president. So the Ebola response was being run by political appointees all the way down, which was not reassuring to anyone who'd been in New Orleans and seen how well political appointees had functioned during Katrina. However, on my second trip back six months later, when I became the national WHO lead for surveillance, I got to know the retired major and Minister of Defense Palo Conteh quite well and was impressed with his hands-on approach.

The NERC was split into multiple pillars that included case management, a public health element that included surveillance and laboratory activities, social mobilization, safe burials, logistics, communications, and a pillar for protecting survivors and addressing their psychosocial needs.

The country had set up a national 117 number to call if someone suspected they were ill, or knew of somebody who was. For job security, and because sometimes the national hotline failed to get the pertinent details, the district teams had a duplicate system based on their own personal cell phones. But at one point Sierra Leone had five hundred cases a week, with five thousand people on the contact-tracing list. And with 149 chiefdoms within the country in fourteen districts, and maybe about six thousand villages or more, there were definitely weak linkages between the national system and what happened at the local level.

Unfortunately, this security-led response produced a situation in which all households in a given compound would be quarantined, and often the village itself, with broad curfews in place. Eventually, the local authorities did narrow down the restrictions from "the entire village" to "certain compounds," and occasionally to individuals, but the shotgun approach had already set the stage for some antagonism between the community and the response, which led to community members often hiding people who were sick, as well as those who had died.

Building this capacity to respond to the outbreak was considered phase one. Phase two—enter yours truly—consisted of trying to get the number of new cases down to zero.

At one of the briefings, I heard about health care workers still getting infected, and no wonder, given the egregious lapses such as people rubbing their eyes after taking off their goggles, smoking cigarettes in the biocontainment unit, and taking cell phones into the red zone so they could receive calls. And given that some health care workers were still taking care of people out in the communities, their infections were not necessarily appropriate to be rolled up into the statistics for the health care setting. On the flip side, classifying these health care workers as community-acquired infections allowed the ruse of blaming the illness of a health care worker on community exposure in order to hide lapses in infection control within the treatment centers.

Back in Freetown, Dr. Delphine Courvoisier, another WHO consultant from Geneva, was helping put the data together and trying to make sense out of it. She told me about the various threads—the laboratory data from the thirteen labs, the viral hemorrhagic fever monitoring system data, and then another district reporting system—and the difficulty in trying to get all of these sources to align. In the end, the data really was a function of who was positive or negative in the lab. But the data systems were outdated, and they were not even accurate: there were samples without people, people without samples, and no standard spelling conventions for names.

These various data streams were supposed to flow into the ministry, and then get mushed together to make one system. But that fell apart, because the system wasn't designed to combine that many records. Everybody had their own data-checking algorithms, which meant that they had different numbers for cases: suspect cases and probable cases. Duplicates were not necessarily deleted within the data, and then there were delays of two to three weeks in data entry for whatever they did get.

As an epidemiologist, my first questions had to do with source and flow of data. Once I got to the district, I realized that all deaths and suspect cases were supposed to be reported to the District Emergency Response Center. The mouths of all corpses should be swabbed and the samples sent for nucleic acid testing. Then the independent surveillance team would get a history and fill out a case report form. Sick persons would be visited by the surveillance team who would fill out a form and, if the person met the case definition for being a suspect or probable case, call the ambulance. The ambulance would take the person to an Ebola treatment unit for a clinical assessment and to draw a blood sample for the laboratory. If the person was a laboratory-confirmed case, an investigation team would return for more in-depth interviews and another form. A contact-tracing team would also come daily for the next twenty-one days to follow all the contacts of the new case—more sets of forms, more different spellings of the same names.

A major challenge was keeping the same case number on all the samples. Later in the outbreak, CDC provided surveillance sheets with three barcodes. If a patient had three samples, you would use one of the three barcodes on each. If the clinicians wanted more samples tested because the patient was still there, they'd just get a brand new surveillance form and put the new barcode on those samples. So a person potentially had multiple identification numbers. Samples were often delayed in reaching the laboratory, especially if it involved the person responsible for collecting death swabs. There was one sample that sat around for eight days before being delivered, and it came up positive.

The epidemiology teams would look at a lab spreadsheet to see who had been declared a confirmed case based on a positive lab test. But sometimes the ministry would say "confirmed case, no, but still a positive lab result." Supposedly this was because they knew that the test was the duplicate of a case known to have been confirmed. More often it was to limit and control the number of cases.

When Delphine updated the database to link the epidemiology with the positive lab data, in one minute she found herself with five hundred additional cases, which was a very disturbing irregularity to a statistician and epidemiologist like me. Most perversely, when I made it down to the districts where this data was being collected, I learned that the local epidemiologists weren't even using the system Freetown had been struggling to clean up.

A similarly fundamental screw-up was pointed out to me by Dr. Yoti Zabulon, medical officer with the Health Security and Emergencies program at the WHO's African Regional Office, now deputy director of WHO for Sierra Leone—a newly created position for him to manage the response for the WHO country office. We'd known each other since the Ebola outbreak in Uganda years before, and nobody knew better how to manage this stuff than he did.

In June 2014, he'd told the powers that be, "What we need is $276,000 to get this outbreak shut down." About 10 percent of that money would be for surveillance. He'd also said they needed maybe sixteen cars, but that kind of support was nowhere to be found at the time he made the request.

Eight months later, in February, as he and I sat in his office, he pointed out the window at the fleet of cars—so many vehicles that they didn't have room to park them in the compound and had been forced to leave them up and down the street. Back when it could have made a decisive difference, WHO, global donors, and the government authorities had not provided the necessary resources. It was only when the first American got sick and needed to be Medexed back to the United States that Ebola in West Africa became a "global emergency" with money pouring in. At the global level, this was reflected in a month's long delay by the WHO in declaring a public health emergency of international concern (PHEIC) despite encouragement of Médicins Sans Frontières and others.

I'd asked Dr. Cleary for a car so I could hit the road, but first I had to get approval from the local security officer. I needed to log in to the UN safety and security system, provide my whole itinerary, what vehicle I was taking, what days I was going to be in the field, and where I'd be staying. I tried to do that online, working with the dodgy Internet access in my room at the Lighthouse, but I spent hours getting nowhere. I thought, There has to be a better way.

So the next day I simply showed up, and it still took hours, but eventually they found Crispin for me, a lovely guy who was local but who'd never seen the rest of his country. He drove a Nissan Pathfinder for a local rental company, and together we were going to head off to see the world, figuring it out along way, winging it on such nontrivial issues as where we were going to get gasoline and where we were going to stay.

The one essential we couldn't leave town without was local currency, because credit cards were not exactly the coin of the realm in the districts where we were heading. So while I stepped out to pick up some post cards and some lunch, Crispin arranged a black market transaction on the street, and when I got back in the car there was this guy with a messenger bag climbing into the back. I handed him US, and he handed me massive bundles of leones, the local currency that trades at about forty-two hundred to the dollar.

Then off we went for four weeks, with poor roads, no running water, usually no electricity, but literally sacks of money. And there are no weapons allowed in WHO cars, by the way. We just had to hope for the best.

Twenty years ago I'd been a young epidemiologist collecting and analyzing the data myself. Now I was here as the senior district epidemiologist for Kono, Koinadugu, Bombali, and Tonkilili, with the responsibility of thinking more strategically about what we were doing with prevention practices, and how we could improve.

Fortunately, the basic science of Ebola transmission and prevention has not changed for more than fifty years. Sick patients infect family members and health care workers; contact with corpses and infection within health care settings or from select superspreaders lead to explosive outbreaks. This transmission pattern dictated the prevention strategy of isolating the sick, safely burying the dead, monitoring the exposed contacts, and improving infection-control practices in the health care settings.

Thanks to Médecins Sans Frontières, the International Federation of Red Cross, Partners in Health, and multiple other clinical partners, this outbreak had a modicum of increased focus on providing care for infected patients and decreasing their death rate. The challenge of the outbreak also remained the same: how to optimally implement the evidence-based practices to drive this outbreak to zero, at the same time communicating the science in a culturally competent way to truly engage the community in their own preventive measures.

We went first to Koinadugu, the farthest northeast district, where the local economy was based on mining diamonds and gold. Even so, and even in Kabbalah, the capital, there was no running water or electricity.

At Wendy's Guest House, the local equivalent of the Ritz, all the rooms had been taken by people from the NGOs. We were relegated to a two-level brick building with maybe a dozen small rooms that opened off a covered walkway, sort of like a Motel 6 without electricity or running water. The owner had plans for such amenities, but those plans remained aspirational.

There was one place in the town where we could get something to eat. My first meal there consisted of some mystery meat swimming in oil with a half a cup of mayonnaise drizzled on top. Also ketchup and a baguette. My first thought was, This is wrong on so many different levels I don't even know where to start. My second thought was, I'm hungry, and they claim it's halal—which was true for most of the food in this Muslim country—so despite violating reams of regs about food safety, I swallowed my dinner quite happily and prayed it got along well with whatever bugs were already resident in my gut.

In my room was a trash can bucket filled with water that you used to flush the toilet and for whatever washing up you could manage. They did have a gasoline-powered generator, and in the evening they used that to produce a couple of hours of electricity—just about enough to charge your phone. There was a fan in the ceiling, but it spun apart when I turned it on, throwing the cover and various forms of shrapnel all over the place, so I decided that still air, as long as it did not include flying machinery, was okay.

I definitely used the bed net around me while I slept, and in the morning I always shook out my shoes. But there was no electricity in the morning, which meant that I washed up in the dark. Then for breakfast I had a boiled egg, with another large dollop of mayonnaise, and another slice of mystery meat.

I thought that "senior field epidemiologist" sounded kind of mundane, and since I was assigned to go to so many districts, I started calling myself a "roving epidemiologist." Then I said no, I was a "free-range epidemiologist," until my colleagues decided that because I had such a broad remit to do and say what I wanted, and didn't hesitate to do so, the term that stuck was "untamed epidemiologist."

So I went from one rural area to the next, consulting with all the field teams: the WHO epidemiologists and their various supervisors. Then I would go out with the burial teams, observe what they were doing, and say, "This is great, let me share it with the other districts" or "Okay, here's a better approach that will help get us to zero." The teams were tired from months of work, and getting to zero—meaning no new cases—became the mantra to try to keep them in the game.

The one big difference between this outbreak and previous outbreaks was that almost everyplace I went, no matter how remote, at the workplace, at least, there was a satellite Internet connection. Unfortunately, they still hadn't found a way to use the interconnectivity to its full potential.

Too often, data collection simply meant someone filling out a form, and then the form going to someone else who had no idea what the form meant except that he or she was supposed to put it into a database. It was just a job, a rote activity as it got rolled all the way up to Freetown, where everybody then looked at it and said, "Oh, what can we find out from this?" Then it got rolled up to Geneva, along with data from Guinea and Liberia, the other two countries most affected, and everybody pored over it.

But, sadly, when you're out in the field you know these numbers are pretty meaningless.

The data had not been double entered, and they had no sense of the contacts, and because there was no ownership by the WHO team or by the local district health team, nobody was willing to vouch for any of it. But in Geneva nobody knew that, and they were assuming these numbers to be rock solid. They were accepting the numbers as gospel even in Freetown.

I discovered that there were silent areas with no reporting, which meant places where there were no dead people. So, evidently, the outbreak of Ebola had also spawned an outbreak of dishonesty—a side effect of people worried about mandatory quarantines, or what would happen to the corpse of a loved one. When somebody died, you were supposed to call a team to come in and swab the individual, but there were all these areas where nobody ever called. We had a running joke that if you wanted immortality, you only had to move to village X or Y or Z.

In other areas, nobody got sick—they just died. During an outbreak like this you have to assume that people are sick before they die, but many villagers, hoping to avoid quarantine or removal of the patient, held back the truth until it was too late.

Equally disturbing was that the local teams didn't seem to fully understand the information flow, even at the local level, and even though that was the data they were supposedly aggregating as the basis for decision making. All they seemed to grasp was that you were expected to have numbers, so everybody spewed out numbers, even though the numbers had no credibility.

Because the databases were incomplete and difficult to use, decisions could never be more sophisticated than figuring out who was positive today, then how this person related to somebody else who was positive. The question being, who were their shared contacts? So it was a very narrow view of the public health response. With better data, the district and national teams could have been more strategic in looking at the arc of the outbreak, and how it was spreading.

But, truth be told, the kind of data mismatch and confusion I saw in Sierra Leone happens in the United States all the time. With all our modern systems, we still collect separate

Excel spreadsheets that have to be collated to see how many cases occur in any given outbreak. We have yet to establish the level of trust we need to create a single database into which everybody can enter his data. The common themes—fog of war, data ownership, data veracity, data sharing, data visualization—remain the same. They're simply starker in a place where the per capita gross domestic product is around $400.

I helped the health workers in my districts think about other critical questions around the disease. We called all of it Ebola virus disease, but very quickly, in the Ebola treatment units, they segregated people into "wet" and "dry" patients, wet being those who were vomiting or had diarrhea or bloody symptoms. I asked the questions, Are these really two different clinical entities? Do these labels indicate that one is more or less likely to die, or to infect more patients or fewer patients? I encouraged them to look at their own data to try to make these more granular, and therefore more useful, determinations.

To say the least, contact tracing and follow-up did not always work well. This was obvious in what I call "missing links" in the chain of transmission. In about 78 percent of cases contact tracers could identify the chain on a contact list and knew the exposure source. But that left the 22 percent of cases for which they could not. Probably over half of those were just because the contact tracers weren't getting a good history, or the patient truly didn't know how they got infected, or they were hiding where they got infected for various reasons. I believe there might have been a tiny portion of individuals infected by somebody who was not very sick. Since that somebody would not have been identified by the infected person, the case was not reported as a possible source of transmission to the public health system.

Disturbingly, there were too many reports of contacts of cases getting sick and dying within a quarantine home, despite the fact that they were supposedly being checked twice a day by a contact follow-up team to assure everybody was fine. In these cases a contact tracer either didn't do a good assessment, or didn't go where he said he did. They were missing people being sick or even missing the number of people within the home, such as children who would be spirited off to get sick elsewhere.

When I returned in August 2015, six months after my first visit, I continued my free-range activities in the three remaining districts of Port Loko, Kambia, and in the Urban region where there were still active cases, investigating the most perplexing among them. For the most part, we'd never seen enough infected people to learn much about the more exotic manifestations. But this outbreak was so large, and so protracted, that over time we were able to see a full range of cases that provided deep insights to the nature of Ebola.

At least one case-pair looked like it was sexual transmission. Weeks after a male came back home, and with no other disease in the community, he infected his partner. This was consistent with lab data and anecdotal evidence, which led us to recommend that people use condoms for ninety days after their onset date. We found many other such compelling case-pairs.

But providing condoms in rural Africa and educating people about their use was not easy. The whole situation was muddled, because in one province males were being imprisoned for potentially infecting their partners, but not everyone in the public health community even believed that sexual transmission was possible. I wrote a paper documenting a handful of pairs of patients where the investigation suggested that the infection was due to sex, trying to raise a warning that this might be more common than we thought. The WHO journal did not want to publish it. A few weeks later, a case of sexual transmission in Guinea was definitively linked by laboratory data and very well publicized. A subsequent study showed that semen could remain potentially infectious for nine months. So even after waiting out two incubation periods— for forty-two days after the last Ebola case—you still needed to be vigilant for nine more months, because there might be a sexual partner of a survivor who would turn up sick. The ability of the virus to survive in the testes was complicated by its ability to survive in other "immunologically protected" sites such as the brain, the eye, and the fetus. The more basic lesson was that the outbreak wasn't necessarily over the first time there was a lull.

One of my investigations ruffled some feathers because it established for the first time that you could get infected with Ebola from somebody with mild, or even no symptoms.

This involved a group quarantined after a family member had a miscarriage. Three days after release from quarantine, two of the folks became ill with Ebola, which called into question the length of the incubation, and whether these people really had been quarantined, even though they had been visited at least twice a day by contact tracers. One of the Ebola cases was the breastfeeding female child of a quarantined contact; the second case was the sister of the child's mother. The mother had no symptoms, or extremely mild symptoms, that went unrecognized by the contact tracers during their twice-daily visits. A blood test on the mother was positive for virus antibodies and her breast milk was positive for active virus infection. Yet the virus of the child and her aunt most closely matched that of the breastfeeding mother, the original case responsible for the quarantine. While the child might have been infected by the breast milk, her aunt clearly was not, suggesting that you can have mild to no illness while infected (not unusual for any infectious disease) but still transmit the virus (disturbing for prevention purposes).

———

Every two to three days we moved to a different district. The next was Bombali, which was the district where the president had multiple homes, and where he came back to visit almost every weekend. Needless to say, the coordinator for that district was a bit high-strung.

We stayed in the capital, Makeni, in a hotel that was lovely even by US standards, which felt like heaven after a week on the road. Since that district was close to my next destination, Tonkolili, I stayed in that same place for a week.

Invariably I would chat with the WHO people, and then I would spend the day with a surveillance team, a burial team, a contact-tracing team, or a case investigator, just to see what they were doing, and to suggest better practices if that was warranted. Then when I came back in the evening, I'd put those thoughts together in order to share them with all the teams in all four districts to say, "These are things you should be considering."

I think the teams appreciated these random musings that appeared every three or four days, because it made them feel listened to, and it reminded them of their role in the larger effort, which made a difference.

Crispin's little Nissan Pathfinder wasn't up to the challenges of the bad road leading to my last district, Kono, a diamond-mining region, so I was assigned a new driver with a four-wheel drive vehicle, but I was told to postpone my trip because there was no place to stay. I said I would sleep in the car and went ahead. It was four hours (about 110 miles) of horrific road conditions to Koidu town, but luckily when I got there, one of the epidemiologists had gone back to help in Freetown, so I was able to spend a few nights in his room at the Diamond Lodge, which was owned by the Sierra Leonian ambassador to China.

When I got back to Freetown we were happy to note a decrease in both cases and deaths. But then suddenly there was a cluster among the fishermen in the Aberdeen area where I'd stayed originally. My old hotel, the Sierra Lighthouse, was in lockdown, and there were soldiers on the street corners, with ropes strung across the intersections to enforce the quarantine. Supposedly there were seven hundred residents in Aberdeen and three toilets. The lull, followed by an isolated spike, was a pattern we'd see repeated until the outbreak was declared over.

From the Aberdeen cluster, one man who'd been isolated for two days in quarantine broke out and fled into Bombali. His friends and family thought he'd been shot (or cursed) by a "witch gun," so they called in the herbalist, and the traditional healer, among others, to try to offset the magic they saw as having made him sick. "Shot by a witch gun" was a local term for a severe curse that reflected the power of guns; a related curse, "a witch plane crash," was used to explain a large number of deaths at once. Most importantly, while you might go to a regular doctor for malaria and other medical diseases, being shot by a witch gun was treatable only by traditional healers.

The afflicted man underwent the treatment of being bathed and having herbs rubbed on his body. It took him thirty-six hours to die, and through all that body contact he exposed a hundred people to the disease, and infected thirty to forty.

I went back out to tour my four districts again, once again starting at Koinadugu. I spent the first night in a chief's hut in the chiefdom that was responsible for 103 of the 106 cases in the district. It was a cinder-block house on a hill, but WHO had put in a generator, and we already had a satellite connection, and they said they were going to put in water tanks (though while I was there we still used buckets). All in all, the chief was going to make out like a bandit from all the WHO- and NGO-provided improvements to his house, proving yet again that it's a very ill wind that doesn't blow somebody some good.

The chief of staff in each district emergency response center was invariably a Ministry of Defense person, with direct connection to the president himself, which meant that in many cases, the district health officers were sidelined or not very visible.

Having a strong military focus gave the effort a lot more traction. There were fewer lengthy discussions of the sort I was used to hearing. The exchanges were crisper, more on point. What was clear, though, was that leadership, if it doesn't have really good support from the district medical team or a good medical input, and if it doesn't understand the full biology of the disease, will make some pretty lousy decisions, because they aren't evidence based.

Many of these districts also had a representative from the new UN Mission for Emergency Ebola Response, set up to respond to this outbreak because of the shortcomings of the traditional WHO-led response. In the revised structure, traditional public health responsibilities were split off from WHO, leaving the UN International Children's Emergency Fund (UNICEF) responsible for social mobilization and the UN Population Fund (UNFPA) responsible for contact tracing. Very quickly, though, it became apparent that these entities didn't really have the technical expertise to support those functions, and WHO in Sierra Leone then had to supplement them with technical experts.

Unfortunately, Sierra Leone's operational effectiveness came at a price. Because the country took an essentially military or law enforcement response, rather than a public health response, it was difficult to get community engagement, and it took more than a year to get the outbreak under control.

The prime example of this coercive approach was the use of forced quarantines, sometimes not just of households but of whole villages. Your house was a two-room mud hut with a thatched roof, with twenty people living there. You had to wait there for twenty-one days to determine if anyone was sick. If one person got infected within the contacts, you had to reset the clock and start over with another twenty-one days in confinement for everybody else.

There were compounds that had been quarantined for three months because people in a household would keep getting infected, and you'd have to keep resetting the clock. In the early days, they didn't even provide food in a timely manner, so quarantine could easily lead to starvation.

The international NGOs working with the authorities got better about providing food, but people would hide cases because they didn't want to stay quarantined, or they would flee quarantine and effectively move the outbreak elsewhere. Could you blame them for wanting to get out of such a desperate situation?

The control of epidemics should take into account not only the numbers but what those numbers mean in terms of daily experience. This means making an effort to understand what people go through, what they believe, what they fear. And then trying to come up with a solution that doesn't push them to hide or flee. If they see us as punishers, they'll run. If they see us as providers of solutions, they'll engage—and to solve an outbreak of this magnitude, we need them to engage. But they will never understand us if we don't first try to understand them.

For all the messaging about what caused Ebola, there still were examples of really poor practice and lapses in judgment by the population, and it really got down to the fact that when you had this long cultural history of doing things a certain way, change was very difficult.

In another of my districts, Kono, there was an Evangelical church with five pastors, of which two had died of Ebola, two were under quarantine, and one was fine. The thought was that this church was doing a lot of laying on of hands, which not unlike the practices of the traditional healers, was a perfect opportunity for transmission. One of the pastors had taken a woman exposed to Ebola and hidden her in a remote village, and he may have even provided her with medical supplies. Eventually, the team was able to find her and bring her in.

In the Koinadugu region a traditional birth attendant got sick with symptoms characteristic of Ebola, and so the local chief in that village asked a motorcycle taxi to come and pick her up and take her to the preventive primary health care unit for treatment. He should have called the central number or alerted the District Emergency Response Center to come and pick her up in an ambulance, and because of his lapse, he got suspended by the paramount chief. At this time, most pregnant women aborted and died, so traditional birth attendants were at very high risk of becoming infected. The woman ended up having Ebola, which put everyone she'd been in contact with in quarantine. The motorcycle taxi guy did fine, but many such drivers got infected and died.

While this woman was in the primary health care unit, she'd had fever, and she'd had chest pain as well as other symptoms, but the nurse didn't put two and two together to say, "You know what. This is probably Ebola." Instead she was telling us, "Oh, no. She got hit on her chest, and that's why her chest was hurting." Then they ended up having to quarantine the nurse and the whole primary health care unit. This was a year into the outbreak and we were still seeing these horrendous lapses.

For all their dissembling, people understood perfectly well how transmission occurred. A young woman died—positive for Ebola—and was referred to the burial team. Her mother had originally said she'd died suddenly and had not traveled anywhere where she could have been exposed. And she had no contacts besides those who lived in the family compound. After a lot of questioning, it turned out the young woman had been sick for several days, then went to a clinic where they told her she was pregnant (by any definition, I would have counted her boyfriend as a close contact!). From there, she had fled into the bush. When she came home, basically it was to die. Subsequent questioning turned up the fact that she had traveled to Freetown, which would explain how she got infected.

Then we contacted the nurse who'd taken care of her at the clinic and said, "We're sorry to tell you, one of your patients has been confirmed with Ebola. That means that you're going to have to go into quarantine."

She said, "Oh, I didn't have contact with any sick people. I'm working in the city. In fact I'll be there tomorrow." Then the next day she was back at the clinic and denied any contact with the case. But the dead woman's mother named her as the nurse who'd taken care of her daughter.

When she could no longer deny her involvement, she said, "Well, I was in complete PPE," meaning complete personal protective equipment.

"So who else was in the clinic?"

"Nobody," she said. "I was the only one there."

But we could see people milling around. There were no services to speak of in these places, but there was always traffic. There was even a man living there.

"So what about the pregnancy test?"

"I showed her how to use it. She took her own urine analysis, dipped it herself, read it herself to know it was positive, and then threw the urine down into the toilet in the back so nobody was exposed. Then once she left, I appropriately took off my personal protective equipment."

It was quite clear that none of this was true, and that this nurse knew exactly how Ebola had been transmitted. She also knew that she had exposed herself, and that she might get sick and die, but she was still trying to make sure that nobody else was implicated and put on the list of contacts. But by prevaricating and withholding information, all she'd done was put many, many people at risk.

This is why the real challenge in an outbreak like this is not the science; it's the social science—the anthropology. We know Ebola doesn't spread by witch guns and magic. Ebola only spreads through physical contact. We also know how to interrupt transmission in the way we take care of the victims, as in not washing corpses and isolating sick people to special Ebola treatment units. But how do you then transfer that knowledge to a community that doesn't have a good sense of germ theory, has long-held cultural practices around magic, and has burial practices that involve lots of hands-on contact with the dead?

The professional anthropologists who came through started off with the term "social mobilization," but in the end I guess they came back and said, "You know what. This is really more about community engagement, empowering the community to take care of these issues themselves." They alerted us to the active efforts to undermine the necessary trust by instituting emergency by-laws, backed by fines and jail time, that imposed penalties for harboring patients and not reporting them in a timely manner, not registering all visitors, and other transgressions.

I rarely saw a true partnership with the community, and I think it was that lack of partnership that explains why the outbreak went on for so long.

Whenever I was out with the teams I reminded them that you must start with the village chief, or whomever the local community leaders are, to make them part of the solution and not just always see them as part of the problem. For that we need to trust them and for them to trust us. And that turns out to be tricky.

When you're trying to work with the community, there's this huge educational and scientific worldview gap. They believe in witch guns. You believe in germ theory. These people in the villages at the center of it are not reading the *New York Times*, and they have no sense of the worldwide global effects. Most of the information they receive is word of mouth.

Then the global community comes in with this arrogance that says, "We know the science, so we know how to shut down this outbreak," which leads to neglecting the unique community issues, even in the United States. We certainly didn't appreciate the unique cultural aspects of the urban outbreaks in West Africa. And this is where we probably should have been engaging the traditional healers from day one, saying to the witch doctors, "Greetings. You are now included in the health care brethren. Here's the secret handshake, and here's your per diem."

Is the concept of a witch gun really that different from the concept of an organism too small to see that attacks your cells? That distinction becomes operative only when it gets down to how you use your theory of disease in treating the person and trying to prevent anybody else from becoming infected.

But in order for these practitioners to listen to what we have to say, first we need to respect them. Within their communities, they are considered wise and experienced. We need to be humble enough to say, "Here is what I know and how I know it. But you know this community far better than I do, so let's work on this together, as a team."

The technology and the pharmacology is the least of it. It's all about obtaining complete transparency; that is, you don't hide, and you don't steal the sick person or the dead person's corpse. Those surreptitious behaviors lead to really big problems when you're talking about something as deadly as Ebola.

But people are accustomed to ritually washing the body, and if you just come and say, "No, you can't do that," you're going to get resistance. The washing is part of their mourning process. So how do you allow them to mourn while you change those practices?

When one of us shows up in a village, head to foot in this protective equipment, the local people will be thinking, Are they from Mars? What's going on?

That's very different from coming and talking to the chief, and to the witch doctor, and making clear that just living in the village doesn't pose a risk. Then you say, "Okay, now, my team is going to put on their equipment and we're going to put the body in the bag. Then we're going to spray the bag with disinfectant before we bury it deep. And once the body is in the bag we can place it outside for your noncontact ritual prayers or customs. That's how we can ensure that there's no risk."

They do recognize patterns of illness and death in their communities, but if you die from Ebola or you die from malaria, you're still dead. This puts a premium on having the health care worker they deal with in the ordinary times—when they're merely dying of malaria—be the same person they see when they're being attacked by something novel.

And yet you have communities all over West Africa that have never seen anybody from their government. And it's not as if they haven't been dying of other diseases like malaria and typhoid. Then, all of a sudden, here's this scary disease, and the government shows up along with lots of outside organizations and the people say, "This seems like all the other things we were dying of. Why are you so interested in this one? And, by the way, where were you when my brother was dying of malaria?"

That same local says, "Why should I get all worried about Ebola? I'll just do what the witch doctor says and maybe it will go away."

"Why?"

"Because when nobody else was there to help my brother, the local witch doctor was there."

The central issue in any environment where there is an outbreak, whether it's an Indian reservation with hantavirus or legionnaire's disease in New York City, is fear of the unknown, and this fear remains irrational regardless of anyone's level of scientific understanding.

A related problem in the early days was that the ministry and the public health folks raised demand without increasing supply. They were out in the field telling people, "Come to the hospital, call us to pick up your dead, and be sure to use gloves within your household if somebody's sick." But there were no gloves available, much less hospital beds. That created distrust between the communities and the power structure that took a long time to resolve. And, by the way, if you're sending out a message that Ebola is invariably lethal—also known as "You are going TO DIE"—what's the incentive to leave your loved ones and go to the hospital?

The distrust was heightened by the fact that everybody seemed to be making money off the outbreak. The NGOs were paying the locals to be cooks, drivers, contact tracers, ambulance drivers, etc., and they were getting top ups on their cell phones. All of a sudden, you had a mini economy established around this one disease, because this was the one the Westerners were worried about.

Then what invariably happened—I've yet to see an outbreak where it hasn't happened—is that people go on strike. They said, "We're not being paid enough." They'd been working for years without being regularly paid, or not being paid enough, and they'd still done it. But all of a sudden, during this time of special urgency (and the special inflow of NGO money), they'd say, "I need to get these special allowances and incentives. If I don't get them, I'm not going to work." At least it highlighted the shameful way in which they're usually treated.

Then there was the issue of, "Why didn't my cousin get that job?" Well, maybe it was because your cousin is in the capital, and not out in the districts where we need the contact tracers. There were plenty of examples of misdistribution, or maldistribution, of resources just because of some corruption in the system. And this was at all levels of the government.

Matt Craven, the operations guy, often raised the question, "How do we change the calculus to make people *want* to stay if they've been exposed, as opposed to fleeing?" It can't all be a stick, in other words. There has to be a carrot part of it.

In Freetown and other places, the national response team was coming up with innovations, such as building trust and providing an incentive by providing medical care to people while they were waiting out their twenty-one days of quarantine. If you were taking care of their colds and headaches and joint aches, then maybe when they really had Ebola they would come to you too, instead of trying to hide it. We also needed to make sure they had food and water. It was pretty basic stuff.

Health data is a powerful mix with politics. Because of the Ebola outbreak, all deaths were supposed to be reported, have an oral swab for Ebola sent to the laboratory, and safely buried. These deaths were usually noted on large boards in the NERCs. As Ebola cases decreased, it became very obvious that most of the deaths were very young children, and this fueled numerous questions. The national health and political leadership acted to discuss the veracity of the data and consider possible solutions. The large number of childhood deaths were completely expected, but giving these children names, ages, and village locations instead of being a little known statistic gave them a voice for change.

Irrational fears and irrational behaviors, of course, are not limited to the Kabala village in Koinadugu. And which is worse, irrationality among people with primitive belief systems who don't know germ theory, or among people who live in sophisticated cities who nonetheless are overloaded with bogus information?

In the West, a faraway Ebola outbreak and Kim Kardashian are equivalent blips on the media screen, and until we develop a longer attention span, and a more measured and appropriate long-term response, we will be lurching from one overblown crisis to the next. In the case of villagers in Sierra Leone, the problem is information scarcity; in highly developed nations, the problem is information overload.

Which is not to say that there is not entirely bogus information—the equivalent of witch guns—in the West. Recently, there was a big measles outbreak in the United States, some of which was owing to affluent parents who wouldn't get their kids vaccinated for fear of giving them autism, a trend fomented by celebrities spouting misinformation on talk shows. And there were the red state governors who somehow were going to set aside the US Constitution to keep Ebola victims out of their jurisdictions. (Very much like those cops who kept the New Orleans residents, at gunpoint, from crossing into suburban Gretna during Katrina, yes?)

It's good to remember that there are many forms of magical thinking, and that the irrationality (and sometimes lack of humanity) of the human species in the face of fear is distributed pretty evenly around the world.

What this means is that we need to be paying attention, and not just when something gruesome sounding happens and suddenly the media swoops in for a three-day feeding frenzy, then moves on to something else. How are we helping to build solid systems of reliable information so that when something really bad happens, we know what's going on, we can distinguish between fact and hysteria, and we can provide support? How do we make sure that people are getting immunizations and other clinical services? How are we providing them information to protect themselves and to promote their health? You can't perk up only when some sexy disease hits the fan and threatens Americans.

Beyond providing new resources for the response, this interest by the high-income countries has multiple silver linings for the local populations in West Africa. We now have a new prevention tool with the vaccine contacts and new drugs to treat Ebola patients.

We need to increase scientific understanding in the West, just as we need to in the developing world. We also need to lower the temperature in the media, reducing the level of junk science entering our brains (along with the level of junk media in general). We need to help people learn to demand actual data as they form their opinions, rather than celebrity sound bites.

When people can get worked up over waves of Mexican "rapists" and "moochers" coming over our southern border, at a time when more Mexicans are leaving than entering the United States, as was the case from 2007–2014, think what's going to happen when there truly *is* a crisis—when something akin to the anthrax attack on Washington or the devastation of Katrina hits on a national scale and there is a true breakdown of civil society.

If you think a village pastor in Africa is behaving irrationally by hiding a victim, wait until you see how the media can stir up an ignoramus culture when there is compelling video of middle-class white people dying in the streets of a major American city. You can't blame African villagers for their ignorance or mistrust. They haven't had a chance. But in the developed world we truly need to get a grip, to demand a little more sophistication in reporting, in analysis, and, no doubt, in our health care systems.

In 2011, during the Influenza H1N1p outbreak, *Fox News* accused the government of rushing the vaccine to market without testing it. Then when there was a shortage, they accused the government of not supplying it fast enough. Or when Playboy bunnies say things like, "The idea that vaccines are a primary cause of autism is not as crackpot as some might wish." Yes, Jenny, it *is* a crackpot idea that you and others of your ilk have promoted that has not a single shred of proof and been refuted by numerous studies. It's a no-win situation when the only metric that some news organizations care about is attracting viewers. And dissemination of these anti-science myths is the type of hype that will not serve us well when an emerging infection decides to really show us who's boss.

10

#JeSuisleMonde

No man ever steps in the same river twice, for it's not the same river and he's not the same man.
—**Heraclitus**

In South Sudan they say that no man (or woman, or child) should step in the river at all, but the reason has nothing to do with ancient Greeks and the inevitability of change. The reason has to do with the life cycle of the Guinea worm, a parasite also known as *Dracunculus medinensis*. The worm's larvae infect humans and cause a painful condition called dracunculiasis, which is Latin for "afflicted by little dragons." The larvae gain access when people drink unfiltered water that contains fleas or copepods infected with the larvae. These microscopic invaders penetrate into the abdomen from the stomach and intestine, mature into adults, and then mate. The male worm dies, and then the female burrows down to the host's lower limbs. There are no symptoms at first, but after about a year a painful burning blister appears in the skin, usually on a foot or leg. The pain causes the victim to seek relief by soaking his or her feet in the water of a river or pond, which releases more larvae into the water through the sores, and the transmission cycle starts all over again.

These worms, which can be one to two millimeters wide and up to one meter long, exit the human body through that sore in the foot or leg during a long, slow, and painful process.

The Sudanese remove the offending worm by rolling it over a stick, something like rolling up the lid of a sardine can on a metal key, but this can take weeks, during which time people may have difficulty working, or even walking, making Guinea worm disease a major impediment to economic development. The pain can continue for months after the worm has been removed, and the ulcers formed by the emerging worm can become otherwise infected.

The only saving grace of this disease is that it affects only humans, and the larvae can survive for only three weeks outside a human host. This means that for the cycle to persist, there's a very brief window during which the larvae need to be ingested by the water fleas. There are occasional infections of dogs, leopards, and other mammals, but these are so rare that if you can interrupt the cycle of transmission to humans, you can eliminate the disease altogether.

In 1986, when there were 3.5 million cases in twenty-one countries, the philanthropic organization run by former president Jimmy Carter, the Carter Center, began trying to make Guinea worm the second human disease after smallpox to be completely eradicated, and the first to be completely eradicated without reliance on a vaccine or medication.

In 2004, I went to Unity State, Sudan, for six weeks as a volunteer to assist the Carter Center health initiative. What I found was a confluence of many of the problems that keep people miserable around the world, and that spawn or sustain the diseases that eventually can find their way to the rest of us back in Omaha or Boston or San Jose. We may live in the land of plenty, and we may enjoy all the comforts of postindustrial capitalism, but the microbes that inflict misery on the poorest members of the human race are only hours away by transcontinental air travel.

Unity State is in the Greater Upper Nile region, which is forty-two thousand square kilometers inhabited by from 1.2 to 2 million people who tend herds of cattle and farm during the rainy season. The capital city, Bentiu, has only nine hours of electricity a day, no telephones, no piped water to homes, no sewers, and no asphalt roads. The "modernization" that's come to the region has not been kind. When oil was discovered in the 1970s, it led to massive displacement of the indigenous population, which was followed by a protracted civil war that has continued into the present. Extortion, abduction, mass rapes and killings, the looting of crops and cattle, and the burning of villages have become routine. Villagers often have to hide from marauding armies in the surrounding bush and swamplands, which leaves them unable to harvest their crops and desperately short of food.

In 2004, the goal of the Carter Center was to bring clean water to a region where people walked miles to find it. It's possible to treat surface water with a chemical called temefos to kill the larvae, but simply filtering through a cloth is often enough to stop the disease. So we went out with the field workers as they tried to develop better wells, and we distributed water filters to the nomads, and educated people about the dangers of putting their infected legs in the water sources they drank from. But we also tried to convey the most basic concepts of project management: how to target goals and monitor results, how to recruit and motivate volunteers, how to communicate with the home office.

While we were there, the Darfur genocide led by the Janjaweed militia and supported by the Sudanese government was well under way. We were some distance from West Sudan, where the worst cruelties were taking place, but we were still confronted with local atrocities in a state that, six years later, would secede to become part of the country of South Sudan. Resident security personnel had to approve all travel outside a locality the morning of travel, and we had to move at night with an armed escort. There were numerous military checkpoints, usually manned by child soldiers with AK-47s.

It's always instructive for a Westerner to get a feel for these kinds of conditions, and to live for a while in a mud hut with a thatched roof, where you wake up with spiders the size of your fist on your bed net, and where during the rainy season it's best to sleep outside to avoid the scorpions that fall down from the rafters during downpours. The defining moment of my visit was the night the rain washed out our latrine and I almost took a dive into the pit.

The kind of hardship and danger the Sudanese endure is what life is like every day in far too many regions of the world. Conditions became so bad in southern Unity that in 2015, even Médecins Sans Frontières had to pull out. But that same year, three decades after the Carter Center began its efforts, there were only twenty cases of Guinea worm disease in all of Africa. This meant that guinea worm was on the path to eradication.

Public health progress *is* possible, then, even in countries that endure the greatest hardships, provided that we provide the collective will, community engagement, and use of common sense and good science, and invest resources at an appropriate and consistent level.

———

There was never a time when humans were not infected with microbes. Even as hunter-gathers in small nomadic populations, we were always susceptible to parasitic infections of the intestine and from microbes circulating in the environment. But the potential for infection increased about ten thousand years ago with the advent of agriculture, when we settled down and started to domesticate animals that could easily pass their infectious diseases on to us. Agriculture also enabled the rise of cities, which meant that there were enough people clustered together to sustain these microbes by purely human-to-human infection.

Flash forward through the millennia, and by the mid–twentieth century germ theory had given rise to vaccines and to improved sanitation. The first international sanitary conference, held in Paris in 1851, focused on the need for quarantine measures for cholera. Hello to the discovery that separating sewage from drinking water and treating it with chlorine not only eliminated typhoid and cholera, but also made the water taste better! This kind of progress gave rise to heady predictions of the demise of infectious diseases.

But as we reduced the baseline of infectious diseases in developed parts of the world, new and reemerging diseases became apparent and tempered that optimism. Adaptation as a means of survival is the name of the game for life on this planet, and as microbes interact with humans, we see them adapt and change all the time.

Beyond the example of influenza viruses genetically drifting, and sometimes shifting, we see the rampant resistance of microbes—bacteria, viruses, fungi, and parasites—to antimicrobial efforts. This resistance to antibiotics and other first-line drugs accounts for the increase in deadly colon infections (*Clostridium difficile*), a blood infection (Carbapenem-resistant *Enterobacteriaceae*), resistant forms of a very common sexually transmitted infection (gonorrhea), multidrug-resistant tuberculosis, and many others.

Each year in the United States, at least 2 million people become infected with bacteria that are resistant to antibiotics, and at least twenty-three thousand people die as a direct result. A significant proportion of these infections stem from the wholesale use of antibiotics to make livestock grow faster, which creates drug-resistant microbes that can be transmitted to humans. But most have to do with inappropriate use of antibiotics in humans, followed by the transmission of those microbes from one human to another, often in health care settings.

In this cycle of mutation and transmission, microbes are like players advancing to new levels in a video game until they have an overwhelmingly potent set of new weapons to make them invincible. Meanwhile, because research on new antibiotics is a riskier business proposition than simply continuing to pump out revised drugs for chronic diseases, we humans are falling behind in the arms race.

If this trend continues, eventually we'll reach a new post-antibiotic age in which we slip back a century or more in terms of health care progress. We can all play our role in slowing the trend by refusing antibiotics for bronchitis, common colds, a sore throat that is not strep, or a simple runny nose, and by completing any regime of antibiotics we've been prescribed so that they can kill, not just "wound," their target organism.

There are plenty of other factors, however, existing at the macro, rather than the micro, scale that increase our threat from emerging infections.

The most potent of these are not scientific but political. Politics underlies poverty and social inequity, which allow certain people to be susceptible to infections and others to be relatively immune—at least for now. Politics is the driver for war and famine, poor public health systems, and biologic, chemical, and radiologic terrorism. As political chaos rages across Africa and the Middle East, just as it has at various times from Burma to Bogotá, disorder leads to displaced populations and mass migrations at risk of contagion, while societal despair and inequity lead to disenfranchised individuals and groups capable of committing bioterrorism.

Responding to political as well as economic pressure, more and more people move to urban areas, creating megacities that dwarf the likes of New York and London, some with peri-urban slums where people live in proximity to livestock. Of the thirty-odd such urban areas that currently exist, the largest, with about 38 million people, is Tokyo-Yokohama. When we consider the health risks of having such huge aggregations of people, however, it is worth remembering that a still greater number live within the megalopolis in the northeastern United States affectionately known as the BosWash Corridor.

Meanwhile, population growth in general, along with the choices people make about land use, has led to increasing encroachment on open spaces and disruption of ecosystems. This leads to increased human contact with wildlife and insects, many of which are new arrivals in certain regions owing to climate change and destruction of habitat elsewhere.

People are also traveling more, and achieving far greater distances faster than previously imaginable. This is also true for the animals and goods that keep our global economy humming, as well as for the microbes that tag along. So it should come as no surprise when, as happened in 2011, a batch of infected sprouts from an organic farm in Germany infected 3,950 people with a severe diarrheal illness and killed 51 persons in sixteen countries.

The microbes being moved from places both isolated and overcrowded to large, densely populated areas where their spread can go unchecked include those that give rise to foodborne outbreaks, to the infections that arise from within health care settings, and to the microbes that are the misbegotten offspring of laboratory misadventures. This category includes irresponsible experiments to create superbugs, as well as simple lab accidents such as the one that led to the 2007 release of foot and mouth disease, an animal ailment, into the British countryside from Pirbright laboratories in Surrey.

To prevent the next pandemic, we need a comprehensive approach that gets beyond a focus on the microbe and that realizes our own role in creating the new "miasma" out of which these events arise.

Perhaps the greatest compounding factor for the spread of existing infectious diseases will be climate change. NASA and the National Oceanic and Atmospheric Administration, in their own separate analyses of the global temperature data, concluded that the year 2015 was the hottest since record keeping began in 1880. The specific effects of global climate change in any given location will vary from drought leading to desert-ification, to rising seawater leading to massive flooding. But, all in all, reports indicate that 400,000 people will begin dying annually from severe weather, heat-related illnesses, and lung diseases and allergies, as well as infectious diseases associated with rising global temperatures and chaotic weather patterns.

Climate change will affect soil moisture, which affects the size of harvest, even as increased heat decreases the nutritional value of foods, including the protein content of wheat and rice. Climate change will also have huge effects on the distribution of the animals that serve as disease reservoirs and vectors, whether we're talking birds, or rodents, or the ticks that cause Lyme disease, or the mosquitoes that cause Zika, dengue, or chikun-gunya. If it's raining, or if it's too hot or humid, these conditions can influence the number of mosquitoes born in a season, or how much runoff of pesticides or parasites will be entering lo-cal streams. Extreme events can cause drowning or heatstroke. Pathogens don't really care about political debates over the cause of climate change: they simply respond to the reality of it. And current projections say that average global temperatures will increase by as much as 3.1–7.2°F by the year 2100.

Changes in climate will also require myriad adjustments in the most mundane details of daily life. If you're the football coach in Decatur, Georgia, and your principal says, "I don't want to see any heatstroke," you pull up the weather data for Decatur and say, "Okay. We're shifting preseason practice in August to four in the morning."

Or if you're the emergency manager at a coastal town in New Jersey, and the mayor says, "Okay, what are we going to do if there's increased coastal flooding?" You go to the US Global Change Research Program data and look at what your risks are, where the floodplains are, and think about what mit-igation strategies you need to implement.

Part of our job in the public health business is to help com-munities understand these kinds of risks by making the data available to them.

The subtle increase in temperature is already causing a rise in the incidence of unexpected disease of the lungs and brain in British Columbia and the US Pacific Northwest from *Cryptococcus gattii*—a yeast that belongs in subtropical and tropical areas. There have been unexpected outbreaks of watery diarrhea and cramps from oysters infected with *Vibrio parahaemolyticus* harvested from the warming waters of Prince Williams Sound, Alaska. In recent decades, there's been an increase in the number and distribution of human cases of tick-borne encephalitis in Central and Eastern European, Baltic, and Nordic countries as the ticks have spread northward and to higher altitudes. In the United States, during the past twenty years, we've seen the ticks that transmit Lyme disease expand their range to include half of all US counties. The number of high-risk counties in the Northeast has increased by 320 percent.

Full disclosure: not all the effects of climate change will be bad from a public health point of view. There are reports that the season for respiratory syncytial virus, a common childhood respiratory malady, is being shortened. And a perversely positive outcome of crippling droughts would mean a decline in the amount of standing water for disease-carrying mosquitoes to breed in. At the same time, however, those bugs will be moving to more temperate climates and to higher altitudes.

———

Early in this book, we mentioned that if any disease entity should keep people like me up at night, it's influenza. At any given time, the influenza viruses infecting birds and pigs are just a few amino acid changes away from causing the next human pandemic. And just for perspective: an influenza outbreak anywhere close to the severity of the 1918 pandemic would require the United States to have 1.5 million body bags ready for our neighbors, friends, and loved ones.

Almost any microbe could gain antibiotic resistance from genetic transfers and then cause bloodstream infections, pneumonia, or other diseases that, owing to poor infection control practices, could then spread into the community. In an age of medical tourism, in which patients travel far and wide to have either higher-quality or lower-cost procedures, this kind of superbug could easily spread worldwide.

Another big one to worry about is SARS/MERS and related viruses, which could spread in hospitals and then cause community-wide outbreaks that could lead to the next pandemic. As I write this, high-level health officials are being fired for their poor response to MERS in the Persian Gulf, and we still don't really understand how it's spreading, though dromedary camels appear to pose a threat that could be neutralized with an effective vaccine.

As we've seen, viral hemorrhagic fevers like Ebola pose a risk for community-based infections from direct contact and likely large respiratory particles. This mode of transmission increases the likelihood of hospital-based outbreaks that can then spread rapidly via global travel. The good news is that it's highly unlikely that Ebola would cause community-based infections in countries with robust public health systems.

Again, within health care settings and also among family members, there are reports of person-to-person transmission of henipaviruses, which cause deadly forms of brain inflammation or pneumonia. These viruses have a bat reservoir in Oceania and Asia, but they can also infect numerous other animals. Having caused a number of recent outbreaks among horses in Australia, they have not appeared on our radar in North America, but chances are they will.

Mosquito-borne viruses associated with mosquitoes that have a very wide geographic distribution, or can jump to a new mosquito vector, continue to cause pandemics, be it from dengue, chikungunya, or Zika virus, the newly newsworthy infection associated with a severe birth defect during pregnancy.

There are also sexually transmitted diseases—think HIV/AIDS—that can spread rapidly and cause an invariably fatal disease decades after infection. A long incubation period allows plenty of time to infect millions before the pandemic is recognized. And the politics of sex makes even routine sexually transmitted infections difficult to treat, as witnessed with gonorrhea infections that have gained antibiotic resistance and spread worldwide.

And then there is bioterrorism. As we've seen, anthrax is not communicable but can cause a devastating outbreak based on the characteristics of the engineered spores. Plague *is* communicable, and is thus a likely choice for a terrorists, as is smallpox. Fortunately, we have more than enough vaccine that could be quickly deployed from the Strategic National Stockpile to vaccinate contacts after the initial cases are recognized. While not strictly bioterrorism, I include sloppy scientists inadvertently releasing deadline microbes in the category as well as unsupervised development of superbugs.

Given the endless dance between microbes and humans, we should continue to expect that new pathogens will emerge and existing pathogens will learn new tricks to exploit changes in their environment. Fortunately, we can prevent the majority of these sporadic infections with better attention to the factors that lead to emergence in the first place. Most of all, we cannot excuse infections as simple public health misadventures. With health care infections and antibiotic resistance of microbes, for example, we can prevent medical tourists bringing back and spreading New Delhi metallo-beta-lactamase-1 superbugs. We can stop feeding pigs in China with antibiotics that lead to the development of MCR-1 (plasmid-mediated colistin resistance) genes that can be spread to human pathogens. We can also prevent Grandma from getting a blood infection at the hospital from a contaminated endoscope. And we can even be more careful of our influence on where many of our emerging infections arrive.

We can also mitigate, if not prevent, most outbreaks. Better compliance with simple sanitary practices, like food workers washing their hands, would prevent a significant portion of the 48 million cases of food-borne illness in the United States each year. The same is true for the estimated annual 722,000 hospital-acquired infections in the US, which lead to 75,000 deaths. These illnesses may be a lot less sexy than many emerging infectious outbreaks, but have a much greater impact.

The outbreaks that do make headlines, such as from Ebola, MERS, and Zika virus, need to be seen *not* as natural accidents, but as the canaries in the coal mine that call attention to weak public health systems.

In the United States we are fortunate to have the Centers for Disease Control and Prevention as our national public health agency, and globally to have the World Health Organization. However, at the end of the day, and even with great guidance and scientific expertisim, public health does not happen in Atlanta or Geneva, but in our communities. It is in our communities that we need to build better public health systems and find ways to engage people in the effort.

While at CDC, I posted a blog about personal preparedness. Instead of using the customary example of a hurricane, I illustrated my message with the scenario of a zombie apocalypse. The tongue-in-cheek post helped reach a massively large audience and made the point that personal preparedness is not just about a kit but making sure that we are all well-informed, have had our vaccinations, have learned CPR, are active in community disaster work, such as with the American Red Cross, and are personally fit. If nothing else, during a zombie apocalypse, we should be able to outrun the zombies!

During a crisis, engagement of health care workers and public health leaders is essential, but it is not sufficient. We need to mobilize the whole community and the entire political structure to interrupt a disease and help the community recover. Large outbreaks and other public health emergencies are political events and need to be recognized and managed as such from day one. The same is true for preparedness and prevention activities. Protecting citizens from these public health emergencies should be seen as no less a core function of government than preventing a foreign army's invasion.

To ensure true global health security through preparedness and proactive responses to pandemics, national disasters, and chemical, biological, and radioactive terrorism, we need to support everyday public health systems in every country. They can't be allowed to limp along in the hope that they can be ramped up as needed in a crisis.

At the global level, we need to create a United Nations undersecretary for health security. This individual should be given the task of mobilizing all global entities to ensure that preparedness and response discussions are at the level of the head of state and not just the minister or secretary of health.

There are already plans under way to support WHO with a contingency fund for emergencies, but we need a global fund to help improve health security preparedness internationally, similar to the global fund for the prevention and treatment of HIV/AIDS, tuberculosis, and malaria. This new global fund could also support nations in developing new medications and vaccines for potential pandemics analogous to the US approach, and establish a global stockpile of some critical materials such as Ebola vaccine. However, new medical countermeasures can never be a crutch to prop up poor public health systems.

Every country needs to define its own critical activities for preparedness and response to epidemics. My suggestion for the core of those activities is to have an emergency operations center that fuses multiple sources of information including media reports and social media, runs national exercises and planning, has routine access to disease-monitoring data, provides medication and coordination during a disaster, and has the ability to manage response teams.

These national improvements will require large new global investments. However, recent outbreaks have proven again and again that the United States is not an island immune to foreign microbes. Our lot is cast with the rest of the world.

The United States is a leader in public health, but it is not in all ways a shining city on a hill. The far too many health care infections and deaths we see are an indication of the poor state of our existing infection-control measures in health care settings. Our rate of infant mortality is an embarrassment for a nation so rich—we rank 167th in the world, on par with some banana republics—and are driven by the marked inequities in health care in this country.

Recently, the Trust for America's Health and the Robert Wood Johnson Foundation issued a 2015 report called "Outbreaks: Protecting Americans from Infectious Diseases." It found that twenty-eight states and Washington, DC, scored five or lower out of ten key indicators related to preventing, detecting, diagnosing, and responding to outbreaks. Meanwhile, the National Association of County and City Health Officials put out a report with results from a survey of their local health directors. Eight of ten health directors said they lacked the expertise to assess the potential impacts of climate change and to effectively create plans. Nine of ten said they lacked sufficient resources.

We simply need to do better, and to organize to combat the kind of foolishness that leads to snowballs being brought to the floor of the US Senate as an argument against climate change. We need to get beyond the pennywise-and-pound-foolish policies that scrimp not just on the physical infrastructure of roads and bridges and airports, but also on the public health infrastructure. We need to move beyond the "disease du jour" approach that manifests in crisis reporting and in requests for emergency funding for critical public health functions. We also cannot afford to neglect the full development of all the human capital contained within our population of 300 million.

And yet denial seems to be the most prevalent state of mind in the union, with some leaders trying to make reality conform to their own self-serving agendas, not unlike China when it refused to come clean about SARS, or WHO when it failed to acknowledge the severity of the 2014–15 Ebola outbreak.

In Florida, the state most vulnerable to rising seawater and an influx of tropical diseases, state officials are not allowed to use the terms "climate change" or "global warming" in any correspondence or reports.

Is that primitive magical thinking, or just primitive third-world logrolling, where narrow self-interest leads to tunnel vision—grab what you can to preserve power or wealth—with no concern for long-term consequences?

I have no idea what the penalty is for using language that conveys the truth. Maybe some politician will shoot me with a witch gun.

The time has come for us to move beyond seeing public health as the ax in the display case, where the sign says IN CASE OF EMERGENCY BREAK GLASS, and into the realm of flame-retardant building materials with fire extinguishers and sprinkler systems. In other words, we need to build preventive measures directly into the infrastructure of our communities and make them resilient. Doing so is dependent on gathering accurate data that lets us identify the underlying causes of problems, develop effective preventive measures, and monitor progress as these measures are implemented to improve health in our communities.

These are the choices we make. And we will see if Louis Pasteur was right when he said, "Gentlemen, it is the microbes who will have the last word."

REFERENCES

CHAPTER 1: FIRST BLUSH

Barry, John M. *The Great Influenza: The Epic Story of the Deadliest Plague in History*, rev. ed. New York: Penguin, 2005.

Bert, Fabrizio, Giacomo Scaioli, Maria Rosaria Gualano, Stefano Passi, Maria Lucia Specchia, Chiara, Cristina Viglianchino, et al. "Norovirus Outbreaks on Commercial Cruise Ships: A Systematic Review and New Targets for the Public Health Agenda." *Food and Environmental Virology* 6, no. 2 (June 2014): 67–74.

Centers for Disease Control and Prevention. "Outbreak Updates for International Cruise Ships." www.cdc.gov/nceh/vsp/surv/gilist.htm.

Khan, A. S., C. L. Moe, R. I. Glass, S. S. Monroe, M. K. Estes, L. E. Chapman, X. Jiang, et al. "Norwalk Associated Gastroenteritis Traced to Ice Exposure Aboard a Cruise Ship in Hawaii: Comparison and Application of Molecular Method-Based Assays." *Journal of Clinical Microbiology* 32, no. 2 (February 1994): 318–322.

Khan, A. S., F. Polezhaev, R. Vasiljeva, V. Drinevsky, J. Buffington, H. Gary, A. Sominina, et al. "Comparison of US Inactivated Split-Virus and Russian Live Attenuated, Cold-Adapted Trivalent Influenza Vaccines in Russian Schoolchildren." *Journal of Infectious Diseases* 173, no. 2 (February 1996): 453–456.

Pendergrast, Mark. *Inside the Outbreaks: The Elite Medical Detectives of the Epidemic Intelligence Service*. Boston: Houghton Mifflin Harcourt, 2010.

CHAPTER 2: SIN NOMBRE

Chapparo, J., J. Vega, W. Terry, B. Barra, R. Meyer, C. J. Peters, A. S. Khan, et al. "Assessment of Person-to-Person Transmission of Hantavirus Pulmonary Syndrome in a Chilean Hospital Setting." *Journal of Hospital Infection* 40, no. 4 (December 1998): 281–285.

Grady, Denise. "Death at the Corners." *Discover*, December 1, 1993. http://discovermagazine.com/1993/dec/deathatthecorner320.

Khan, A. S., J. Mills, B. Ellis, W. Terry, J. M. Vega, J. A. Toro, Z. Yadon, et al. "Informe final de las activides realizadas por la Comisión Conjunta—Centers for Disease Control and Prevention de Estados Unidos de América, Ministerio de Salud, Organización Panamericana de la Salud y ANLIS Argentina—en relación por hantavirus en Chile." *Revista Chilena de Infectologia* 14, no. 2 (1997): 123–134.

Ksiazek, T. G., C. J. Peters, P. E. Rollin, S. Zaki, S. T. Nichol, C. F. Spiropoulou, S, Morzunov, et al. "Identification of a New North American Hantavirus That Causes Acute Pulmonary Insufficiency." *American Journal of Tropical Medicine and Hygiene* 52, no. 2 (February 1995): 117–123.

Montoya-Ruiz, Carolina, Francisco J. Diaz, and Juan D. Rodas. "Recent Evidence of Hantavirus Circulation in the American Tropic." *Viruses* 6, no. 3 (March 2014): 1274–1293.

Toro, J., J. D. Vega, A. S. Khan, J. N. Mills, P. Padula, W. Terry, Z. Yadón, et al. "An Outbreak of Hantavirus Pulmonary Syndrome, Chile, 1997." *Emerging Infectious Diseases* 4, no. 4 (October–December 1998): 687–694.

CHAPTER 3: THE FACE OF THE DEVIL

Khan, A. S., G. O. Maupin, P. E. Rollin, A. M. Noor, H. H. Shurie, A. G. Shalabi, S. Wasef, et al. (1997) "An Outbreak of Crimean-Congo Hemorrhagic Fever in the United Arab Emirates, 1994–1995." *American Journal of Tropical Medicine and Hygiene* 57, no. 5 (November 1997): 519–525.

Khan, A. S., F. K. Tshioko, D. L. Heymann, B. Le Guenno, P. Nabeth, B. Kerstiëns, Y. Fleerackers, et al. "The Reemergence of Ebola Hemorrhagic Fever, Democratic Republic of the Congo, 1995." *Journal of Infectious Diseases* 179, suppl. 1 (February 1999): S76–86.

Rodriguez, L. L., G. O. Maupin, T. G. Ksiazek, P. E. Rollin, A. S. Khan, T. F. Schwarz, R. S. Lofts, et al. "Molecular Investigation of a Multi-source Outbreak of Crimean-Congo Hemorrhagic Fever in the United Arab Emirates." *American Journal of Tropical Medicine and Hygiene* 57, no. 5 (November 1997): 512–518.

CHAPTER 4: A POX ON BOTH YOUR HOUSES

Foege, William H. *House on Fire: The Fight to Eradicate Smallpox.* Berkeley: University of California Press and Milbank Memorial Fund, 2011.

Hutin, Y. J., R. J. Williams, P. Malfait, R. Pebody, V. N. Loparev, S. L. Ropp, M. Rodriguez, et al. "Outbreak of Human Monkeypox, Democratic Republic of Congo, 1996–1997." *Emerging Infectious Diseases* 7, no. 3 (June 2001): 434–438.

Kile, J. C., A. T. Fleischauer, B. Beard, M. J. Kuehnert, R. S. Kanwal, P. Pontones, H. J. Messersmith, et al. "Transmission of Monkeypox Among Persons Exposed to Infected Prairie Dogs in Indiana in 2003." *Archives of Pediatric and Adolescent Medicine* 159, no. 11 (November 2005): 1022–1025.

Likos, A., S. Sammons, V. Olson, M. Frace, Y. Li, M. Olsen-Rasmussen, W. Davidson, et al. "A Tale of Two Clades: Monkeypox Viruses." *Journal of General Virology* 86, pt. 10 (October 2005): 2661–2672.

McCollum, A. M., and I. K. Damon. "Human Monkeypox." *Clinical Infectious Diseases.* 58, no. 2 (January 2014): 260–267.

Mukinda, V. B. K., G. Mwema, M. Kilundu, D. L. Heymann, A. S. Khan, and J. J. Esposito. "Re-emergence of Human Monkeypox in Zaire in 1996." *Lancet* 349, no. 9063 (1997): 1449–1450.

CHAPTER 5: A HIGHER FORM OF KILLING

Centers for Disease Control and Prevention. "Killer Strain: Anthrax." Animations and Videos. www.cdc.gov/anthrax/news-multimedia/animations-and-videos.html.

Dewan, P. K., A. M. Fry, K. Laserson, B. C. Tierney, C. P. Quinn, J. A. Hayslett, L. N. Broyles, et al. "Inhalational Anthrax Outbreak Among Postal Workers, Washington, D.C., 2001." *Emerging Infectious Diseases* 18, no. 10 (October 2002): 1066–1072.

Jernigan, J. A., D. S. Stephens, D. A. Ashford, C. Omenaca, M. S. Topiel, M. Galbraith, M. Taper, et al. "Bioterrorism-Related Inhalational Anthrax: The First 10 Cases Reported in the United States." *Emerging Infectious Diseases* 7, no. 6 (November–December 2001): 933–944.

Willman, David. *The Mirage Man: Bruce Ivins, the Anthrax Attacks, and America's Rush to War.* New York: Bantam Books, 2011.

CHAPTER 6: MIGRATIONS

Plague in New York City

Auerbach, Jonathan. "Does New York City Really Have as Many Rats as People?" *Significance* 11, no. 4 (October 2014): 22–27.

Chase, Marilyn. *The Barbary Plague: The Black Death in Victorian San Francisco.* New York: Random House Trade Paperbacks, 2004.

Inglesby, T. V., D. T. Dennis, D. A. Henderson, J. G. Bartlett, M. S. Ascher, E. Eitzen, A. D. Fine, et al. "Plague as a Biological Weapon: Medical and Public Health Management (Consensus Statement)." *Journal of the American Medical Association* 283, no. 17 (May 2000): 2281–2290.

Sullivan, Robert. *Rats: Observations on the History and Habitat of the City's Most Unwanted Inhabitants.* New York: Bloomsbury, 2004.

West Nile Virus

Centers for Disease Control and Prevention. "West Nile Virus." www .cdc.gov/westnile.

Rossi, S. L., T. M. Ross, and J. D. Evans. "Emerging Pathogens: West Nile Virus." *Clinics in Laboratory Medicine* 30, no. 1 (March 2010): 47–65.

Bird Flu Virginia

Centers for Disease Control and Prevention. "Highly Pathogenic Asian Avian Influenza A (H5N1) Virus." www.cdc.gov/flu/avianflu/h5n1 -virus.htm.

Centers for Disease Control and Prevention. "Outbreaks of Avian Influenza in North America." www.cdc.gov/flu/avianflu/outbreaks.htm.

Fung, T. K. F., K. Namkoong, and D. Brossard. "Media, Social Proximity, and Risk: A Comparative Analysis of Newspaper Coverage of Avian Flu in Hong Kong and in the United States." *Journal of Health Communication* 16, no. 8 (September 2011): 889–907.

Kawaoka, Y. "H5N1: Flu Transmission Work Is Urgent." *Nature* 482, no. 7384 (February 9, 2012): 155.

CHAPTER 7: DIRECT FROM THE METROPOLE HOTEL

Centers for Disease Control and Prevention. "Outbreak of Severe Acute Respiratory Syndrome—Worldwide, 2003." *Morbidity and Mortality Weekly Report (MMWR)* 52, no. 12 (2003): 241–248.

Gopalakrishna, G., P. Choo, Y. S. Leo, B. K. Tay, Y. T. Lim, A. S. Khan, and C. C. Tan. "SARS Transmission and Hospital Containment." *Emerging Infectious Diseases* 10, no. 3 (March 2004): 395–400.

Normile, Dennis. "The Metropole, Superspreaders, and Other Mysteries." *Science* 339, no. 6125 (March 15, 2013): 1272–1273.

Schrag, S. J., J. T. Brooks, C. Van Beneden, U. D. Parashar, P. M. Griffin, L. J. Anderson, W. J. Bellini, et al. "SARS Surveillance During Emergency Public Health Response, United States, March–July 2003." *Emerging Infectious Diseases* 10, no. 2 (February 2004): 185–194.

CHAPTER 8: AFTER THE DELUGE

Brinkley, Douglas. *The Great Deluge: Hurricane Katrina, New Orleans, and the Mississippi Gulf Coast.* New York: Morrow, 2006.

Centers for Disease Control and Prevention. "Infectious Disease and Dermatologic Conditions in Evacuees and Rescue Workers After Hurricane Katrina—Multiple States, August–September, 2005." *Morbidity Mortality Weekly Report* 54, no. 38 (September 30, 2005): 961–964.

Sharma, A. J., E. C. Weiss, S. L. Young, K. Stephens, R. Ratard, S. Straif-Bourgeois, T. M. Sokol, et al. "Chronic Disease and Related Conditions at Emergency Treatment Facilities in the New Orleans Area After Hurricane Katrina." *Disaster Medicine and Public Health Preparedness* 2, no. 1 (March 2008): 27–32.

Watson, J. T., M. Gayer, and M. A. Connolly. "Epidemics After Natural Disasters." *Emerging Infectious Diseases* 13, no. 1 (January 2007): 1–5.

CHAPTER 9: SIERRA LEONE

Henao-Restrepo, Ana Maria, Ira M. Longini, Matthias Egger, Natalie E. Dean, W. John Edmunds, Anton Camacho, et al. "Efficacy and Effectiveness of an rVSV-Vectored Vaccine Expressing Ebola Surface Glycoprotein: Interim Results from the Guinea Ring Vaccination Cluster-Randomised Trial." *Lancet* 386, no. 9996 (August 29, 2015): 857–866.

Moon, S., D. Sridhar, M. A. Pate, A. K. Jha, C. Clinton, S. Delaunay, V. Edwin, et al. "Will Ebola Change the Game? Ten Essential Reforms Before the Next Pandemic: The Report of the Harvard-LSHTM Independent Panel on the Global Response to Ebola." *Lancet* 386, no. 10009 (November 28, 2015): 2204–2221.

World Health Organization. "Report of the Ebola Interim Assessment Panel—July 2015." www.who.int/csr/resources/publications/ebola/ebola-panel-report/en.

CHAPTER 10: #JESUISLEMONDE

Johnson, Steven. *The Ghost Map: The Story of London's Most Terrifying Epidemic—and How It Changed Science, Cities, and the Modern World.* New York: Riverhead Books/Penguin Group, 2006.

Trust for America's Health. *Outbreaks: Protecting Americans from Infectious Diseases 2015* (Robert Wood Johnson Foundation, December 2015). http://healthyamericans.org/assets/files/TFAH-2015-OutbreaksRpt-FINAL.pdf.

Watts, Nick, W. Neil Adger, Paolo Agnolucci, Jason Blackstock, Peter Byass, Wenjia Cai, Sarah Chaytor, et al. "Health and Climate Change: Policy Responses to Protect Public Health." *Lancet* 386, no. 10006 (November 2015): 1861–1914.

The White House. *National Action Plan for Combating Antibiotic-Resistant Bacteria* (March 2015). www.whitehouse.gov/sites/default /files/docs/national_action_plan_for_combating_antibotic-resistant _bacteria.pdf.

WHO Collaborating Center for Research, Training and Eradication of Dracunculiasis, CDC. "Memorandum: Guinea Worm Wrap-up #237." November 17, 2015. www.cartercenter.org/resources/pdfs/ news/health_publications/guinea_worm/wrap-up/237.pdf.

INDEX

ABOUT THE AUTHORS

Courtesy of UNMC

DR. ALI S. KHAN is the former director of the Office of Public Health Preparedness and Response at the Centers for Disease Control and Prevention. In more than twenty years at CDC, his career focused on emerging infectious diseases, bioterrorism, and global health security. Now dean of the College of Public Health at the University of Nebraska, he continues this work worldwide to protect communities from all public health threats.

Photo by Carolyn Savarese

WILLIAM PATRICK has collaborated on numerous memoirs with subjects ranging from Academy Award Winner Sidney Poitier to the Jet Propulsion Laboratory's Adam Steltzner. He is also the author of two well regarded suspense novels dealing with biological threats.